Stephania Bonilla

Odious Debt

GABLER RESEARCH

Ökonomische Analyse des Rechts

Die ökonomische Analyse des Rechts untersucht Rechtsnormen auf ihre gesellschaftlichen Folgewirkungen und bedient sich dabei des methodischen Instrumentariums der Wirtschaftswissenschaften. Sie ist ein interdisziplinäres Forschungsgebiet, in dem sowohl Rechtswissenschaftler als auch Wirtschaftswissenschaftler tätig sind und das zu wesentlichen neuen Erkenntnissen über Funktion und Wirkungen von Rechtsnormen geführt hat. Die Schriftenreihe enthält Monographien zu verschiedenen Rechtsgebieten und Rechtsentwicklungen.

Stephania Bonilla

Odious Debt

Law-and-Economics Perspectives

With a foreword by Prof. Dr. Hans-Bernd Schäfer

GABLER

RESEARCH

Bibliographic information published by the Deutsche Nationalbibliothek
The Deutsche Nationalbibliothek lists this publication in the Deutsche Nationalbibliografie; detailed bibliographic data are available in the Internet at http://dnb.d-nb.de.

Doctoral thesis, University of Hamburg, Graduiertenkolleg Recht und Ökonomik, 2010

1st Edition 2011

Editorial Office: Stefanie Brich | Sabine Schöller

Gabler Verlag is a brand of Springer Fachmedien.
Springer Fachmedien is part of Springer Science+Business Media.
www.gabler.de

Cover design: KünkelLopka Medienentwicklung, Heidelberg
Printed on acid-free paper
Printed in Germany

ISBN 978-3-8349-2993-8

Foreword

If a private creditor gives a loan to a private person, knowing that the money is used to finance a crime, a civil court would declare the credit contract as nil and void. Contract law provides legal rules such as „void for illegality“ and principles of "good faith“ or "boni mores" to deal with such odious debts. This level of civilization achieved in private law has never been reached in international relations. If a sovereign state takes up an international credit to finance an aggressive war, an apparatus of oppression or to channel the money into the private coffers of office holders the rule of succession requires that a subsequent government has to honor the debt. This applies even if the creditor was aware of how the money was used and no matter what hardship this implies for the people in the debtor country. There are exceptions to this rule, which states treat like black boxes. After the Spanish Cuban war of 1898 independent Cuba was forgiven the debt from Spanish Government bonds, as they were odious as stated in the peace treaty between the USA and Spain. The same argument applied for German bonds used in territories, which became part of the new Republic of Poland after World War I. And after the dethronement of Saddam Hussein in Iraq creditors forgave most of their debts to Iraq under heavy political pressure from the IMF and the USA. However, these cases -regardless of how legitimate the outcomes may be- reflect not so much decisions based on the rule of law but more the distribution of power after a war. South Africa was not forgiven any of its international debts, even though some of the money financed apartheid and everybody knew it. South Africa after apartheid did not want to agonize creditors and a judicial routine to cope with the problem did not exist. When it comes to odious debts international relations are better conceptualized by an analysis of the Hobbesian state of nature than by a concept of law, based on fair rules and principles.

Over the last decade the scientific community and especially scholars of law and economics have rediscovered this problem anew. It lay almost idle for about 60 years after a discussion in the 1920s on the legitimacy of the Soviet Union's decision to cancel Czarist government bonds. Stephania Bonilla's doctoral thesis is an important contribution to the current debate. She wrote it as a student in the doctoral law and economics program "Graduiertenkolleg Recht und Ökonomik" at the University of Hamburg. The research was financed by the German Research Foundation. Many of the issues discussed in this book in the context of odious debt are key issues, which will need to be addressed in order to move towards a more sustainable financial system, including ethics in finance and most notably, the issue of responsible lending and borrowing and finding solutions, which address the problem effectively without hampering the mechanism of international credit relations.

Odious debt is also a timely topic as it touches on the complicit role of creditors and the issue of lender responsibility, while also raising the question about how to deal with repressive and autocratic borrowing governments who act against the interest of their people. These are timely issues particularly this year as the Middle East revolutions are taking place. Among other issues, one will see how new governments and regimes in these countries will deal with their past financial obligations.

This book analyzes, why sovereign debtors generally tend to service their foreign debts, whether odious or not and how states consider their reputation in the sovereign debt field and in international law when making their decision. It looks at the incentives of parties and different creditors in distinct sovereign debt relations, and the implications that the incentive structures can have on reputation and odious debt.

The book also provides an economic analysis on distinct facets of the odious debt issue, which are relevant for international economic governance as a whole. It looks at the players and the drivers of change at the policy level in the field of sovereign debt and in the current odious debt debate.

It also deals with the question of whether an ex ante or ex post approach is more feasible to solve the problem efficiently. The latter would –as in private contract law-cancel an odious debt contract after a government has taken up the credit. This might lead to legal uncertainty for a considerable span of time and might negatively influence international credit. The former would legitimize an international body to declare future credits to a particular country as odious. It is obvious that the ex ante approach would impose the least legal uncertainty and not much disrupt international credit markets.

The book is highly recommendable for lawyers, economists and political scientists working in the field. But it is also attractive for a larger audience interested in an important aspect of international financial relations.

Prof. Dr. Hans-Bernd Schäfer

Acknowledgements

This book is the result of my research at the Doctoral College of Law-and-Economics (Graduiertenkolleg Recht und Ökonomik) of the University of Hamburg. My first acquaintance with law-and-economics began as a student of the European Master of Law-and-Economics (EMLE) and it paved the way for my PhD and my continued passion for the field.

First of all, I would like to thank my thesis supervisor Prof. Dr. Hans-Bernd Schäfer, who initially provided me with the idea of writing on the fascinating topic of odious debt. I have witnessed and have been inspired by his passion for law-and-economics and his quest for learning. I am grateful for his continuing support, encouragement and excellent guidance.

I would also like to thank the other professors at the Institute of Law and Economics, particularly Prof. Dr. Thomas Eger who provided me with support and encouragement throughout my time as a student and with helpful criticism at the PhD seminars where I presented earlier versions of my work. I would also like to mention my time working at the International Review of Law and Economics working with Prof. Dr. Claus Ott. My thanks go to the editors of the scientific series "Okonomische Analyse des Rechts" for giving me the opportunity to publish my thesis here.

Writing a doctoral thesis is both an intellectual and an emotional journey, one which is undoubtedly more difficult without a good support group. My experience would not have been as rewarding if it weren't for the friendship and motivation of my fellow PhD students at the Institute in particular my officemate Tammy de Wright as well Jan Peter Sasse, Katherine Walker, Peter Cserne, Susan Russell, Jan Matauschek, Stephan Wittig, Henning Frässdorf, Frank Müller-Langer and honorary member of the Institute and friend, Lena Ekelund.

I would further like to express special gratitude to Prof. Avery Katz and the University of Columbia for having hosted me as a Visiting Research Fellow in the Spring of 2008. I am indebted to Prof. Anne van Aaken for having listened to my presentations on odious debt countless times and whose positive criticism and enthusiasm have been invaluable. I am grateful for the comments that I received from Prof. Mitu Gulati, Prof. Eric Posner, Prof. P.G. Babu, Prof. Thomas S. Ulen, Prof. Thomas Ginsburg and Prof. Andrew Guzman on earlier drafts of my Papers. Of course, the opinions expressed and errors made are all mine.

One of the best parts of doing research is to be able to share it and discuss it with others. I would like to thank participants of the law-and-economics conferences in Madrid, Copenhagen, Rome, Kassel, Prague and the summer schools in Gerzensee, St. Gallen, Corsica and our own Institute's Summer School in Law-and-Economics in

Hamburg. Special thanks to Ido Baum and Ohad Soudry for organizing an invaluable summer school experience at the universities of Haifa and Tel-Aviv in 2005.

I acknowledge and am grateful for the generous financial support provided by the German Science Research Foundation (DFG) for my research both in Germany and the United States and for allowing me to travel and present it across Europe.

Finally, I wish to thank my husband Greg, for his unconditional love, support and patience, particularly during the 4 years of long distance relationship during my studies.

I wish to dedicate this book to my parents and my sister, who have never seized to inspire me, support me and guide me.

Table of contents

1 Introduction

The ability of sovereigns to borrow serves an important role in the sound management of national affairs. Indeed, the credit system is an important pillar of capitalism and allows governments, as well as enterprises and households, to invest in opportunities for promoting valuable objectives that they would otherwise be forced to pass up. Despite the positive effects that cross border financial flows have on recipient governments, they can also bring about dramatic negative consequences. Many developing countries, for example, repeatedly find themselves in debt crises after having acquired debt that has grown beyond sustainable and manageable levels. The political and moral debates that stem from the debt problem of developing countries are indicative of the power that debt has to provoke highly emotive reactions. This book focuses on another negative facet of sovereign debt which has witnessed an international moral outcry, namely; the problem of odious debt.

The international debate on odious debt touches on many fundamental issues, including the intersection between ethics and finance, the moral responsibility of parties to international contracts and of sovereigns to their constituents. Further, it is indicative of the increased interdependence of states due to globalisation and the collective interest in addressing problems that can have long term cross border repercussions.

Odious debt can be understood as an obligation incurred in the name of a sovereign nation by a despotic or illegitimate government, the proceeds of which only enrich the despot, or fund the repression of his subjects.[1] Some governments take up these types of debts, only to leave them to the people and the successor government to repay them once they are out of office or overturned. The 'odious' label has been attributed to the activities related to the looting of international funds in many forms; from ill advised investment projects, Swiss bank account of heads of state, the financing of inefficient and corrupt projects, to the indiscriminate use of state

[1] Feibelman 2007, 2

treasuries by dictators including Marcos in the Philippines, the Duvaliers in Haiti, Mobutu in the Congo and the Abachas in Nigeria.[2]

The interest in the subject first re-emerged in the context of the fall of the Apartheid government in South Africa when the Truth and Reconciliation Commission recommended canceling certain odious debts in 1998.[3] Then, in 2003 Saddam Hussein was ousted from Iraq and subsequently left the Iraqi people saddled with debt which many argued was odious.[4] The U.S. House of Representatives introduced a bill in June of the same year, the Iraqi Freedom from Debt Act, which called for the cancellation of Iraq's debt, given that based on "international precedent, debts incurred by dictatorships for the purposes of oppressing their people or for personal purpose may be considered odious."[5] Iraq, however, ultimately refrained from invoking the odious debt argument. Nevertheless, nothing short of a social movement was already well underway.

The momentum has all but diminished in the last several years. Odious debt has become a fashionable term not only in NGO but also academic and policy circles. Several university conferences have been devoted to odious debt[6] and a growing body of scholarship has developed.[7] Prominent legal and economic scholars such as Robert Howse[8] and Nobel laureate Joseph Stiglitz[9] have written on the subject. The official sector, through the initiatives of several states and international financial organizations, has also become involved in the cause. For example, institutions such as

---

[2] Hanlon November (1998) (available at: http://www.jubileeresearch.org/analysis/reports/dictatorsreport.html last visited on October 13th, 2009); Sack 1938; Foorman and Jehle (1982); Hoeflich (1982); Frankenberg and Knieper (1984); Adams (1991); Majot (1994)

[3] See King (2007), at 623 (citing Truth and Reconciliation Commission Report (1998), mentioning the 1976 International Monetary Fund loan that helped finance the security state)

[4] These included both anti-debt campaigner as well as the United States government. See for example, Julia(2002), 215, 236 and Steffan (2001) at 125-128 Footnote Michalowsky note 5

[5] This applied to the debt of Iraq as, " a significant amount of Iraq's outstanding loans were taken out at the behest of Baath Party leadership and rather than being used for the benefit or the well being of the Iraqi people were used for building lavish palaces, secret police, prisons and illegal weapons programs. However, the debt reduction process of Iraq was ultimately conducted mainly under the auspices of the Paris Club and through bilateral agreements with creditor countries that do not form part of the Paris Club. See www.clubdeparis.org/en/press_release/page_detail_commupresse.php?FICHIER=com11011125170

[6] For example, Conference on Odious Debt and State Corruption held at Duke University on January 26th, 2007; Workshop on Odious Debt held at the University of North Carolina at Chapel Hill on February, 2007; Harvard University Conference on obtaining political support for an odious debt proposal, January 2009

[7] See for example: Buchheit, Gulati et al. (2007) ; Stephan (2007) ; Adams (1991); Khalfan, King et al. (2003); Gelpern (2005); Jayachandran and Kremer (2006); Choi and Posner (2007); Gelpern (2007); Tarullo (2007); Rajan December (2004); Stiglitz November (2003)

[8] Howse (2007)

[9] Stiglitz November (2003)

UNCTAD[10] and the World Bank[11] have recently published papers on odious debt and have held conferences[12] and workshops[13] addressing the issue. Furthermore, governments such as those of Norway[14] and Ecuador[15] have been active in promoting the odious debt cause and initiatives are underway in other countries such as the Philippines and Mali. In the United States, President Barack Obama expressed interest in "leading a multilateral effort to address the issue of odious debt" in a white paper on economic development in 2008 during his presidential campaign.[16] Meanwhile, civil society continues to push an odious debt agenda and increase awareness of the problem.[17]

The widespread attention that has been devoted to the problem of odious debt in international finance is a reflection of the dissatisfaction by the international community with debt governance. This dissatisfaction is fueled by the persistent debt problems of many countries across the world and the fact that many morally repugnant activities are being financed by reckless lending and irresponsible sovereign borrowing. In view of the recent global financial and economic crisis of and the aftermath that ensued, the importance of introducing equitable considerations and responsibility in international finance has becomes more prominent, and interest in the subject is surely to continue to increase.

---

[10] Howse (2007); Paulus (2007)

[11] Nehru (2007)

[12] UNCTAD Sixth Debt Management Conference in 2007 included odious debt as one of central themes See http://r0.unctad.org/dfmas/docs/DM6thAgenda_En.pdf Again, in 2009, UNCTAD's 7th Debt Management Conference included two panels addressing the issue of illegitimate debt. See http://www.unctad.org/templates/Meeting.asp?intItemID=2068&m=1710&info=&lang=2 In 2010, during UNCTAD's World Investment Forum in China, officials met to discuss draft principles on sovereign lending and borrowing See http://www.unctad.org/templates/webflyer.asp?docid=13836&intItemID=5267&lang=1 and UNCTAD discussion paper on the topic: http://www.unctad.org/en/docs/osgdp20102_en.pdf

[13] Panel on New Expertise on Odious Debts 2008

[14] Norway takes historic step 2006

[15] hoy.mec.ec 2008; Zeledon 2009

[16] See www.barackobama.com 2007 Since then, this initiative has moved from a broader, multilateral promise envisioned towards a country specific approach considered in the form of loan sanctions which have been considered for North Korea and Iran. See http://www.politifact.com/truth-o-meter/promises/obameter/promise/211/create-loan-sanctions-to-stop-private-creditors-fr/

[17] See http://www.jubileeiraq.org/tribunal.html, www.odiousdebt.org, www.cadtm.org, Transparency International

1.1 The traditional doctrine of odious debt

In essence, the concept of odious debt challenges the present international rule of state succession of obligations which requires that states and governments inherit the debts incurred by their predecessors (hereinafter, 'the rule of repayment').[18] While the renewed interest in odious debt is relatively recent, the concept dates back to the writings of Aristotle[19] and has since been mainly developed in the work of Anglo-American jurists.[20] However, the odious debt qualification to the rule of repayment is most often associated with Alexander Nahum Sack, who wrote in the 1920's on the subject, when he lived in Paris as a Russian expatriate. Drawing from the writings of scholars such as C.C. Hyde[21] and Gaston Jèze[22] as well as on some (rare) examples of state practice which he regarded as evidence of custom, Sack formally developed what has come to be known as the doctrine of odious debt. While he adhered to the strict rule of repayment, he argued that some debts are odious and therefore unenforceable. He classified odious debts into three categories, namely "war debts", "subjugation debts" and "regime debts."[23]

1.1.1 War debts

Sack defined "war debts" as debts which are incurred by a government of a state "with a view to waging war against another state."[24] There are several instances of state

[18] The leading treaties are: Feilchenfeld (1931); O'Connell (1967) and most recently Cheng (2006) For a commentary see Khalfan, King et al. (2003) and Hoeflich (1982)

[19] "(When) a democracy tak(es) place of an oligarchy or despotism...some persons refuse...to meet the contracts in hand on the ground that it was not the State, but the despot who entered upon them." Aristotle (1877) cited in Cheng (2007), 12

[20] See Bedjaoui (1977)

[21] See Hyde 1945 See also Khalfan, King et al. 2003, 40 (citing an example of when Sack cites Hyde in the American Journal of International Law as writing, "Where a debt is shown to have been incurred for purposd to be fairly deemed hostile to the purposed of a particular district or territory, in case of a change in sovereignty wrought, for example, by revolution, is not likely to be regarded as burdened with the fiscal obligation, irrespective of the design of the original debtor."

See Bedjaoui 1977, 67 and King 2007, 623

[22] Sack drew on the public finance theory and international legal work of the French scholar Gaston Jezé. Jèze 1921; Jèze 1922 See also Khalfan, King et al. 2003, 40 and King 2007, 623 (discussing Jèze's influence on Sack).

[23] He did not regard these as strict categories, but rather as examples of different contexts when the odious debt doctrine had been invoked.

[24] "Ce sont les dettes conclus par le gouvernement de l'Etat en vue d'une guerre avec un autre Etat." Sack 1927, 165 See Buchheit, Gulati et al. 2007, 1212(Explaining the war debts qualification, "...if the rebels get inside the presidential palace, they are not obliged to honour the loans incurred by the prior occupants to purchase the bullets employed in the effort to dissuade the rebels from the recent enterprise." See also King 2007, 629 (discussing war debts as an established type of odious debt, supported by the writings of scholars such as Cahn, Westlake, Feilchenfeld and O'Connell).

practice, where a successor state has rejected war debts contracted by its predecessor to sustain its war effort against the former. Notably, one example can be traced back to the British annexation of the Boer Republics in 1900.[25] The British, after having won, announced that they would take up the debts of the South African Republics which were contracted *prior* to the hostilities, but refused to take up those debts which followed after the Boer War had already begun.[26] Another case in point is that of the peace treaties which were negotiated after the First World War, where the Allies excluded war debts from distribution against the ceded territories. They insisted that the debts were to be borne by Germany, Austria and Hungary.[27] The Fourteenth Amendment of the Constitution of the United States reflects a similar approach applied to the debts incurred by the rebellious Confederate States of America.[28]

Notwithstanding these cases of state practice in support of Sack's war debts qualification, there is an overwhelming body of examples which militate against it. Indeed, history points to a significant number of states which have assumed the war debts of their predecessor states, such as the assumption of a percentage of the Austrian war debts by the former Czechoslovakia after the First World War.[29] Other examples include post revolutionary France, Mexico, Ecuador, Brazil and Costa Rica. As a result of this rather uneven state practice, prominent legal scholars such as Feilchenfeld, who nonetheless support the war debts qualification as a "natural demand of justice"[30], have thus argued that no specific international customary rule has emerged exempting war debts from assumption in the case of annexation or dismemberment.[31]

---

[25] Feilchenfeld 1931, 393-395.

[26] "The British Government denied all legal responsibility for such "odious" debt, denied the Republic's capacity to have issued such debt validly, and announced that the British Government would not honour the bonds upon presentation." See Hoeflich 1982, 59 Feilchenfeld 1931, 380-381 See also Khalfan, King et al. 2003, 26 (noting that the British Government later did pay, ex gratia, ten percent of the value of the bonds).

[27] A compromise agreement was reached with Austria and Hungary since the entire burden would have resulted in complete bankruptcy. See Khalfan, King et al. 2003, 18-19

[28] See the Fourteenth amendment to the Constitution of the United States, enacted in 1868 after the Union victory in the American Civil War. Section 4 of the Fourteenth Amendment begins by reaffirming the validity of the public debt of the United States. It then goes on to decree that: "...neither the United states nor any state shall assume or pay any debt or obligation incurred in aid of insurrection or rebellion against the United States...but all such debts, obligations and claims shall be held illegal and void." U.S. CONST. Amend. XIV (cited in Buchheit, Gulati et al. 2007, 1213)

[29] See Bedjaoui 1977 (cited in Nehru 2007, 9)

[30] Feilchenfeld 1931, 394

[31] Feilchenfeld 1931, 718-21

1.1.2 Subjugation debts

Sack's second odious qualification to the strict rule of repayment involves "subjugation debts" which he defined as debts which a government contracts "to subjugate the population of part of its territory or to colonize it by members of the dominant nationality."[32] He also derived this qualification from examples of state practice, in particular the case of the repudiation by the United States of Cuba's debt owed to Spain following the Spanish-American War.[33] During this war, the United States supported Cuba's fight for independence from Spain and ultimately won. Spain ceded to it its sovereignty over Cuba, the Philippines, Puerto Rico and other territories. Relying on the traditional rule of repayment in state succession, Spain argued that the United States was bound to repay the outstanding debt of the territories being transferred. The Americans, in turn, refused to assume responsibility for the debts, in particular those which the Spanish Crown had incurred in its own name but for which Cuban revenue streams had been pledged.[34]

The United States put forth several justifications for its reluctance to honour the debts. One of its main arguments emphasized the fact that the proceeds of the loans had been used for purposed which were harmful to the citizens of Cuba: the suppression of their independence movement. In other words, they were considered "hostile" to the very people expected to repay them.[35] Secondly, the Americans argued that the Cuban people had not consented to the debts, but rather that these had been imposed on them by Spain. Finally, the third justification put forth that, in the context of sovereign lending, reasonable expectations are not always based on the borrower's ability and willingness to pay, but sometimes they are based on the probability that the incumbent regime will remain in power long enough to repay the debt.[36] One can gather than the intuition being this reasoning is that, under certain circumstances, debts are personal to the regime or the rulers in power.

The arguments by the United States seemed to have been upheld in the 1898 Treaty of Peace which ended the dispute, in that neither the United States nor Cuba assumed the subjugation debts contracted by Spain. Although it has been widely cited

[32] "Lorsque le gouvernment contracte des dettes afin d'asservir la population d'une partie de son territoire ou de coloniser celle-ci par des ressortissants de la nationalité dominante. " See Sack 1927, 158

[33] See Sack 1927, 159 Khalfan, King et al. 2003, 25 Michalowski 2007, 34-35 Cheng 2007, 15

[34] Feilchenfeld 1931, 324-343

[35] Buchheit, Gulati et al. 2007, 1214

[36] The creditors knew that the pledges of Cuban revenues to secure the loans had been given in the context of efforts to suppress a people struggling for freedom from Spanish rule. The creditors, then "took the obvious chances of their investment on so precarious a security." See Feilchenfeld 1931, 341 (cited in Buchheit, Gulati et al. 2007, 1215)

by the proponents of the odious debt doctrine as evidence of state practice,[37] others have treated it rather as evidence of the power relations at the time,[38] and it remains questionable whether a customary international rule allowing the repudiation of subjugation debts really exists.[39]

1.1.3 Regime debts

Sack wrote extensively on the treatment of state debts in the event of regime change. Within this context, as opposed to the context of state succession where he treated war debts and subjugations debts, he developed the third category of odious debts; regime debts. The argument here is that, despite the continuity of state, there has been a change in government and the successor government refuses to honour the debts contracted by the predecessor regime on account of their having been contracted in the exclusive interests of the predecessor regime, and not to the benefit of the state or its population. His definition of regime debts is generally regarded as the most comprehensive definition of odious debt. It comprises three elements: absence of consent, absence of benefit and creditor awareness of both:

When a despotic regime contracts a debt, not for the needs or in the interest of the state, but rather to strengthen itself, to suppress a popular insurrection, etc., this debt is odious for the population of the entire state. This debt does not bind the nation; it is a debt of the regime, a personal debt by the power that contracted it, and consequently it falls with the demise of that power. The reason why these "odious" debts cannot be considered to burden the territory of the state is that they do not fulfill one of the conditions determining the regularity of State debts, namely that State debts must be incurred, and the proceeds used, for the needs and in the interests of the state.

Odious debts, contracted and utilized, for purposes which, to the lenders' knowledge, are contrary to the needs and the interests of the nation, are not binding on it – when it succeeds in overthrowing the government that contracted them – unless the debt is within the limits of real advantage that these debts might have afforded. The lenders have committed a hostile act against the people, they cannot expect a nation, which has freed itself of a despotic regime, to assume these odious debts, which are the personal debts of the ruler. Even if one despotic regime is overthrown by another, which is despotic and which does not follow the will of the people, the odious debts

---

[37] Another example often cited is that brought forth by O'Connel in his Treatise "State Succession in Municipal Law and International Law." In 1919, the Treaty of Versailles exempted Poland from the repayment of debts which were incurred to contribute to the German and Prussian colonization of Poland. What was emphasized was the notion that the debts were aggressive or 'hostile' to the interests of the nation. See O'Connell 1967

[38] See for example Kaiser and Queck 2004 available at: www.erlassjahr.de/content/publikationen/dokumente/is_200402_irakstudie.doc (last visited on October 27th, 2009)

[39] For a brief discussion on how this qualification has been contested and of inconsistence in state practice See Nehru 2007, 9-10

contracted by the fallen regime remain personal debts and are not binding on the new regime.[40]

As an example of regime debts, Sack relied on arbitration between Great Britain and Costa Rica which lends support to the odious debt argument.[41] The background of the case involves a former Costa Rican dictator, Federico Tinoco. Towards the end of his two year government, Mr.Tinoco managed to borrow some money from the Royal Bank of Canada. Subsequently, the entire proceeds from the loan left the country at the same time that Mr. Tinoco did. The arbitration which followed involved William Howard Taft as sole arbitrator.[42] Great Britain claimed that the successor government of Costa Rica was bound to honour the loans extended by the Royal Bank of Canada. While Jutstice Taft adhered to the rule of repayment, he refused to order Costa Rica to repay the Tinoco loans on the basis that the transactions were not used for a legitimate governmental purpose and were not of "an ordinary nature" but were "full of irregularities." He further added that the Royal Bank of Canada knew that this money was to be used by the retiring president, Mr. Tinoco, for his personal support after he had taken refuge in a foreign country and would therefore not benefit the state or the people of Costa Rica.[43] This last point is important in that Taft emphasized the awareness of the bank in his decision, as opposed to the questionable legitimacy of the Tinoco government.

1.1.4 A note on the doctrine

Sack's doctrine of odious debt has been the subject of much attention and has received both widespread praise as well as criticism. Those who advocate the doctrine appear to adhere to its moral underpinnings.[44] They champion its potential to remedy gross injustices imposed on the debtor nation's population and identify its normative basis as a question of human rights. Interestingly, however, many of them enlist the terminology, but not the content of the doctrine. These proponents often take for granted that the doctrine holds a place in international law, and appear to

---

[40] Adams 1991, 3 (translating Sack 1927, 157)

[41] Arbitration between Great Britain and Costa Rica 1923

[42] Great Britain and Costa Rica jointly chose Justice Taft. See Choose Taft as Arbitrator November 2nd, 1922 See also Buchheit, Gulati et al. 2007, 1216 footnote 40, (discussing why from Great Britain's perspective, however, it was an unhappy choice as sole arbitrator given his acute distaste for political corruption in developing countries.)

[43] "Arbitration Between Great Britain and Costa Rica" 1924, 168 See also Buchheit, Gulati et al. 2007, 1216 (discussing that Mr. Taft ruled that the bank "must make out its case of actual furnishing money to the government for its legitimate use. It has not done so."

[44] See for example http://www.odiousdebts.org (citing Sack's doctrine and stating that; "The South makes compelling moral arguments to cancel its foreign debts. But, it also has an indisputable legal case because the overwhelming majority of those debts are odious in law.") (last visited on November 4th, 2009)

misappropriate it, applying it not only to debts, but to entire regimes.[45] Buchheit et al. point out that it would astonish Alexander Sack today to learn that his "odious" adjective had, in the twenty first century, become, "the rallying cry of groups advocating the wholesale forgiveness of the sovereign debt of countries victimized by despotic or kleptomaniacal regimes."[46] Indeed, Sack advocated a very strict application of the rule of repayment and considered any debt repudiation on the grounds of odiousness to be a rare exception to that rule. He therefore would have been against branding debts as odious in a discretionary manner.[47] For example, he has openly ridiculed the argument of the Soviet government in the U.S.S.R. in 1918 that it, as the government of the "workers and the peasants", had the legal right to repudiate the debts incurred by prior Russian governments of the "landlords and the bourgeoisie."[48]

Those who criticize the doctrine, on the other hand, point to the fact that state practice which supports it is at best inconsistent[49] and that expert opinion on it is far from a consensus.[50] While almost everyone can agree that it seems fundamentally unfair to demand that a population repay its inherited debts which were used against its general interest, the principal question is whether the moral imperative embodied in the doctrine of odious debt can be translated into a workable legal theory. Many argue that Sack's doctrine fails at this task due to the vague and unworkable criteria

---

[45] See Buchheit, Gulati et al. 2007, 1222 (stating that "some recent commentators are prepared to assume that all odious regimes behave odiously all the time and therefore all of the their debts must be odious." See also for example Hanlon November 1998 (emphasizing the odiousness of the regime as the primary reason to nullify the debt)

[46] Buchheit, Gulati et al. 2007, 1223

[47] Sack envisioned an international tribunal which would be responsible for making the determination of odiousness, and the burden of persuasion would rest with the new government seeking to repudiate its inherited debts. The new government would be required to establish that the proceeds of the borrowing were used for purposes contrary to the interests of the population of the country and that the lender, at the time the loan was extended, knew this to be the case. See Sack 1927, 163 See Kaiser and Queck March 2004 (discussing that Sack's doctrine of odious debt is not applied unilaterally and is strictly based on a multilateral agreement, i.e. a convention or international treaty, or on an ad hoc multilateral procedure). Available at: http://www.erlassjahr.de/dev/cms/upload/englisch/dokumente/international_claims_on_iraq/200403_iraq:paper.pdf (last visited on October 28th, 2009)

[48] Sack 1938, 1, 10 (cited in Buchheit, Gulati et al. 2007, 1224)

[49] See for example Stephan 2007, 11 (arguing that the last thirty years has seen the collapse of authoritarian or Soviet-style governments across the continents which were all frought with human rights abuses and political injustices, yet none of the successor regimes sought debt relief by adhering to the doctrine of odious debt.) See also Gelpern 2005, 406 (arguing that the lack of state practice in support of the doctrine is puzzling and evident given a century of Hitler, Stalin , Mobutu, Abacha, Somoza and Marcos as well as socialist revolutions, capitalist restorations and decolonizations.)

[50] See for example Stephan 2007 (discussing the possibility of whether the "invisible college" could bring forth the doctrine to have a place in customary international law. The invisible college conception argues that expert opinion provides better evidence of an existing international consensus than do the observations of non experts. He concludes that even under this conception, the doctrine would not find a place in custom, as academic and expert opinion is far from a consensus on the subject.)

embodied in his definitions of odious debt such as 'absence of consent' 'absence of benefit' and 'creditor awareness' which are difficult to observe and verify by third parties.[51]

Perhaps Sack considered these criteria to be self evident in certain cases. Indeed, the particularity of the examples of state practice that Sack based himself on in his writing reflects the limits of the doctrine as a diagnostic tool generally applicable to more complex and modern cases of odious debt. For example, wars, independence movements and revolutions are unique events which are easily observable at low cost. Sack consequently stressed the importance of 'creditor awareness' and the reasonable expectations of creditors when extending loans in the face of such events.[52] They knew, or should have known, of these circumstances and accordingly priced the risk in the contract. [53] Likewise, the odious nature of the Tinoco loans and the fact that they would not benefit the State or the people of Costa Rica was also observable at low cost, both by the creditor, the Royal Bank of Canada, and by a third party such as Justice Taft. In this sense, the Tinoco case is particular in that Mr. Tinoco appropriated the *entire* amount of the debts for his personal use. Most cases of 'odiousness', in contrast, are not so blatantly obvious today and creditors are not necessarily well positioned to detect them. Governments are not 100% odious all of the time and the money that they borrow is not entirely used for odious purposes. The condition of having every cent used against the interests of the people is difficult to fulfill even with modern day corruption.[54] Consequently, attempts at developing a general, relevant and workable legal theory based on the categories of odious debt identified in Sack's doctrine have faced significant obstacles.

---

[51] For a discussion See Michalowski 2007, 49-59 See also Buchheit, Gulati et al. 2007, 17 (Stressing the fact that the three criteria are linked with connectives. They argues that aside from being theoretically attractive, as soon as one tries to apply the criteria in practice, the doctrine's "limits as a diagnostic tool" become apparent.)

[52] Likewise, some of the early legal opinions which followed Sack emphasized the complicit role of creditors. For example, with regards to war debts, Westlake argues that creditors enter the war on a particular side. See Westlake 1904 Fischer, in turn, reinterprets this argument as an "all or nothing" bet by the creditors on the outcome of the war. See Pufendorf 1967, 11 (discussing John Fischer's argument, "A creditor who advanced money to a belligerent during a war, to some extent adventures his money on the faith of the borrower's success.") Others, including O'Connell and Hyde argue that creditors should be regarded as having taken their chances with the investment. Hyde 1945, 442 O'Connell 1967, 462

[53] Furthermore, from an incentive point of view, there is no reason why the victor should assume the debts of a defeated nation, as this would reduce the cost of credit for future enemies because creditors would feel confident that they would get repaid regardless of whether the debtor wins the war. The victor has no reason for giving creditors this incentive.

[54] Furthermore, the fungibility of money means that even if the loans are used legitimately, resources would then be freed up which could be used for odious purposes.

1.2 The literature

1.2.1 Legal proposals

The international legal literature has been particularly active in treating the odious debt problem and allowing for its transition from the rallying cries of activist groups to the academic realm. By and large, the legal scholarship has moved from specifically focusing on Sack's doctrine,[55] to finding an alternative legal basis for the odious debt argument.

Some commentators turn to other doctrines of international law which sovereigns can recur to when challenging the enforcement of their debts.[56] Similarly, in a draft article proposed for the Vienna Convention on Succession of States in respect to State Property, Archives and Debts (the Vienna Convention), Special Rapporteur Bedjaoui proposed that a group of debts should be regarded as odious if they are not in conformity with international law and, in particular, with the principles of international law embodied in the Charter of the United Nations.[57] Under this approach, a debt would be odious if it was contracted, "in order to purchase arms that were used to flout human rights through genocide, racial discrimination or apartheid" or " to finance a policy of subjugating a people and colonizing its territory, or, in general, any policy contrary to the right of the peoples to self determination." [58] While a doctrine based on *ius cogens* violations provides clearer criteria than the traditional doctrine of odious debts, it leaves open a whole new set of questions that would have to be addressed before it could have a chance of becoming operable.[59] For this reason, and do to the fact that the International Law Commissioners concluded that state practice did not support the discontinuity of oppressive debts, the article never made it into the Vienna Convention[60]

Other legal scholars have looked to general principles of law to draw support for the odious debt argument. To this end, they examine existing national tools and solutions which can contribute to the repudiation of odious debts in one of the venues

---

[55] At Duke University Conference on Odious Debts and State Corruption, something which rarely occurs in an academic setting happened, everyone was in agreement...at least with regards to the fact that advancing Sack's odious debt doctrine was undesirable. One notable exception is King (See Khalfan, King et al. 2003 and King 2003) whose extensive work focuses on advancing the odious debt doctrine.

[56] Khalfan, King et al. 2003

[57] Bedjaoui 1977, 70

[58] Bedjaoui 1977, 134,135

[59] For a discussion of the potential of the proposal see Michalowski 2007, 69-96

[60] For a discussion of how the article was ultimately rejected from inclusion in the Vienna Convention on Succession of States in Respect of State Property, Archives and Debts See Cheng 2007, 19 and "Compare Summary Records of the 1425th Meeting U.N. Doc A/CN.4/SER.A/1977" 1977

chosen by the contracting parties themselves.[61] Gulati and Buchheit, for example, look to commercial/corporate law as a defense.[62] They propose that odious debts might be found unenforceable under contract law as against public policy,[63] under the doctrines of fraud and unclean hands,[64] under agency principles or by incurring to defenses analogous to corporate veil-piercing. [65] Furthermore, others have looked to the doctrine of unjust enrichment[66] and to the familiar problem in law of allocating liability among secondary contributors and examining contributory negligence and comparative benefit.[67]

The list of national tools available to potentially back up an odious debt claim highlights the fact that the innate elements of the odious debt problem are not intangible and have a place in national law. However, the exercise of addressing odious debts in domestic courts using private law is not as simple as the above discussion suggests. As one commentator argues, domestic analogies to the odious debt problem, may be at best just that, analogies.[68] One of the main limitations is that

---

[61] The municipal courts of New York and London are the venues most often chosen in international debt contracts.

[62] See Buchheit, Gulati et al. 2007, 28-48

[63] Id., 28-30

[64] Id., 30-32

[65] Under American law of agency, a principal is generally bound by the actions of its agent if the agent was acting with authority – actual or apparent – to bind the agent. An agent may not have authority to bind the principle, if it is clear to a third party that the principle derives no benefit from the transaction with its agent. See Restatement Second of Agency cited in Buchheit, Gulati et al. 2007 The authors combine this argument with a defence analogous to corporate veil piercing. Under corporate law, the obligations of a corporation generally do not extend to its shareholders. Under some circumstances, however, a creditor can reach the assets of the corporation's shareholders. American law considers that if innocent parties are being injured as a result of respecting the continuing legal fiction, an exception may be justifiable. Such an exception in corporate law is referred to as "piercing the corporate veil". These authors argue that the underlying rationale of the PVC is applicable to the odious debt situation. This would be the misuse of the separate identity status. See Buchheit, Gulati et al. 2007, 37-39

[66] See Bonilla February 7th, 2007, 38 (discussing the common law of unjust enrichment as a useful analogy to the problem of odious debt when the creditor has been unjustly enriched as a result of repayment it received for odious loans which cause harm to the debtor's population. Also considers the equivalent to unjust enrichment in German law) available at: http://papers.ssrn.com/sol3/papers.cfm?abstract_id=946111

[67] "See Ben-Shahar and Gulati 2007 (arguing that there is a paradox in punishing either the creditor or the populace for odious debt since both are innately victims of the despot who stole from them. They argue that fault should be understood as a relative judgment and what is left for the law to determine is the relative culpability of the disputing parties, the populace and the creditor. Accordingly, the comparative benefit of the respective parties should be taken into consideration, such as the population benefiting from the use of some of the odious loan proceeds.

[68] See for example DeMott 2007 (focusing on the limitations of applying the agency doctrine as a defence for odious debt) See Also Ben-Shahar and Gulati 2007 (discussing the collective action problem on the part of municipal courts in bringing forth private law doctrines to address odious debt. Neither would want to be seen as the court that attracts the borrowing business of odious debtors/creditors).

such arguments may never get their day in court given that debtors would only have a chance to use them if their creditors decide to sue them in domestic courts, which, although an increasing practice, remains rare. Furthermore, the option is only available in the cases of bank loans and bonds, excluding official credit.

1.2.2 Other proposals

While the vast majority of the literature has focused on litigation strategies to address the problem of odious debt, there are namely two noteworthy exceptions. The first is a contractarian approach offered by Feibelman. Under his approach, the creditors of a sovereign debtor would include a definition of "odious debt" in their contracts with the debtor. If the obligations were later challenged as odious, the issue would be resolved by a creditor vote. The obligations would be disallowed if a majority of supermajority of creditors viewed them as odious.[69] Although the proposal is subject to some obvious limitations,[70] and, as with domestic courts is only limited to private debt-obligations, the idea of using private contract, as opposed to an institutional, top down solution, is promising.

Finally, economists Kremer and Jayachandran have proposed an on-going international institution, such as the United Nations Security Council, which would have the ability to impose loan sanctions on odious regimes. Loan sanctions would be accompanied by legal changes that would prevent the seizure of odious debtor's assets for non repayment of debt incurred after it was designated as odious. Loan sanctions eliminate the penalty to a country from repudiating odious debt, and anticipating this, most creditors would presumable avoid lending to sanctioned regimes, or at least charge a much higher interest to do so. Gelpern notes that such as scheme would, "remove some reputational damage to a country from repudiating odious debt, would shield the country from lawsuits, and would enable meaningful risk assessment by creditors. Most importantly, it may discourage lending to oppressive governments and free their people from responsibility for the debts."[71] Despite these advantages, the proposal faces important obstacles pertaining to its implementation, not least because it takes a significant leap from assessing debts, to assessing entire regimes.

1.3 Approach and outline of this book

As rich and extensive as the literature is, a solution to odious debt is yet to be found. Indeed, odious debt is still a major policy problem. None of the above proposals have made the transition from an academic idea to real world implementation. For the most part, this may be due to the non-negligible practical, conceptual, legal and political

[69] Feibelman 2007

[70] For a discussion See Bolton and Skeel 2007, 93-94

[71] Gelpern 2005, 413

obstacles that many of the proposals involve. Furthermore, despite a general acceptance that sovereigns should not incur odious debt and that successor regimes should not have to pay truly odious debt, it is accompanied by a fear that the medicine for odious debt may in fact prove deadlier than the disease. As Bolton and Steel point out, "even a policy intervention that is clearly desirable in a first-best world may actually have perverse effects in a second best world."[72]

Against this background, the aim of this book is to further the analysis of the intriguing and complex topic of odious debt by offering a new perspective, that of law and economics. Rather than attempt to propose a perfect solution to the problem, it takes a step back: How does odious debt come about? What are the dynamics of the status quo which the odious debt literature is trying to change? Who are the players that are capable of bringing about change? At the same time, this book also takes a step forward, and applies a consequentialist approach: What would be the repercussions for a debtor if it defaults on its debt on the grounds that it was odious? Who would win and lose from an odious debt solution? These are some of the questions that will be discussed in the chapters to follow. Although central to the overall analysis, no specific definition of odious debt is provided. Rather, the book seeks to address different aspects and manifestations of the odious debt problem.

Drawing from the economic analysis of international law, the first two chapters of this book focus on the dynamics of sovereign debt relations. In contrast to some of the legal odious debt literature, they explicitly hold the lack of formal third party enforcement in international law at the center of the analysis. **Chapter 1** argues that any attempt to alter the status quo of sovereign debt relations must begin with a full understanding of it and the mechanisms that sustain it. Before considering a purported odious debt exception to the rule of state succession, it is necessary to analyze the incentives that drive debtors to ever pay back their debts, given that no Leviathan exists to coerce them to do so. In doing so, it considers the traditional legal and economic theories as well as more recent dynamic economic models of reputation applied to sovereign debt and international law. The chapter looks at how a sovereign debtor's concern for its reputation in the sovereign debt context and its reputation in complying with its international legal obligations, both push it in the same direction towards repayment of its debts generally. More specifically, the first act of repayment or default by a new state or a transformed regime will have a greater marginal impact on its reputation. Consequently, a successor regime's policy concern for addressing past odious debt will have to be weighted against a greater marginal effect of default on its reputation and access to future international credit.

While reputation sustains sovereign debt relations between parties that are primarily motivated by profit, what is the role of reputation when parties have other interests? The extensive literature devoted to sovereign debt, by and large, does not offer a comprehensive account of the range of different contractual relations that are

[72] Bolton and Skeel 2007, 87 referring to the General Theory of Second Best by Lispey and Lancaster 1956

encompassed by the term 'sovereign debt.' Although they all fall within the same umbrella heading, and have in common a promise to repay, beyond that the differ substantially in form and substance. The incentives and interests of the parties differ in each type of relationship, as does the role of reputation. Some relationships are characterized by arm's length transactions sustained by a debtor's reputation to repay. In others, the reputation mechanism is obstructed by outside factors such as hegemonic interests. Less transparent creditor-debtor exchanges also exist, where reputation is based not on whether a debtor repays, but on whether it cedes policy control. Still others are based more on dependency and control than on reputation at all. Accordingly, this is the focus of **Chapter 2** which takes a more extensive view of creditors who lend to sovereigns and a closer look at reputation in sovereign debt relations. Further, it looks at the implications of this analysis for odious debt and looks at whether and how odious debt stems from these different relationships.

Following the first two chapters which focus on the nature of the sovereign debtor-creditor relationship in its various forms, **Chapter 3** focuses on the general question of whether an ex ante approach or an ex post approach would be more suitable to tackle odious debt. Assuming that an international solution is desired, it addressed the trade offs involved in each approach. It draws from Shavell's seminal analysis of ex ante regulation versus ex post liability in the context of tort and applies it to the sovereign lending context and the risk of odious debt. Neither approach can completely eliminate the risk of odious debt. Efficient ex ante incentives are needed to prevent perverse incentives of both creditors and lenders and encourage responsible lending and debt management. Ex post mechanisms are needed when odious debt does occur. Finally, the loan sanctions proposal offered by Kremer and Jayachandran is considered.[73] Their approach, in effect, lies somewhere in between the ex post and ex ante approaches and is therefore interesting to examine in this respect.

Chapter 4 focuses on the rational argument that a solution to odious debt will not come about as a result of the benevolent interests of parties in international finance. Indeed, one of the reasons why the odious debt problem has not been addressed may be due to an unwillingness of the major actors to take action and drive change. Alternatively, it may be due to collective action problems at the international level. Furthermore, the opportunity costs of devoting efforts and political capital to addressing odious debt must not be underestimated. Accordingly, the drivers of change in international debt governance are analyzed. The chapter looks at the web of international economic governance that surrounds debt and looks at its role in shaping the current discourse on odious debt. Whether the debt regime as it stands will move towards addressing the problem of odious debt will largely depend on the actors that are capable to drive change within it. In this light, it examines the three main branches of players surrounding the odious debt cause, namely: the official sector (states and international organizations), NGOs devoted to debt issues, and the epistemic community, composed mainly of academics from the legal and economic fields. The

[73] Jayachandran and Kremer 2006

possibility of introducing odious debt within the context of debt renegotiations is considered. On the one hand, the widespread practice of renegotiation and the use of venues such as the Paris Club, as opposed to legal venues, may be one of the reasons international law regarding debt is relatively under-developed. On the other hand, the legal discourse, norms and precedents of debt governance are being shaped within the renegotiation context.

2 Reputation and Odious Debt

Any attempt to alter the status quo of sovereign debt relations must begin with a full understanding of it and the mechanisms that sustain it. The concept of odious debt essentially challenges the present international doctrine of state succession, which requires for the continuity of rights and obligations, including the obligation to assume debts, when there is a change in government. Before addressing the purported exception of odious debt, it is necessary to analyze the incentives that drive debtors to pay back their debts upon succession.

Accordingly, the first two sections of this Chapter begin by tracing back the traditional legal and economic rationales explaining why states repay their debts generally and upon succession more specifically. The former emphasizes the notions of state identity and personality as well as the classical theories of benefit and burden. Most importantly, the sanctity of contracts and duly acquired rights of creditors justify repayment. The latter stems from the axiom that unless default imposes costs on the debtor, not only will the debtor not pay back the debt, but the lender would not make the loan in the first place. The dominant view in the economics of sovereign debt is that the primary cost of default to the sovereign is the exclusion from future borrowing.

While both rationales are able to justify why states do repay their debts, their limitations lie in their lack of explanatory power to predict when and why, despite legal and economic incentives to repay, governments sometimes default. They further fail to explain why a government may choose to repay at one point in time, and default in another.

Consequently, the rest of this Chapter is devoted to addressing the limitations of the traditional rationales and obtaining a better understanding of the dynamics of sovereign debt relations, through insights from new reputation theories. It draws from the work of Michael Tomz, whose reputation model is applied to sovereign debt and that of Andrew Guzman, which is used to explain a state's behaviour in complying with international law. What these two models have in common is the fact that they allow for reputation change and assume incomplete information between parties in the international context. They both argue that a state's reputation in the eyes of observers is a function of its past behaviour as well as its current behaviour in context.

Against this background the dynamic reputation approach to sovereign debt is explained and odious debt is then placed within the reputation analysis. The last section goes on to address the role of law in sovereign debt relations and how it implicates reputation. The chapter concludes that a state's concern for its reputation in the sovereign debt context and its concern for its reputation with complying with international law pull it in the same direction towards repayment. Put differently, a debtor's decision to default on the basis of the purported doctrine of odious debt would have a negative impact on its reputation in both issue areas.

2.1 The Legal Approach

2.1.1 Legal Rationales to Succession of Obligations

Pacta Sund Servanda is one of the most widely accepted doctrines in international law and the foundational rule that treaties must be obeyed. It is the main legal rationale behind state succession of debt obligations.[74] Nevertheless, looking back at legal history and contemporary international relations theory, these show that there has constantly been a conflict between competing definitions of state and regime and the respective obligations upon succession. There have also been different interpretations of the 'sovereign' in sovereign debt, each having different implications on the succession of debt.[75] In effect, the debate over odious debts, which attempts to reconcile continuity and respect of legal agreements with equitable and moral considerations, has its roots here.

The concept of 'sovereign debt' and the notion of state were developed in the classical writings of Grotius and Pufendorf.[76] They moulded what is known today as the 'rule of succession in debt obligations' in international law. Their writings were in part shaped by the Roman law of inheritance and the generally accepted rule of universal succession of obligations.[77] Their theories brought forth legal rationales for such a rule which are still applied today. Before Grotius, the maintenance of public debts referred to debts of individual rulers and princes, as opposed to debts of nations, and had not been based on the conception of the modern state.[78] He developed the notion of state identity and argued that the state remains identical despite the

[74] The leading treaties are Feilchenfeld 1931; O'Connell 1967; Cheng 2006

[75] See Lienau 2008, 63

[76] Pufendorf 1967

[77] The concept of inheritance in civil law is a derivative of Roman law and states that the *heres* (appointed successor) acquires not only the single *res* but also the aggregate rights and liabilities *ius universitas*. See Craven 1998

[78] Feilchenfeld 1931, 30

immigration or emigration of its nationals and changes in the form of its government.[79] A change which is merely political does not affect the identity of the state and its fiscal liabilities as debtor. Today, this is referred to in law as the "legal personality" of the state, much like that of a domestic corporation which remains bound to its contractual obligations even as it management and board of director changes.[80]

Pufendorf later brought the 'Permanence of Burden' and 'Benefit' theories to support the rule of succession.[81] The former holds that the debtor state did not acquire debts in its capacity as such, but that the debts have their foundation in the fact that the debtor possessed certain assets. It follows then, that the debts must logically be passed on to each subsequent possessor of the assets. The benefit theory, in turn, argues that a state remains permanently liable for all the money which has been used for the benefit of the population.[82] Indeed, the root of the odious debt problem is found in this theory, as it implies that successive populations that did not benefit from the debt should not be liable to repay it.

Both Grotius' and Pufendorf's theories were considered as arguments which supported the continuity of obligations upon state succession, rather than exclusive rationales to it. They explicitly adhered to the sanctity of contracts and the duly acquired rights of creditors. They believed that countries ought to respect their debt contracts because creditors should not lose the acquired rights which they obtained from a lawful ruler.[83] The argument continues, even if some contracts may have been subject to moral objections, this does not affect their legal validity.

At this point, some clarification of terminology may be necessary. The classical writings of Grotius and Pufendorf did not explicitly differentiate between state and regime. Today, positivists define the two differently. State succession involves a change in the territory or international legal personality of the state.[84] At present there are no clear customary rules or multilateral treaties in force governing whether and when a successor state is responsible for the debts of its predecessor state. Scholars and jurists are divided on whether the "clean slate" approach or the "universal succession" approach is applicable.[85] State practice has also been inconsistent.

---

[79] Feilchenfeld 1931, 27

[80] Buchheit, Gulati et al. 2007, 4

[81] Pufendorf 1964, 1345-6

[82] See Buchheit, Gulati et al. 2007, 1224(explaining how the U.S. Property and Inheritance Laws reflect the benefit/burden theories) See also, RESTATEMENT OF PROPERTY 537 (1944)

[83] Feilchenfeld 1931, 30

[84] See Cheng 2007

[85] The clean slate approach argues that the new state is never bound by the obligations of the predecessor states. The universal succession approach, on the other hand, arues that the successor state is generally bound by the

In contrast to state succession, governmental succession involves a change in government and does not change the state's legal personality. While state succession is more contested, public international law is particularly strict when it comes to government succession.[86] Under positivistic international rules, a successor government is always responsible for the debts of its predecessor government.[87]

Buchheit et al. describe government debts in the sovereign context as 'congenital' and 'adhesive' in the sense that each generation of citizens inherits a responsibility to contribute towards repayment of the old debts merely by being born in the state.[88] They go on to argue that sovereign debts are also 'ineradicable' and it is these three factors considered together which makes for intergenerational conflict. This approach has roots in the "strictly statist" conception of the sovereign, which views states as a "unitary black box."[89] The implications of this approach to sovereign debt as well as foreign obligations in general, is that they remain the obligations of the state, regardless of changes in regime, the nature of the political form or uses of the proceeds of the loan.

However, there is a growing competing school of thought which conceives a more popular definition of the sovereign. It seeks to link a state's internal respect for democratic ideals and individual rights to the validity of its external, international actions.[90] This approach draws from agency theory in which the head of state is a representative of the interests of the population and it is the consent of the sovereign people which provides legitimacy to the state and authority for its external interactions.[91]

---

obligations of its predecessor state. Another indication that the rule is not clear is the Vienna Convention on Succession of State in respect of State Property, Archivesa and Debts of 1983, which has not yet been ratified

[86] See Feilchenfeld 1931; O'Connell 1967; Cheng 2006

[87] Cheng has argued that although positivists explicitly make the distinction between state and government succession, in practice, the definitions have been blurred. There is a wide and complex range of different types of successions including independence from colonial rule, fall of Soviet-style regimes and acquisition among many others and it is difficult to come up with a clear distinction. Cheng argues that both government and state succession should be justified or criticized on the same grounds and rationales. See Cheng 2006 Furthermore, Ernst Feilchenfeld (cited in King 2007, 648) argues that, with regards to addressing debt succession and odious debt, any distinction between state and government succession would be entirely arbitrary.

[88] Buchheit, Gulati et al. 2007, 1208

[89] Such an approach assumes the continuity of sovereign obligation across successive regimes and therefore mandates the payment of all debt, regardless of its political legitimacy. Conventional wisdom holds that this strictly statist conception of sovereignty is entirely consistent with a fully functioning sovereign credit market. See Lienau 2008

[90] As such, this approach rejects international legal positivism's separation of law from moral and political considerations. See Lienau 2008

[91] See DeMott 2007

2.1.2 Lack of Explanatory Power

Once authority is given to be bound by a treaty, the State is bound to respect it in accordance with the principle of pacta sund servanda[92] By definition, this principle applies to sovereign debt contracts. Indeed, pacta sund servanda and the rule of repayment are straightforward obligations under international law. The legal literature, however, does not provide clear guidance to determine when these obligations can breached.[93]

Therefore, in order to understand when and why states decide to repay their debts and when they do not, we must first address the main difference between law in the domestic and in the international context, and subsequently turn to economics. None of the traditional legal rationales for state succession in international law explicitly account for the fundamental difference between the domestic and international platforms of exchange; namely the lack of coercive third party enforcement in international law. Indeed, the fundamental characteristic of sovereign debt is the lack of contractual enforcement mechanisms analogous to those that exist at the level of domestic corporate debt. Litigation is unusual and often ineffective and creditors do not have strong legal enforcement means at their disposal to secure repayment from the borrowers they lend to.

Without a global Leviathan and effective third party enforcement, how then are sovereign debt relations sustained? And what, if any, is the role of international law if not to enforce contracts between parties? How does the law influence a regime's decision to comply with its inherited obligations upon succession? Before proceeding to analyse how new reputation theories answer these questions, the next section first provides a brief overview of the traditional economic approach explaining sovereign debt.

2.2 The Economic Approach

2.2.1 Why Does Sovereign Debt Exist?

The economics of sovereign debt builds on the following axiom: unless default imposed costs on the debtor, not only will the debtor not pay the debt, but the lender will not make the loan in the first place. Accordingly, economists have suggested two main explanations to sovereign debt; the reputation theory and the enforcement theory.

---

[92] Article 26, The Vienna Convention on the Law of Treaties May 23,1969

[93] For a taxonomy of sovereign debt See Buchheit, Gulati et al. 2007, 6-18

2.2.1.1 The Reputation Theory

In their seminal contribution, Eaton and Gersovitz were one of the first to address the question of why creditors lend to governments, given limited formal enforcement mechanisms at their disposal.[94] They argued that the primary cost of default to the sovereign is the exclusion from future borrowing. Most countries need to borrow repeatedly, as opposed to only once, to meet ongoing domestic demands such as economic development, national defence and domestic consumption. Their theory is based on the assumption that national economies are cyclical and that people prefer to consume evenly across cycles.[95] Countries then decide to borrow on the downward cycle to fund consumption and repay the loans with returns generated on the upward cycle. Investors adopt a history-contingent strategy. They penalize countries that default by barring them from new loans or by charging them higher interest rates in subsequent years.[96] Consequently, a sovereign debt market can exist even if creditors have no direct control over debtors and their only means of retaliating in the event of default is through the denial of future credit. For this to be true, some assumptions need to hold, namely that default entails permanent exclusion from credit markets and that borrowing is the only means available for debtor to ensure against output shocks.[97]

While Eaton and Gersovitz' reputation theory subsequently became the dominant view in economics and was highly influential, it has been criticized from distinct angles. One line of criticism focuses on their first assumption; that default entails permanent exclusion from credit markets. Theoretically, the problem lies in the fact that a lending equilibrium sustained by the threat of a permanent embargo on future lending is not 'renegotiation proof.' Both parties – creditors and debtors – are generally worse off than in a situation where lending resumes. In other words, following a default, both parties potentially benefit from reaching an agreement involving positive lending. Intuitively, if such an agreement is anticipated, then this undermines the threat of exclusion which was sustaining the lending relationship in the first place.[98] Until recently, research did not support the notion that investors adopt a history contingent strategy when lending to governments. On the contrary, several studies have found that, by and large, international investors have ignored history.[99]

Vinod Aggarwal argues that one of the main reasons that investors do not pay attention to the historical behaviour of debtors is ignorance. He states that, "almost

---

[94] Eaton and Gersovitz 1981

[95] In Eaton and Gersovitz's model, the insurance motive comes through concativity in the utility function, that is, risk aversion: the country prefers smooth consumption to choppy consumption.

[96] Tomz 2007, 5

[97] Eaton and Gersovitz 1981, 32 Sturzenegger and Zettelmeyer 2006

[98] See Kletzer 1994

[99] Tomz 2007, 5,6

without exception, modern bankers have made mistakes as a result of their unfamiliarity with the turbulent history of international lending. Few lenders in the 1970s, for example, knew that sovereign countries had frequently defaulted on their debt payments in the past."[100] Other scholars emphasize the role of irrational exuberance on the part of investors, who "are drawn into speculative manias and, without systematically weighing the consequences, have lent to countries with records of default."[101]

Furthermore, the assumption that default entails permanent exclusion from the credit markets suffers from another theoretical problem pertaining to inter-creditor coordination. For a creditor to completely bar a defaulting debtor from the international credit markets or punish it via higher interest rates, it would need the cooperation of a majority of current and future lenders around the world. In the years where syndicated bank lending dominated the market, it was relatively easy for banks to collude in punishing defaults.[102] For most of financial history, however, the supply of sovereign credit has come from tens of thousands of scattered investors who are not easily coordinated and who lack incentives to coalesce into a punishment cartel. It is unclear why profit seeking bondholders and banks would collaborate in punishing a government for defaulting on someone else's loans.

Consequently, given that permanent exclusion from the credit markets is implausible, that creditors can ignore history and that renegotiations and coordination problems exist, several questions remain; why do sovereigns ever repay their debts? Furthermore, why do creditors lend to sovereigns in the first place? A second main strand of literature has focused on the enforcement theory to answer these questions.

2.2.1.2 The Enforcement Theory

The enforcement theory, offered by Bolow and Rogoff,[103] stems from their criticism of Eaton and Gersovitz' assumption that borrowing from international markets is the only way countries can smooth consumption in response to shocks in output. They argue that other ways are possible, including storing output, purchasing insurance, or investing a portion of one's wealth abroad so that it can be recurred to in times of need. Essentially, a sovereign faces a choice at the end of an upward cycle, after having incurred debt in its previous downward cycle. It can either repay the debt, or it can default and invest the capital. If an investment opportunity is available, it would prove rational for the sovereign to default and obtain a higher return available from

[100] Aggarwal 1996, 15

[101] Tomz 2007, 6

[102] See for example Wright 2002

[103] Bulow and Rogoff 1989

saving and investing than that which is available from borrowing and repaying.[104] This would decrease a state's dependence of international credit for insurance purposes.

The implication from this theory is that even if a sovereign needs a future source of finance, it may still rationally repudiate its debts. Consequently, because the threat of exclusion from access to international credit is not sufficient, it follows that sovereign debt cannot be sustained on pure reputation enforcement and creditors must have other means to inflict cost on the debtor to enforce their claims.

Some scholars have focused on the role of direct punishments for non repayment in sustaining creditor-debtor relationships. They have highlighted the role of non financial, "extrinsic" sanctions which involve punishment on an issue distinct from the one that sparked the dispute.[105] This is in contrast to the "intrinsic" sanctions involved in the reputation theory which involves punishment in the same issue area in which the borrower cheated in the first place.

One such punishment, highlighted by Bulow and Rogoff, can come from the creditor's ability to seize a debtor's foreign assets in case of non repayment. They admit that this ability is limited because defaulting sovereigns do not leave any obvious assets around for creditors to grab. However, they argue that the exercise of international creditor evasion carries indirect costs. Even if these are small in relation to their GNP, they are still large enough compared to the defaulted interest and consequently render repudiation undesirable.[106]

Other related extrinsic sanctions can come through military intervention or through trade sanctions. The former option has been the focus of the "gunboat diplomacy" hypothesis which involves the use of arms to extract repayment. Although empirical evidence is mixed,[107] this mode of enforcement has been argued by some to have been imposed in roughly one third of cases of sovereign default between 1870 and 1913.[108] The latter option involves a tactical link between finance and trade. If a debtor defaults on its debt, a creditor, with the help of its home government, may retaliate by imposing an embargo on commercial relations with the defaulting state. Theoretically, should be particularly relevant and effective today as globalisation has made countries dependent on each other through various relationships in different

[104] Buchheit, Gulati et al. 2007, 15

[105] Lipson 1981, 630

[106] Bulow and Rogoff 1989, 43-47

[107] For a review of empirical studies See Tomz 2007, 7

[108] See Mitchener 2005 (cited in King 2007, 11-12) The issue of using force to enforce sovereign debts les to the formulation of the Calvo Doctrine in 1868 (the assertion by the Argentinian jurist, Carlos Calvo, that there was no right in international law for one state to use military intervention to collect on private pecuniary claims against another state) and the Drago Doctrine in 1902 (stating that the issuance of foreign debt is a sovereign act and that the use of military force to collect upon it was not justified in international law or the domestic law of nations such as the United States). For a discussion, See King 2007, 12

issue areas. Although issue linkage between trade and finance is "widely accepted" amongst economist theorists,[109] surprisingly, the existing empirical literature on the subject is inconclusive.[110] Moreover, trade sanctions theoretically suffer from the same collective action problem existent in the reputation theory. A single country, unless it is a significant trade partner of the country being sanctioned, would not be able to exclude a defaulting borrower from international trade. Finally, another limitation is offered by Bratton and Gulati who argue that it is not clear why lenders would want to interfere with the trade of defaulting debtors, especially in distress defaults, as this would only prolong the distress and lower/delay any future repayment prospects.[111]

2.3 The Comeback of Reputation

The two classical theses suggest that incentives to repay sovereign debt might include a combination of credit market incentives and concerns about retaliation in the form of trade or other non financial sanctions. Pure credit market incentives may not be as critical as had been initially assumed by Eaton and Gersovitz, and the general point made by Bulow and Rogoff that the importance of access to external borrowing is diminished if governments have other ways of transferring income across time, is valid.

Nevertheless, reputation theories not only continue to be influential in explaining the dynamics of sovereign debt and cooperation in the international realm more generally, but they have recently made a comeback. This section highlights how reputation has been brought back to the forefront of theories explaining sovereign debt[112] and cooperation in the international context, more generally. This sets the stage for the next section which places odious debt within the reputation analysis.

2.3.1 Incomplete Information and Changing Preferences

One of the key premises that traditional reputation theories are based on is the assumption that lenders know all of the relevant characteristics of individual borrowers. In other words, lending takes place under conditions of complete information and creditors know the type of debtor that they are confronting. [113] As shown by Grossman and van Hyuck and, more recently Tomz, this assumption does

[109] Tomz 2007, 9

[110] Tomz August, 2004

[111] Bratton 2004, 16

[112] This Chapter focuses on how reputation sustains the private market for sovereign debt and deals with relationships between sovereigns and profit maximizing creditors. For a discussion on the distinct incentives of different creditors who lend to sovereigns and how reputation is affected in their relationships See Bonilla 2009b

[113] See Eaton and Gersovitz 1981 and Aggarwal 1996

not always hold in practice. Investors have ways to learn about a particular debtor's *ability to pay,* such as economic indicators, but they ultimately lack information on its *willingness to pay* which depends on a debtor's preferences. These preferences are unobservable to investors. Consequently, investors must make loans with only partial information about a key variable in the investment equation.

A debtor's willingness to pay depends on its preferences. The traditional reputation models generally assume that the preferences of parties are static.[114] While this standard assumption in economics is suitable for private, profit maximizing bondholders, it is less realistic and useful when dealing with governments, whose incentives are influenced by a wide range of public choice considerations.[115] Tomz is one of the few to have included this assumption into a rational economic model.[116] He does not explain how preferences change, but allows for the possibility that they can change. Similarly, Guzman has followed with a reputation model explaining states' behaviour in the international context which, using an institutional approach, seeks to reconcile the tension present in the analysis of state behaviour. This tension involves the choice between including relevant public choice issues which are determinant in a state's decision making process, and creating a general model with useful predictions. He resolves this tension by including domestic political issues in an ad hoc way to provide explanatory power to the behaviour of states when they are most relevant. [117]

The specific context of sovereign debt is indeed one where domestic politics are extremely relevant and can therefore provide much explanatory power with regards to states' decision to repay or default. Recent research by both Frieden and Tomz shows that a country's external debt can be a source of tension domestically, especially in

[114] For a review see Mailath and Samuelson 2006

[115] The relevance of public choice considerations on the behaviour and decisions of states have traditionally been included in liberal and public choice theories who relax the assumption that the state is the primary actor. For a discussion See Guzman 2008, 16-22 For a prominent example of liberalist approach Slaughter 2004 (arguing that the state is "disaggregated", in the sense that informal networks of government officials engage in international governance.

[116] A small economic literature exists which explores the consequences of changing types. See Cole, Dow et al. 1995; Mailath and Samuelson 2001

[117] See Guzman 2008, 129 Guzman argues that the economic analysis of law argues that the inclusion of public choice concerns is useful as a form of positive analysis in a specific context, but are less helpful in general models. He adopts an ad hoc way to incorporate domestic political issues, which allows both a functioning predictive model to exist and allows consideration of domestic issues where these are most relevant.

The discussion of how the problem of modelling domestic activities intersects with the study of international law is not new. The practical outcome has been, by and large, for analyses to treat the state as a unitary actor. For a detailed discussion on how one can handle public choice issues when writing in international law See Guzman 2002, 900-04

times of crises in developing countries, because debt repayment creates economic winners and losers.[118]

A government's preferences about debt are likely to shift from regime to regime, due to factors such as; shifts in pro or anti debt coalitions, elections or coups d'état, among others. Consequently, these political factors can determine how leaders balance debt repayment against other priorities and in turn, whether they are willing to elevate foreign debt above other domestic concerns.[119]

Theories of reputation that include asymmetric information and political change help explain why countries with favourable reputations sometimes default, and conversely, why countries with bad reputations suddenly decide to settle with their foreign creditors. In contrast, with static preferences, it is difficult to explain why a long standing player would begin defecting during good times, and why a previously intransigent defaulter would make great sacrifices to settle its debts.[120] It follows that one of the implications from changing payoffs and preferences is that a state's decision to comply or not comply with an international obligation at one point in time, does not mean that it will do so at another point in time. Accordingly, it also implies that a state's reputation can change and this, in turn, allows for both market exit and market re entry for borrowers.

Russia is a case in point. As its preferences changed, its reputation changed in the eyes of investors and at one point in history led to the exclusion of Russia from the international credit markets, and later, to its re entry. Following the Revolution, the new Bolshevik government repudiated the debts accumulated by the tsarist government on the grounds that they were illegitimate and the personal debts of the tsar.[121] By repudiating on their debt, the Soviet leaders shattered their long standing good reputation[122] and investors refrained from providing new flows of credit.

Interestingly, the grounds for default, in effect, are those of the odious debt argument. However, this is irrelevant to reputation theories about sovereign debt. Default, regardless of the reason for justifying it, is interpreted as an indication that the regime in place is not willing to elevate external debt above other policy considerations. Similarly, Guzman's theory attributes this behaviour to lower expected

---

[118] See Frieden 1988; Frieden 1989; Frieden 1991; Tomz 2005

[119] Tomz 2007, 15

[120] P. 12 the traditional theories explain default as a result of exogenous shocks. Still, they fail to explain break downs of cooperation and defaults during good times.

[121] Guzman 2008, 89

[122] Before this, Russia had already fallen out with Germany, one of its major creditors at the time. See for example, Kindleberger 1984, 226 - 228 This is consistent with the arguments made by some scholars, See for example Guzman 2008 arguing that, although not completely separate, a state's reputation can be separated by contracting partner and dyad.

payoffs from repayment, an indication that maintaining a good reputation was not considered essential to the regime.[123]

Russia's payoffs and concern for its reputation in the sovereign debt arena, were much different upon the collapse of the Soviet Union in 1991. The new Russian government announced that it would honour existing Soviet debt. This was a costly signal to the international financial community, that the new Russian government valued its reputation. Contrary to the Bolshevik regime in 1917, developing financial ties with the west and improving its reputation were important to Russia. [124]

2.3.2 Repayment Record and Diminishing Returns

A debtor's willingness to pay is unobservable to investors who must infer it through a learning mechanism based on the information that is available to them. Including asymmetric information transforms the standard repeat play model into a dynamic model of reputation where investors continually update their beliefs about the type of government they are confronting. Put differently, investors engage in a Bayesian updating of their estimates of a borrowing state's reputation. Consistent with economic theories, the new reputation models assume that investors interpret information in rational ways.

One important source of information that investors consider when developing judgments about a potential borrower's reputation is its past repayment record. Contrary to the traditional reputation theories which argued that investors do not adopt a history contingent approach, new studies, such as Tomz' empirical work over three centuries, find that investors look at a debtor's behaviour and past record of repayment when developing beliefs about its reputation.[125] Similarly, Guzman's reputation model of state decision making in the international context, argues that observers use a state's past behaviour to predict its future behaviour.[126]

Investors will have little or no information to base themselves on when evaluating the reputation of new states, or states with new regimes. Accordingly, Tomz finds evidence that new borrowers with no past repayment record for investors to base their beliefs on, have historically faced higher yields because they had not yet demonstrated

---

[123] In his capitulation of the history of Soviet Russia, Carr explains that in the early days of the regime, the Bolsheviks expected a communist revolution to overwhelm Europe in the wake of World War I. See Carr 1985 Faced with the expectation of a new international order taking over in the near future, Soviet Russia's preference with regards to repaying its external debts to its Western creditors changed. Its ability to pay did not change, but its willingness to pay did as a result of its expected future benefits from repayment being lower. See Guzman 2008, 89

[124] Guzman 2008, 89 The media at the time interpreted Russia's declaration to pay back Soviet-era debt as a sign that Russia wanted to restore relationships with the West See for example, Conway August 22, 2006; Finn August 22nd, 2006

[125] Tomz 2007

[126] Guzman 2008, 73

their willingness to honour debt contracts. The premium that investors demanded is a result of their uncertainty regarding a new borrower's type.[127] If the borrowing country then acts consistently over a period of time, such as by repaying its debts punctually, the process will be subject to seasonal effects and each additional act of repayment will enhance its reputation by a smaller amount.[128] Guzman's model concurs. It shows that because observers have only weak priors about a new state's willingness to comply, each individual compliance decision has a larger impact on a new state's reputation. Subsequently, the process is subject to diminishing returns.[129]

2.3.3 Context

Besides looking a debtor's record of repayment, investors also look at the context of a state's decision to repay or default. Grossman and Van Huyck's economic model first showed how the same decision to default could have different reputation consequences for a debtor, depending on whether it was considered as an "excusable default" or a "strategic default" by investors. The former involves a default in bad economic times or due to an exogenous shock, while the latter type of default is considered opportunistic because it is not due to factors affecting a debtor's ability to pay. They showed that debtors whose defaults were judged as excusable were able to regain market access faster than debtors who defaulted for strategic reasons.[130] Tomz' recent model takes into consideration whether states repay and default during "adverse conditions" or "favourable conditions."[131] Finally, Guzman's reputation model in the context of international law also differentiates between what he calls "non reputational" and "reputational payoffs."[132]

Although the models differ from each other,[133] they all imply that a debtor's reputation is not based purely on whether a debtor repays or defaults. Rather, investors care about the circumstances that a state faces when deciding to behave in one way or another and infer its reputation type, in part, from the context of its decision. In effect,

---

[127] Tomz 2007, 90-93

[128] Tomz 2007, 19,20, 27,28, 40-47,

[129] Guzman 2008, 90

[130] Other reputational models followed in other fields, such as Mercer's social psychology approach who models a state's reputation for resolve and similarly considers both a state's "situational" and "dispositional" attributes at the time that it makes its decision. See Mercer 1996

[131] Tomz 2007, 19

[132] Guzman 2008, 74-77

[133] Grossman and Van Huyck argue that debt contracts implicitly take these types of contingencies into account. Guzman's reputational theory also argues that agreements implicitly include the expectations by parties that a state will not comply in circumstances such as war, for example. Guzman 2008, 78-82 See also Alesina 1988 Although similar, Tomz's model argues that investors judge a how a state responds to similar unfavourable conditions, such as exogenous shocks and this implicates their reputation.

the context provides investors with a signal about the difficulty of a debtor's decision and this allows investors to differentiate between different debtor reputation types as well as to infer when these change.[134] When speaking about context, the rest of this chapter will refer to Tomz's model which argues that investors judge how different states respond to similar unfavourable economic conditions, such as exogenous shocks, and this implicates their reputation.

Reputation theories, therefore, continue to be the most influential in explaining sovereign debt and international cooperation more generally. Building on the seminal work of Eaton and Gersovitz, recent models, such as that of Tomz, include new assumptions, namely changing reputation types and incomplete information. Accordingly, reputation is able to go beyond explaining why cooperation comes about in the optimal equilibrium and predict when cooperation can break down and how it can be restored.

2.4 Implications for Odious Debt

Against this background, this section will place odious debt within the context of the reputation analysis. In doing so, it will draw insights as to how reputation concerns give incentives to new regimes to repay their inherited debts generally, whether odious or not. It will look at the two factors that investors look at when developing their beliefs about a debtor's reputation and analyse how odious debt can affect them. These are past repayment record and context respectively.

2.4.1 Repayment Record

As discussed in the previous section, the process whereby investors look at a debtor's past actions to develop beliefs about its reputation is subject to seasonal effects. Put differently, the signals offered to investors from a debtor's behaviour are subject to diminishing returns. Therefore, all else equal, a new state that is concerned about its reputation in the sovereign debt arena has a higher propensity to repay its debt.

New regimes, if drastically different from the past regimes in the country, will also be "new" in the eyes of investors and there will be uncertainty with regards to its

---

[134] For example, Tomz classifies debtors into three types, each assigned a different value to maintaining good relations with creditors ; stalwarts, fair-weathers and lemons. "Stalwart governments benefit the most from future access to foreign capital, relative to the short term costs of repayment. They stand ready to service their debts in good times and bad. Lemons, on the other hand, find the costs of keeping faith with creditors too much to bear. They default in bad times and may even do so when economic conditions are favourable. Finally, fair weather governments have intermediate preferences. The net value they attach to future loans is sufficient to motivate repayment in good times but not during bad ones. Investors further understand the possibility of political change: a government in office today may have different preferences from its predecessors. At each moment, investors hold beliefs about whether they are dealing with a stalwart, a fair-weather, or a lemon, and revise their beliefs through a process of contextual inference." See Tomz 2007, 224

reputation type.[135] For example, Mexico's Institutional Revolutionary Party (PRI) ruled the country for more than 70 years, until the National Action Party (PAN) replaced it in 2000. Although the Mexican state did not change, the change in political party represented a significant transformation. Another example is arguably that of Chile's Pinochet, whose regime succeeded that of Allende by way of coup d'état and represented a drastic change. Consequently, new states, or substantially new regimes, have more at stake when they make compliance decisions. Any individual action will have a larger marginal impact on their reputation.[136]

This of course applies to all new states and new regimes generally, regardless of whether the debt that they inherited is odious or not. All else equal, although there are certainly moral reasons to want to repudiate odious debt upon succession, these will have to be weighed against a higher marginal impact of non repayment on reputation in the sovereign debt context.

In contrast, the decision of old states who have acted consistently for long periods of time will have an ever smaller effect on their reputation. If subsequent regimes are not drastically different from each other, particularly with regards to their view on international finance, each new regime will not be building a new reputation on its own. Rather, investors will judge it on the basis of the past repayment record of the state as a whole. Indeed, whether a democratic or a republican party is in power in the United States may make a difference with regards to issues such as the enlargement of Free Trade Agreements in the Americas or its role in the Middle East conflict, but its behaviour and reputation in the realm of international finance will likely stay intact. Therefore, if the regime in power continues to honour its external debt obligations, it will not improve the reputation of the state, but merely maintain it. However, if the successor regime defaults, investors would infer that this action signals a change in preferences and a decrease in its reputation.

A successor regime may inherit both odious debt and a good reputation from the previous government. This would be the case if the previous government borrowed from abroad to finance repression or looting, but nevertheless maintained good financial relations with its creditors and regularly paid back its debt, at least until before it left office, leaving a portion of unpaid debt to the successor government. The successor regime, therefore, would be obliged to repay its inherited debts, if it wanted to maintain the creditworthy reputation of the state.

Conversely, a successor regime can also inherit both odious debt and a poor reputation. Indeed, to the extent that odious activities such as genocide negatively affect the economy, it is likely that a successor regime that inherits odious debt also inherits an economy in shackles. At the same time, due to a poor reputation in the financial markets, it will also inherit strained relations with investors and an exclusion

---

[135] Guzman 2008, 106

[136] Guzman 2008, 90

from the international credit markets. Investors will be very reluctant to extend any credit to this country because of its poor economic condition and its poor reputation. If the successor regime wants to improve the reputation of the state, it will have to engage in costly actions that signal to investors that its reputation type has changed, such as repaying its outstanding debt and compensating investors. This signal would be particularly costly if repayment occurs in difficult economic times.

Evidently, rebuilding a reputation is difficult and takes time, and it may prove too costly or infeasible for the successor regime. Indeed, it is because signals are costly and hard to imitate that they are effective in signalling. Conversely, the regime could engage in what game theory refers to as "cheap talk" and declare its intention to improve its economy, settle its relations with foreign creditors and repay its debt, while setting out a time plan. It is therefore sending a signal by which it can be held accountable by investors.

In summary, new states and new regimes have strong incentives to repay their inherited debt, whether odious or not, because the act of repayment has a high marginal impact on their reputation in international finance all else equal. Successor regimes which inherit their state's reputation can maintain it by acting consistently. Conversely, they have the power to either shatter or improve the state's reputation by acting radically different.

A successor regime which is concerned about its reputation in international finance will therefore have incentives to repay its inherited debt, including odious debt. Only successor regimes who value other competing policy concerns more than reputation, will default. The next subsection discusses this further by looking at the relevance of context.

2.4.2 Context

A borrower's reputation in the eyes of investors is a function of its behaviour, past and present, as well as the context of its behaviour. Creditors care about factors beyond repayment and default and seek to obtain contextual inferences about whether a state's decision is a reflection of its ability to pay, or its willingness to pay. As discussed earlier, investors tend to judge a debtor's ability to pay based on its economic situation, which is observable. This can include knowledge about a borrower's economic resources, as well as earnings from international trade and level of outstanding debt as well as its GDP. Together, these provide an indication of the borrower's economic capacity. Investors will also be able to observe any adverse exogenous shocks that can affect a government's ability to repay. These can be economic shocks such as changes in the prices of tradable goods or in the international interest rate, or natural shocks such as droughts and hurricanes.[137] Different

[137] Investors may not have an exact measure of a debtor's ability to pay, but what's important is that it is what investors use to make their judgment. Ultimately, because it is investors who judge a debtor's reputation, what matters is how they interpret a debtor's ability to pay based on the available information.

governments respond to exogenous shocks and a low ability to pay in different ways, depending on their preferences and the value that they accord to their reputation. They could, for example, increase taxes. A debtor's preferences are not easily observable, and the economic context, therefore, provides signals to investors about them. In effect, investors look at how different borrowers respond to similar economic circumstances. This information is then used by investors to determine a borrower's specific reputation type.

In each period that investors judge a debtor's actions, they observe the actual payment, ($P = q \times A$) and the economic context of the payment, which is its ability to pay (A). Therefore, they are able to infer the amount the debtor is willing to pay, ($q \in [0, 1]$).

If a debtor who has constantly only paid during favourable economic times, (when A is high), suddenly decides to pay during adverse economic times (when A is low), it is engaging in a costly signal that indicates to investors that its reputation has improved. As analysis in the economics of contracts tells us, the more costly a signal, the more effective it is. A signal must be cheap enough for the sender to decide to proceed with it, but expensive enough so that the target updates its prior beliefs.

To acquire and maintain the highest type of reputation, a borrower must repay at all times, whatever the value of A, in both favourable and adverse economic circumstances.

2.4.3 Default and odious debt

What happens when a debtor defaults on its inherited debt on the grounds that it was odious? In 1917, when the Bolshevik government defaulted on similar grounds, investors did not pay much attention as to *why* it decided to default, and instead focused on the fact that it defaulted and the economic context at the time. Put differently, investors observed actual repayment which was zero ($p = 0$), they observed the country's economic ability to pay (A), which was high, and inferred that the amount it was willing to pay (q) was low. They compared this to its past behaviour and concluded that its reputation type had changed, and was lower. Taking the recent default by Ecuador as an example, investors seem to not have become more susceptible to the odious debt argument almost a century later.

Ecuador's Rafael Correa essentially used the odious debt argument when he fulfilled a promise made during his presidential campaign to default on past debts which were considered "illegal" and "illegitimate." On November 15th, 2008 his government delayed a $30.6 million interest payment on part of its foreign debt of $10 million. Five days later, it released the report a committee which was set to audit the country's debt contracts between 1976 and 2006. The committee said it found widespread evidence of malfeasance, particularly in three sets of bonds with a total value of 3.9 billion.[138] While the audit and Correa's government focused on the odious debt argument, investors focused more on whether the economic situation of the country justified default, which most argued that it did not. At the time, *The Economist* wrote, "It is hardly as if the government cannot pay now. The public debt amounts to only 21% of GDP, and until recently the government was flushed with oil revenues." Claudio Loser, the former director of the International Monetary Fund's western hemisphere department concurred, "The financial need wasn't so great that it was forced to declare default."[139] Moody's Vice President Gabriel Torres concurred, "Despite the drop in oil prices, the decision not to pay a $31 million interest payment due on its external debt was a political one as Ecuador has ample financial resources and the payment dues was very small since"[140]

Ecuador's decision to default on its debt, despite economic circumstances that allowed it to pay it back, has hurt its reputation. Although the default was followed by a relatively smooth repurchase of 91% of the defaulted bonds – at 35% of face value – Ecuador remains locked out of voluntary capital markets.[141] Igor Arsenin, an emerging market strategist at Credit Suisse Group in New York stated that "the default, while reducing Ecuador's debt load, was still a mistake because Correa won't be able to sell bonds in foreign markets for the foreseeable future."[142] One of the reasons the repurchase was so successful, is because the value of the bonds had decreased to a third of their value in the markets. Indeed, there was suspicion that Correa purposefully used the odious debt argument and default to drive down the value of the bonds.[143]

The justification for default based on the grounds that the past debts were "illegal" and "illegitimate" was interpreted as opportunistic. Some commentators described the odious debt argument as "ideologically driven"[144] and "a ridiculous ideology."[145] The Ecuador Bondholders Group, commenting on the matter, "Some of us have less than a year since we bought these Global Bonds, we trusted in the Ecuadorian economy knowing very well that compared to other countries their debt was quite low. Ecuador being a land full of resources we never thought that they would put their own economic future at risk just to make a political point." In 2010, S&P rates Ecuador

[138] Can pay, might not November 27th, 2008

[139] Kueffner December 12th, 2008

[140] Moody's December 22nd, 2008

[141] Ecuador's winning strategy June 17th, 2009

[142] Pimentel June 16th, 2009

[143] Can pay, might not November 27th, 2008

[144] Can pay, might not November 27th, 2008

[145] Pimentel June 16th, 2009

CCC+, seven levels below investment grade and the second-lowest in the Western hemisphere. According to the director of sovereign ratings at S&P, the country's rating is in part based on question about its "willingness to pay debt."[146]

While investors abroad and domestically have reacted negatively to it, Correa's decision to default was very popular with the population at large, especially the poor. The odious debt argument appeared to be part of a larger populist agenda that made Correa win the Presidency by a landslide and subsequently got him re elected. It is unclear whether Correa's decision to default was based on an honest concern to address the odiousness of Ecuador's past debts, or a means to increase his political popularity. Most likely, it is both. Regardless, what is clear is that he valued other policy concerns higher than maintaining good relations with his external creditors. The decision to default provided a signal to investors that the country no longer held external debt above competing domestic concerns. This signal is particularly strong, given that Ecuador found itself in favourable conditions, where the economic costs of repayment were low.

2.4.4 Repayment and odious debt

The literature on odious debt generally cites Nelson Mandela's government which succeeded the apartheid era in South Africa as an example of a regime which inherited odious debt. Indeed, Nelson Mandela inherited debt whose proceeds were used, in part, to repress the black majority in his country. Unlike Correa in Ecuador, however, Nelson Mandela's government actively disassociated itself from the calls of NGOs and civil activist groups, both at the domestic and international level, to repudiate the debt that it inherited from the apartheid regime on moral grounds. In its official response to lawsuits against foreign multinationals and banks which were alleged to collaborating in crimes against Black South Africans during the apartheid, justice minister Penuell Maduna stated that;

> "We are not supporting the claims for individual reparations.
>
> We are talking to those very same companies named in the
>
> lawsuits about investing in post-apartheid South Africa.
>
> The focus is on getting those companies to keep investing in
>
> South Africa to benefit the entire population as a whole."[147]

It had several reasons to do so. On the one hand, Mandela's majority elected government represented a significant transformation from its predecessor regime and

---

[146] See Business Week, "Ecuador Default 'Clear and Present Danger' S&P Says Update 1)" January 28, 2010 http://www.businessweek.com/news/2010-01-28/ecuador-bond-default-a-clear-and-present-danger-s-p-says.html

[147] S. Africa Shuns Apartheid Lawsuits November 27, 2002

investors were therefore judging it, in part, as a new regime. Its decision to repay or default would therefore have a strong impact on its new reputation. The editorial page of The Economist was very clear as to what it considered would be the consequences for South Africa if it repudiated its apartheid era debt; "(South Africa's) credit rating would be wrecked as it came to be lumped with other deadbeats. Foreign investors would be deterred and South Africa would have to pay more for future borrowing."[148]

On the other hand, besides establishing its reputation as a new regime, the new South African government also sought to differentiate itself from the behaviour of the apartheid regime which had gained a reputation as a global pariah generally and from its reputation in the sovereign debt context specifically when it entered a partial debt standstill in the mid 80s.[149] The decision by Mandela's regime to repay in rather unfavourable conditions sent a costly signal to investors and marked a change with the past. A statement by the South African Government upon making the final debt repayment from the debt standstill notes that it, "....marks the end of an era and the elevation of the South African credit."

In summary, investors observe whether any exogenous shocks affected the debtor's capacity to pay and from this they infer its willingness to pay. Justifying default on odious debt grounds is interpreted by investors as a claim that the debtor cares more about redressing past grievances than it does about its future borrowing prospects. The reason for default is not in itself important, but the economic context at the time is. Putting odious debt, or any other policy concern, above repayment during good economic times is considered graver than during bad economic times.

2.5 Insights from the Economic Analysis of International Law

Amidst the different and complex payoffs that a state faces at any given point in time, concerns about its reputation in the financial realm provide it with an incentive to repay its debts. If sovereign debt relations are mainly sustained by reputation, what, then, is the role of law in the sovereign debt context? Differently put, does the law have a role in the enforcement of sovereign debt contracts? This is the focus of this section, which argues that the law indeed plays a role in enforcement, by implicating a state's reputation. The law provides a marginal pull to repay debt, even when there may be strong reasons not to, such as its odious character.

2.5.1 The Role of Law in the International Context

The fundamental difference between the domestic and international platforms of exchange is their respective enforcement mechanisms. Contract theorists recognize a distinction between the formal and informal enforcement of contracts. The former

---

[148] South Africa's Debt: Unforgivable April 24th, 1999

[149] "South Africa Makes Final Debt Repayment in Debt Standstill Net" September 3d, 2001

involves enforcement of contracts by courts, while the latter involves enforcement of contracts through reputation and similar non legal mechanisms. This distinction is relatively clear cut in the domestic context, but not so in the international context.[150] While international courts and forums exist, and some scholars have argued that odious debt claims could be brought before them,[151] without a world government or a global Leviathan, there is no analogy to the domestic court, with its power of coercion.

Therefore, analyzing international law through the lens of domestic law is not only inadequate, but the comparison often undermines the function of international law, as it deems it ineffective in comparison. Gottlieb was one of the first scholars to recognize the limitations of the traditional analysis of international law.[152] He viewed international law, not as ineffective, but rather as providing for much explanatory power regarding the dynamics of relational contracts with no coercive third party enforcement. Since Gottlieb, many scholars, including many from the law and economics literature, have addressed the role of law in the international context.

Dunoff and Trachtman argue that international law agreements mainly serve to determine the information that will be exchanged in negotiations once breach has taken place.[153] The information exchanged, in turn, affects the bargaining power of parties during negotiations. As Gottlieb explains, "In sustained and inextricable relations, a principal use of contracts is to provide the basis for renegotiations once a defective performance occurs."[154] He goes on to explain that loan agreements are nothing more than worst case scenarios. In practice, creditors do not often sue, or seek litigation as a first recourse. He also argued that a legal agreement will prevent a party to the agreement from asserting in good faith that it is at liberty to terminate it or modify it unilaterally.

It is this last argument by Gottlieb which this section focuses on. It highlights the fact that merely the act of entering into an agreement and making a promise can have important implications and can implicate a state's reputation. Indeed, this is one of the main insights from Guzman's recent reputation model explaining why states comply

---

[150] However, some scholars argue that this distinction also exists in the international arena. For example, Stephan and Scott argue that "informal enforcement" of international law is when states comply with international law because they fear retaliation from the victim of breach or they seek to avoid acquiring a reputation for disregarding international commitments. "Formal enforcement", in turn, is when an independent tribunal orders a state that has violated international law to come into compliance or engage in remedial action such as paying reparations. They classify the ICJ, the WTO's Dispute Settlement Mechanism with other forms of informal enforcement, and they consider the ICC and NAFTA review tribunals and domestic courts as providing formal means of enforcement. See Scott and Stephan 2006 For a critique and review of their work See Posner 2007

[151] For example, see Chapter two "Sites and Strategic Legal Options for Addressing Illegitimate Debt" in Khalfan, King et al. 2003, 53-82

[152] Gottlieb Spring 1983

[153] Trachtman 1999

[154] Gottlieb Spring 1983, 573

with international law.[155] International law acts as one of the many factors that affect the incentives and payoffs of states, and it operates at the margin. When a state decides to repay or default its sovereign debt, therefore, it will consider its reputation in the sovereign debt context, as well as it reputation in complying with international legal obligations more generally. The next subsection goes over how the increased formalisation in the sovereign debt context implicates reputation.

2.5.2 How law Implicates Reputation

If reputation is the main enforcement mechanism sustaining the private sovereign debt, the increased formalisation of the market seems puzzling.[156] The first step in this direction took place in the second half of the 20th century upon the erosion of a state's immunity from lawsuits when in breach of commercial contracts with foreign parties.[157] This represented a significant evolution of the notion of the state, which under capitalism, became a specific type of juridical person with rights and obligations, and does not benefit from an inviolable legal status ordinarily attributed to sovereign states.[158]

Since the erosion of a sovereign's immunity from lawsuits, more salient developments have continued to advance the commercial market for sovereign debt towards a more formalist direction. Sovereigns engage in detailed commercial contracts with investors which include covenants,[159] private investors are increasingly willing to sue sovereign debtors,[160] and debtor states, in turn, often go out of their way to justify their actions legally. For example, 3 years after Argentina's default in 2001, nearly 40 individual lawsuits had been filed in New York seeking repayment of Argentina's obligations, and judgments in favour of plaintiffs had been entered in seven cases entailing some $740 million. In addition, more than a dozen class action

[155] See Guzman 2008

[156] One interesting question would be to analyze whether this increased process of formalization complements or interferes with the reputation mechanism. For a discussion of why increased formalization in international is not necessarily efficient as it may negatively interfere with existing informal methods of enforcement See Scott and Stephan 2006

[157] In the United States, the interpretation of sovereign immunity began to change in the 1950s,partly as a result of the Cold War and American reluctance to grant sovereign immunity to Soviet-Union state owned companies operating in the United States. In 1976 the Foreign Sovereign Immunities Act allowed private parties to sue a foreign government in a U.S. courts if the complaint relates to commercial activity. The United Kingdom adopted similar legislation in 1978, and most other legislations have followed suit. For a review See Buchheit 1986

[158] Hattori 2008, 5

[159] Upon examining more than thirty different sovereign issuers having done recent issuances , Triantis and Gulati 2007 found that they all included three standard creditor covenants: the negative pledge clause, the cross default clause and the pari passu clause.

[160] The Argentina default of 2001 was followed by the largest bondholder run to the courts in history. For a discussion See Gelpern 2005; Porzecanski 2005-2006; Gelpern 2005a

lawsuits had been filed against the Argentine government, and one of the plaintiffs had been granted the motion to certify its complaint involving two series of bonds with a face value of $ 3.5 billion.[161] Interestingly, the Argentine government, responded with a legal defense, arguing that it had no assets in the United States used for "commercial activity", such as would provide a legal basis for an attachment or execution under the Foreign Sovereign Immunities Act.[162]

Nevertheless, despite the increased formalization, the decision to default, repay and how much to compensate creditors ultimately remains in the hands of the debtor. In practice, the right of investors to sue a debtor is limited by persistent limits on private creditor control over debtor assets to secure repayment. Even with a favourable court decision, it is difficult to force a government to pay against its will, due to the fact that most of the assets or income streams that could be used for repayment are located inside the country.

What, then, is the function of this increased formalization, in the face of a persistent lack of third party enforcement? The fact that states invest resources and effort to write contracts, respond to legal suits against them and justify their arguments legally indicates that they care about the law. The economics of international law tells us that parties indeed care about law in the sovereign debt context because they are concerned with their reputation in complying with international legal obligations generally.

2.5.3 Interpreting the Law: The Odious Debt Doctrine is Dead

The implication of the previous analysis is that when states are evaluating their payoffs with regards to repaying or defaulting on their debts, their concern about their reputation with complying with international law will add an additional benefit from repayment. Interestingly, this logic is in stark contrast to what the advocates of the purported doctrine of odious debt argue. Because the doctrine of odious debt has received much attention in the odious debt literature as well as in NGO odious debt campaigns, this section briefly goes over it. It concludes that the assumption that the doctrine of odious debt is part of international law is flawed. Consequently, repudiating on these grounds not only hurts a state's reputation in the sovereign debt context, but also its reputation about complying with international law more generally.

The doctrine of odious debt was formalized by Alexander Nahum Sack in the early 20th Century. It requires that public inherited debts fulfill three criteria in order to qualify as odious and consequently should not be paid back. These criteria include namely: 1. that the debts were incurred without the consent of the people of the state 2. that the money owed was used against the general interest of the people of the state and 3. that the creditors who made the loans were aware that the money was used for

---

[161] For a discussion, See Porzecanski 2005-2006, 326-27

[162] Porzecanski 2005-2006, 326-27

illegitimate purposes.[163] Proponents of the doctrine passionately advocate its potential to remedy gross injustices imposed on the debtor nation's population and identify its normative basis as a question of human rights.

Some, such as Patricia Adams, promote adherence to the doctrine by debtor countries as it stands.[164] Others have tried to advance the doctrine by developing it and better defining the terms in it.[165] This strand of literature is characterized by an assumption that the odious debt doctrine does or potentially could play a role in international law.

In essence, proponents see repudiation on the basis of the doctrine of odious debt as complying with international law. Indeed, a strict positivist interpretation of the doctrine implies the cancellation of oppressive debt *ipso jure* upon succession. The fallacy lies in the assumption that just because the doctrine exists, that it is part of the legal expectations of parties in international law. The implications from this assumption are that default on the grounds of the odious debt doctrine would be in compliance with international law, and, it would consequently improve a state's reputation with complying with international law. Consequently, a state's concern for its reputation in the sovereign debt context and its concern for its reputation for complying with international law would pull it in opposite directions, the former pulling it towards repayment and the latter towards default. This highlights an important point: a state's reputation about complying with international will depend on how observers interpret the law.

Guzman argues that, because reputation sanctions are the result of an updating of beliefs by observers, what ultimately matters is the interpretation of observing parties about what the law is. If the legal rules are uncertain, effects on reputation will be determined by how observers interpret the violation. Therefore, even if the doctrine of odious debts has a place in international law and is invoked in good faith by a debtor government, what matters is whether the international community at large formally recognizes it.

The question that follows, therefore, is whether there is indication that the international community recognizes the doctrine of odious debt. The evidence speaks to the contrary. The sources of international law are principally treaties, customary law as determined by widespread state practice and *opinon juris* (a belief in the existence of rules), general principles, and *jus congenus* (peremptory norms).[166] Although an exception to the continuity of legal obligations was included for odious debts in the draft article of the Vienna Convention on Succession of States in Respect to Property,

[163] Sack 1927; Adams 1991

[164] Adams 1991; Adams 2004

[165] Khalfan, King et al. 2003

[166] See Statute of International Court of Justice, Art. 38

Archives and Debts, it was ultimately omitted in the final version of 1983.[167] As for the doctrine being considered as part of customary international law, state practice is at best inconsistent and overall, there has been a widespread reluctance of regimes to invoke it. Stephan notes that the last 30 years have seen the collapse of authoritarian or Soviet style governments across the continents which were all frought with human rights abuses and political injustices, yet none of the successor regimes sought debt relief by adhering to the doctrine of odious debt.[168] As opposed to the uncertainty regarding the doctrine of odious debts, the customary international rule of *pacta sund servanda* is widely recognized. Guzman argues that when parties create international agreements they are purposefully adhering to the rule that treaties must be respected.[169]

Consequently, a debtor state's concern for its reputation in both the international law arena and the sovereign debt context will pull it towards repayment of its sovereign debts. This is the case generally, as well as upon succession and in the case of odious debt.

2.6 Conclusion

This chapter began with the traditional legal and economic approaches explaining the rule of state succession of obligations in international law. The former emphasized the sanctity of contracts and the duly acquired rights of creditors. The latter argued that the fear of exclusion through reputation sanctions is the main reason why states repay their debts.

Although both explain why states *do* repay their debts, they provide limited explanatory power as to why they sometimes *don't* and why. Accordingly, insight drawn from new reputation theories which allow for political change and incomplete information, show that this reputation concerns in the context of sovereign debt are weighed against other policy concerns that a state has. Put simply, when the benefits of maintaining a reputation in the sovereign debt market are larger than the benefits obtained from elevating other policy concerns above external debt, a state will repay its debt. Therefore, reputation is the main enforcement mechanism sustaining sovereign debt relations and explaining the succession of state obligations generally. Only states that value addressing odious debt more highly than their access to future credit in the international markets will default on their odious debt.

Against this background, the last section of this chapter addressed the role of law in sovereign debt relations and argued that a state's decision to repay its sovereign debt implicates its reputation in complying with international law generally. Conversely,

[167] Cheng 2007, 24,25

[168] See Stephan 2007

[169] Guzman 2008, 204

because the doctrine of odious debt is not recognized in international law, defaulting on the grounds that debt is odious harms a state's reputation both in the sovereign debt context and international law.

Indeed, the problem of odious debt cannot be viewed in isolation. Proponents who seek for debtor governments to repudiate their odious debts hold odious debt at the centre of the argument. Looked at alone, odious debts are morally repugnant and, all else equal, successor governments and the population should not be held accountable for the odious deeds of previous dictators. But all things are rarely equal, and the problem of odious debt is one of many concerns and payoffs that a government has to assess upon succession.

3 A Focus on Creditors and Odious Debt

The extensive literature devoted to sovereign debt, by and large, does not offer a comprehensive account of the range of different contractual relations that are encompassed by the term 'sovereign debt.' While reputation is widely accepted to play a dominant role in sustaining creditor-debtor relations in the international sphere,[170] the strength of its role and the degree to which it is obstructed, vary from one type of sovereign debt relation to another. The aim of this Chapter, therefore, is to address the distinct relationships that different creditors have with sovereign debtors. Although they all fall within the umbrella heading of "sovereign debt" and have in common a promise to repay, beyond that they differ substantially in form and substance. The incentives and interests of the parties differ in each type of relationship, as does the role of reputation. Some relationships are characterized by arm's length transactions sustained by a debtor's reputation to repay. In others, the reputation mechanism is obstructed by outside factors such as hegemonic interests and influences. Less transparent creditor-debtor exchanges also exist, where reputation is based not on whether a debtor repays, but on whether it cedes policy control, or provides access to strategic resources. Still others are based more on dependency and control than on reputation at all.

This Chapter concludes by looking at the implications of this analysis for odious debt. Specifically, it looks at whether and how odious debt stems from and can affect these different relationships. It argues that odiousness can be the result of externalities from the sovereign debt contract. Other times odiousness can directly affect the risk of the contract and will therefore implicate reputation. Conversely, odious activities can be embodied in the mutual exchange involved in the creditor-debtor relationship. By looking at what distinguishes government debt contracts with different creditors, this chapter attempts to fill an analytical gap in the odious debt literature, which has primarily treated the odious debt problem within the private sovereign debt context. Focusing solely on the private market for sovereign debt excludes many developing countries, in particular the least developed countries from the analysis, as they are by and large financed by other states. Arguably, the consequences of odious debt are largest in these countries. Furthermore, many so called "rogue" states such as Iraq

[170] See Eaton and Gersovitz 1981; Sturzenegger and Zettelmeyer 2006; Tomz 2007

under Saddam Hussein, Iran and North Korea have little or no debt owed to private creditors. At the same time, while the diverse incentives of official creditors sometimes contribute to the problem of odious debt, they may also be the most conducive to a solution. The official incentives to lend for humanitarian and macroeconomic concerns, for example, will often implicate addressing odious debt.

The Chapter is structured as follows: following this Introduction, the next section goes over the particularities common to all sovereign debt. Section 3.2 then goes on to highlight the differences between different types of sovereign debt relations. It focuses mainly on the differences between creditors, namely; official creditors and private creditors including banks and bondholders. 5 factors which can obstruct the reputation mechanism are then identified and explained and their role in the different types of sovereign debt relations analyzed. Implications for the causes of odious debt are drawn in the last section.

3.1 Particularities of Sovereign Debt

Before proceeding to address the differences that exist within the range of relationships characterized as "sovereign debt", this section briefly goes over the characteristics that are common to all. In doing so, it looks at their counterpart in the domestic sphere for comparison.

3.1.1 Principal-Agent Problem

The principal agent problem explains the inherent tension that exists in all debt relations, including sovereign debt. The sovereign borrower has better information about its economic prospects than the lender and it can alter the risks of the loan after the funds are advanced. The former illustrates the problem of hidden action, the latter illustrates the problem of agency. For example, in the corporate context, the quintessential example of agency costs raised by managerial prerequisites is the corporate jet. Similarly, sovereign borrowers can engage in inefficient incentives that may raise the risk of default. Indeed, the problems of hidden action and agency may be more prevalent when a sovereign is the borrower, due to its political nature. A sovereign engages in a broader range of actions under more complex decision making structures than do corporations.

3.1.2 Succession of Obligations

Furthermore, the political economy of sovereign borrowing, which implicates the short sightedness of governments, explains the inter generational conflict inherent in sovereign debt. Indeed, a government negotiates on behalf of its citizens and can bind them, and future governments, to the interest obligations. This is because, like a corporation, the state is a legal entity which remains responsible for the rights and obligations of its different regimes that come and go.[171] Thus, like managers, governments may be willing to bind their future taxpayers to the obligation of paying higher interest in order to fund self interested and inefficient actions. In the corporate sphere, debt covenants constrain the freedom of borrowers to engage in activities that are clearly or even possibly inefficient, yet similar provisions are absent from sovereign contracts.[172]

3.1.3 Limited Scope of Judicial Remedies

The fundamental distinction that explains the difference between corporate and sovereign debt contracts is their respective enforcement mechanisms. Corporate creditors sue and use the judicial process to enforce judgments for accelerated obligations against the assets of their debtor. Conversely, they can threaten to sue, and thereby extract either payment or a change in the governance of the debtor. In contrast, creditors of sovereigns have limited legal recourse. Sovereign debt is characterized by the lack of formal enforcement mechanism analogous to the one present in the domestic corporate context.

In line with the experience of the last decades, the Argentine default of 2001 and the largest bondholder run to the courts that ensued, exemplifies the limits of the formal approach in the sovereign context. Although suits against Argentina were filed in various legislations and some court decisions were rendered in favour of the creditors, they have by and large resulted in fruitless endeavors and the majority of bondholders in the end have chosen to accept Argentina's exchange offers, while others are still waiting to receive a penny.[173]

Sovereign debt relations, instead, are enforced by non legal sanctions, primarily through a reputation mechanism. The threat of a damaged reputation makes default costly and gives an incentive for the debtor to repay and lenders the assurance to lend.[174] While it is the main mechanism sustaining sovereign debt relations, reputation can deteriorate, be obstructed or ultimately break down.

3.1.4 Lack of Bankruptcy Regime

Finally, a formal legal mechanism is lacking not only to enforce the original sovereign debt contract, but also the restructuring process that ensues in the event of default. While the domestic debt context is associated with an organized system of repayment

---

[171] Feilchenfeld 1931 ; For a review of the rationales for state succession See Bonilla 2009

[172] For a comparison of corporate and sovereign debt see Triantis and Gulati 2007

[173] For a discussion on litigations against Argentina following its 2001default *see* Gelpern 2008, 111; Federico Sturzenegger 2006, 75; *see also* Porzecanski 2005-2006

[174] For an overview of reputation theories of sovereign debt see Bonilla 2009

priorities, this is largely missing in the context of sovereign debt.[175] Insolvent countries have no recourse to a bankruptcy process that could give them meaningful financial relief and their creditors reasonable assurance of equitable treatment. In practice, sovereigns engage in ad hoc prioritization when repaying their creditors. During this process, how much and in what order, creditors receive compensation in the form of restructuring offers implicates a debtor's reputation.[176]

3.2 Different Creditors, Different Incentives

3.2.1 Private Creditors – Bondholders

3.2.1.1 Brief Background to Bond Lending

Historically, bond based lending has dominated the supply market for private credit to sovereign states. The market was shut down for over 60 years in the 1930's after depression era defaults.[177] Private lending to states then resumes in the 1970's, but in the form of bank loans. During the 1970's and 80's, bank significantly increased their relative exposure in the market, as a result of a combination of excess liquidity and lax domestic regulation in developed countries.[178] The debt crises that ensued led some banks to subsequently seek to reduce their exposure to foreign sovereigns by selling off parts of their loans at a discount and writing off the difference as a loss. At the same time, under the Brady Plan, commercial banks agreed to repackage the remaining loans into bonds offered to the public and freely tradable on secondary markets.[179] It was during the rapid expansion of the secondary market that followed that bonds regained their dominant role in the private sovereign credit market.[180].

Bonds are standardized financial instruments that are usually traded on markets. Their increased popularity as a funding instrument is due to their highly liquid nature. They are tradable, and hence very liquid, which makes them attractive to a broad range of potential lenders. The negotiability of bonds means that bondholders have greater flexibility in dealing with their bonds than banks have in managing loan agreements, for example.

---

175 See Gelpern 2004

176 Tomz 2007

177 For a discussion see Macmillan 1995

178 See Kapstein 1994; Tomz 2007

179 In the early 1990s, banks agreed to exchange bad loans for Brady Bonds, named after the U.S. Treasury Secretary who helped broker the solution. For a summary see Birdsall and Williamson 2002, 14-15

180 See Vasquez 1996; Hughes-Verdier 2004

Usually, the first markets in financial instruments to develop in a country are the markets in government paper, beginning with short term notes and eventually involving longer term bonds. The government is the best known and the least risky issuer in every domestic market. The buyers of its bonds are usually domestic financial institutions, such as banks, pension funds and insurance companies, as well as individuals.

An international market for government bonds in 'hard' currencies first reemerged in the postwar era with developed country issuers in the Euromarket. Today, the Eurobond market is no longer the only bond market that is genuinely international in character. "Over the years, the traditional domestic bond markets have attracted increasing international investor interest as a result of factors such as improved communication technology and dismantlement of exchange controls."[181] Foreign demand has begun to grow for government bonds issued on the financial markets of the larger developing countries, albeit first for dollar linked domestic currency bonds and other types of securities, and then local currency bonds themselves. The increased willingness of international financial investors to hold currency bonds of emerging economies represents a major step in financial globalisation.[182]

3.2.1.2 Incentives to Lend

Private creditors are motivated, above all, by economic gain. Commercial loans are a form of economic exchange with interest as the time value of money. The profit maximizing incentives of bondholders are transparent. As Gelpern describes it, "They want to get out as soon as possible with as much money as possible."[183] International investors generally see government bonds as part of a portfolio of securities they hold. The aim of any portfolio manager is to strike an appropriate balance among a variety of financial assets with different risk and return characteristics so as to earn some targeted average yield in exchange for an overall level of risk.

Different categories of creditors have distinct appetites for risk and investment strategies, but they are all motivated by profit. For example, the buy side actors in the market for emerging market debt is composed of 'dedicated' and 'cross over' institutions, active trading accounts and 'buy and hold' investors. Dedicated investors include funds such as a Latin America or Southeast Asia Fund, which commit to put all or some of their money in risky emerging market debt. Cross over investors are often highly regulated companies such as insurance and pension funds which are more risk averse and can only hold bonds on 'investment grade.' They may invest a portion of their portfolio in emerging markets to boost returns when yields are low on mature

[181] Scott and Wellons 2002, 727

[182] For a discussion, see for example BIS 2003, 45-63

[183] Gelpern 2007, 98

market assets. Other investors, notably hedge funds, are attracted by riskier debt and look for a quick profit in arbitraging price and interest rate differences worldwide.[184]

3.2.2 Private Creditors - Banks

3.2.2.1 Brief Background to Bank Lending

Large scale international bank lending only emerged as a major form of international financial transfer to developing countries in the 1970s. It primarily took the form of international bank loans in foreign currency to governments. Banks had traditionally lent to governments to finance capital-equipment exports, such as airplanes or locomotives.[185] These export credits were, and still are, guaranteed by an official agency of the exporting country, however, and have thus been a low risk to banks. But, as of the 1970s, banks began to make large scale multi-bank loans to governments for purposes such as general fiscal deficit financing, or to replenish foreign exchange reserves, among other purposes. Most of the large scale bank lending was conducted in syndications in which many banks, sometimes up to 100 banks, would participate. Large governments would typically have several syndicated bank loans outstanding at the same time. This type of lending, however, has been largely superseded by bond financing.

Today, several of the major internationally active commercial banks of the 1970s and 80s now make up some of the most important intermediaries in the emerging economy sovereign bond market. In this business, the commercial banks have joined in the core business of investment banks, which advise governments on how, where, and when to issue their bonds, help them structure bond offerings, take care of the initial marketing of the issue, and underwrite the issue as they effect their sale to first buyers.

3.2.2.2 Incentives to Lend

Like bondholders, banks extend private credit to sovereigns and are by and large motivated by profit. Lending to sovereigns is often one of the many ongoing activities that a bank will have with a debtor country which provides it with a steady flow of income. For example, banks often invest in the domestic sector of the debtor country, have branches there and are engaged in multiple, ongoing activities which provide them with a steady flow of income. They want to be able to gain as much profit from all of their multiple relations with the debtor country. They have the long term interest of their relations to protect, and by the same token may be concerned with the long run economic condition of the debtor country.

---

[184] See Gelpern and Gulati 2007, 9

[185] See Herman 2007

3.2.3 Official Creditors: States

3.2.3.1 A Brief Background to State to State Lending

Private sources of credit to sovereigns long preceded large scale official lending.[186] In fact, the type of large scale official lending that we witness today is a relatively new development. Furthermore, the wide range of purposes that official lending serves in the present time is in stark contrast to the few interests that previously motivated governments to lend to other governments. These included, notably; loans to finance war, such as when the United States lent to its World War I allies, as well as loans for export finance, whose purpose was to promote national exports and were destined for importing countries.[187] Several developments, including the Cold War and the escalation of anti colonial struggles, sparked a new era of sovereign financing which was backed by creditor state policy interests that went largely beyond targeted military and export credits.[188] Countries like the United States and the Soviet Union began financing friendly governments directly on a large scale.

3.2.3.2 Incentives to Lend

The incentives of official creditors differ from those of private creditors. They do not have a uniform or primary interest in profit maximization. Unlike private debt, official debt is never extended at arm's length or for direct economic gain. At any point in time, states have a complex and intertwined set of preferences, priorities and policy objectives. Lending is an important policy tool and the range of policy interests in the countries that they lend to is vast and can be benign or odious, ranging from supporting economic development to propping up dictators in developing countries.

While countries are not motivated by direct economic gain, this does not rule out economic considerations altogether. The mix of official and commercial aspects is different across different official sovereign debt relations. The interest in lending may be in the form of an indirect economic interest. For example, official export promotion is aimed to boost economic growth and job creation in the creditor country. Furthermore, while repayment may not be the main motivation behind the creditor states' incentive to offer credit, there may nevertheless be an explicit underlying fungible exchange existing in the relationship. This is the case if a state lends to a debtor to obtain strategic access to its natural resources. Some analysts argue that China's increasing need for raw materials underlies its generous and 'zero conditionality' loans to Africa as well as the Caribbean. [189] Other times, the relationship involves less liquid exchange, such as when the goal of the creditor is to

---

[186] For a review of sovereign lending see, Hoeflich 1982

[187] Gelpern 2007, 94

[188] Ibid.

[189] See for example Goodman December 23, 2004; McGreal February 8th, 2007; Settling the China Question: A Caribbean Challenge May 2nd, 2008

obtain influence over the borrower. Examples include the interests of the United States in lending to Turkey and Pakistan, as part of its fight against terrorism.[190]

Despite the fact that official transfers of the kind outlined above are substantially different from what is traditionally understood as 'debt', they nonetheless fall within the umbrella heading of 'sovereign debt.' Hattori compares state to state loans in the international sphere to loans between friends or family members.[191] While they are still a form of economic exchange, they differ from commercial loans in that they are, at least in part, motivated by social considerations as opposed to the potential for economic return. Friends and relatives lend then no one else will. Likewise, the poorest and least creditworthy countries, which do not have access to the private markets for credit, are usually dependant on official creditor 'friends' for funds. Creditor governments will often lend to them even in the face of dire economic circumstances and when repayment prospects are dim.[192] States usually lend to non enemy states. As Hattori explains, "Just as loans between strangers are unlikely, so loans between enemy states are unlikely."[193] Nevertheless, this does not necessarily involve credit relations between countries of equal standing. On the contrary, official lending often involves loosely hierarchical relations where power plays an important role.[194] For example, take the case of the poor country which does not have access to the private credit markets and which is lent money by a friendly government large enough to have the funds to do so. By definition, the relationship involves two parties of very different economic power.

3.2.3.3 Types of Official Lending

A large part of sovereign debt is contingent, wherein the creditor government guarantees the loan of a private lender, which is usually a bank, officially promising that the guaranteeing government will cover the obligations should the borrowing government default. When states guarantee the debts of private creditors, they are implicitly providing an insurance mechanism to them to cover the risk that the debtor will not repay. If the debtor defaults on its debt, the bank will be repaid by its home government which provided the guarantee, and the government will subsequently take over the debt obligation and become creditor. Like all insurance mechanisms, official debt guarantees create moral hazard on the part of the insuree, who may take excessive risk or be more negligent as a result.

[190] Triantis and Gulati 2007, 9

[191] Hattori 2008, 13

[192] Gelpern 2007, 83

[193] Hattori 2008, 14

[194] Id.

Just as direct state to state lending is a relatively new development, so is official interference with the financial activities of private creditors abroad, which was previously limited to guaranteeing export finance. Some of the incentives of states to guarantee private lending are the same as those that guide them to lend directly to other states. This is the case when states use the private sector as a tool to advance policy and imperialist goals. Other interests can include promoting free market, international competition of the private sector, containing contagion and the stability of financial systems.[195] Accordingly, sometimes the guarantee is an incentive for banks to lend to risky borrowers for political reasons ex ante. Other times, intervention is an ex post response to the risk of contagion.[196]

States also indirectly engage in another form of official lending through the international financial institutions (IFIs), such as the International Monetary Fund (IMF) and the World Bank. These IFIs pool together the deposits of their members to provide multilateral credit to other member countries, for a variety of purposes, including the financing of specific projects in developing countries as well as providing financing to help members suffering from balance of payment problems.[197] The same states which have sufficient means to engage in large scale direct lending to other countries, such as the member states of the Organization for Economic Co-operation and Development, also provide the large bulk of deposits to these IFIs. Likewise, developing states who usually borrow from official credit markets become members of IFIs to obtain "easy" access to credit, and receive the bulk of deposits.[198]

Given that the larger economic states maintain, and often replenish, substantial deposits at the IFIs, it is interesting to analyze what motivates them to do so. There are three primary reasons. First, as is the case with official lending in general, policy interests drive states to deposit funds in the IFIs. It was the major depositing states which originally created the IFIs and pushed towards a liberal international economic order.[199] IFIs also serve institutional functions that could not be fulfilled by an

---

[195] See Raffer 2007

[196] Id, 89

[197] See Articles of Agreement of the International Monetary Fund available at http://www.imf.org/external/pubs/ft/aa/index.mth (last accessed; 23d of June, 2009)

[198] The economic gap that separates creditor states from debtor states is translated into a power gap within these institutions. For example, the International Bank for Reconstruction and Development, the oldest institution of the World Bank, is structured like a joint stock company in which all member states are shareholders. Shares determine a member country's decision making power and are allocated among member states according to a formula, which reflects their relative position in the international economy. Similarly, in the IMF, each member is assigned a quote which determines, among other things, the amount that the country deposits in the IMF as well as its voting power. See:
http://web.worldbank.org/WBSITE/EXTERNAL/EXTABOUTUS/0,,contentMDK:20122644~menuPK:278902~pagePK:51123644~piPK:329829~theSitePK:29708,00.html (last accessed: 23d of June, 2009) See Also, Gold 1984

[199] See Hattori 2008

individual, or even a few states. These include tasks such as the monitoring of consistency between the national policies, such as adequate liquidity, stable exchange rates and a smooth adjustment mechanism.[200] Underlying these reasons, however, is the primary interests of states in having IFIs play an intermediary role as facilitators of finance between lenders and sovereign borrowers.[201]

3.3 5 Factors Affecting the Dynamics of Sovereign Debt

A fundamental characteristic of sovereign debt is the lack of contractual enforcement mechanisms analogous to those that exist at the level of corporate debt. Reputation, therefore, functions as an alternative enforcement mechanism that sustains sovereign debt relations. Its role and strength, however, vary across the relations that a sovereign has with its different creditors.

The different incentives of creditors determine, in part, the dynamics of the sovereign debt relation and the strength of the reputation mechanism that sustains it. This section focuses on 5 interrelated factors which can affect reputation. These factors stem from the nature and incentives of different types of creditors. These factors are, namely; 1) the outside influences that creditors and the debt relation are exposed to 2) the number of different types of relations that a creditor has with a borrowing country 3) the gap between form and substance of the debt agreement 4) the amount and type of information that creditors have access to and 5) coordination problems between creditors. While this section focuses on creditors, the last section will then go on to look at the implications that this has for the incentives of debtors and odious debt.

3.3.1 Outside Influences

Palzer argues that sovereign debt contracts are unique in the sense that they involve a complex combination of both external and internal interests.[202] In other words, while debt contracts can embody the interests of the main parties to the contract, namely the debtor and the creditor, the interests of third parties can also be implicated either directly or indirectly. This is true for all sovereign debt to different degrees, and depends on how susceptible parties are to outside influences.

---

[200] See Germain 1997

[201] See Sgard 2004

[202] See Palzer 1988

3.3.1.1 Private Creditors: Bondholders

Hegemonic Influences

The dispersed nature of bondholders and their small size relative to other types of creditors, such as banks, makes them less susceptible to direct influence.[203] Individually, they do not hold enough capital to be able to engage in large scale 1970s style bank lending to developing countries in order to fulfill the policy goals of their home governments. Collectively, they hold an enormous amount of capital, but the fact that they are scattered across the world, and the fact that bonds are highly liquid and are constantly changing hands, makes it difficult for a government to engage with them and subject them to arm twisting.

Furthermore, the nature of bondholders makes them relatively immune to other types of influences as well, such as moral or equitable considerations. For example, official creditors often attempt, with limited success, to use moral suasion to convince private creditors to provide debt forgiveness to poor countries.[204]

Bonds are not relational contracts, they are arm's length transactions between strangers. It is not a relationship which underlines the contract, but mutually exchange and the self interests of parties. Just as it is much harder to influence a stranger to do something than it is to ask a friend, it is harder for governments or any outside parties to influence the millions of anonymous investors holding sovereign bonds at any point in time. Their relative impermeability to outside influence that could interfere with their risk assessment and with their interests in getting repaid strengthens the reputation mechanism underlying the bond contracts. Having said that, during a period in the mid 1990s, the dynamics of sovereign bond relations were perversely obstructed by the official sector's provision of emergency funds to sovereigns in default. The next subsection discusses this issue briefly.

IMF Bailouts

The interests of the IMF in providing bailouts to countries in default were aligned with its interest in maintaining stability in the international financial system and preventing contagion as a result of a deterioration of a sovereign debtor's economic situation. For example, emergency credit provided by the IMF cured the liquidity crisis of countries like Mexico and the East Asian Tigers during the 1990s.[205] IMF bailouts created the same trade off that official bailouts to banks pose today in the midst of the financial crisis: greater macroeconomic stability at the expense of long run moral hazard.

---

[203] The description is stylized. Some syndicated include hundreds of banks, while some bond issues are closely held.

[204] See for example Guyana's Experience with Paris Club and Commercial Creditors 2006

[205] Bratton 2004, 9

Indeed, bailouts produced a two sided moral hazard problem: both on the part of the sovereign and on the part of investors. As Bratton and Gulati argue, the IMF found itself in a "bailout trap."[206] On the one hand, it led sovereign debtors to prefer outright default to negotiating and restructuring with its creditors.[207] This was because rehabilitation was achieved much more quickly thanks to the IMF's financial backing. Furthermore, a sovereign's incentives to engage in prudent borrowing were diminished as a result of the assurance that the IMF was going to come in with cash.[208] On the other hand, on the part of the creditors, because some of the IMF's emergency funding went directly into the pockets of the bondholders, this created perverse lending incentives as well. The reputation mechanism was therefore grossly disrupted.

These incentive problems have diminished to a large extent, as exemplified by the defaults of Argentina and Russia which occurred without the benefit of an emergency credit from the IMF, thereby terminating the expectations that all large economies, and their creditors, would be bailed out.[209] Nevertheless, bailouts still exist. For example, in 2002, Brazil, Paraguay and Uruguay received IMF bailouts.[210] More recently, in the midst of the financial crisis of 2008, the IMF also bailed out developed countries such as Iceland.[211] The status quo is nonetheless relatively more efficient, because although bailouts still occur, neither creditors nor debtors can completely rely on them nor predict them. This discretionary mechanism has been described as 'constructive ambiguity.'[212]

The increased reluctance of the IMF to provide emergency funds to countries upon default marked a significant change in the rules of the game of sovereign lending. It indicated to private creditors that, from then on, they would have to proceed at their own risk when lending to sovereigns and would have to engage in restructurings in the case of default and thereby make concessions.[213] This increased burden and risk sharing by private creditors is referred to in the literature as 'private sector involvement.' Less official bailouts, therefore, meant more restructuring by the private sector. As a result, investors who traded instruments wanted to be able to price restructuring risk. Indeed, the order and predictability of restructurings and how

[206] Bratton 2004, 9

[207] Brown 2005, 3

[208] Bratton 2004, 9

[209] Ibid.

[210] For discussion see Tarullo 2001, 631-31, 649-51

[211] See Power and Sigurdardottir October 21, 2008

[212] See for example Eichengreen 2001, 3

[213] See Eichengreen 2001

different investors classes fare implicate a debtor's reputation and affect the terms of bond contracts.

3.3.1.2 Private Creditors: Banks

The prominence of bank lending to sovereigns in the 1970s came about as a result of several interrelated factors. This period is indicative of the salient role that outside influences can have on the nature of bank lending, in particular hegemonic influences and regulation.

Hegemonic Influences

Unlike bondholders, commercial banks are subject to a wide range of influences, primarily from their home governments, which interfere with their lending activities. There are several reasons why commercial banks are particularly susceptible to such influences. One reason, highlighted by Tomz, involves the capacity of banks to engage in large scale, defensive lending.[214] This makes them a particularly important tool for their home governments, which can exploit this ability to pursue both domestic and foreign policy interests. When a debtor defaults on its debt, creditor country governments can exploit the capacity of their banks by asking them to provide the debtor with new loans. Secondly, governments can easily communicate with bank officials and may even develop close relationships with them, making both sides more susceptible to 'arm twisting.'

Drawing from the American banking context, Perez and Weissman find that banks are subject to the constraints of policy imperatives and the national interests of the states in which they operate. The influences of national governments on banks can be indirect in the form of discretionary oversight or implicit assurances for the loans that they make. They argue that nowhere do these issues reveal themselves with greater clarity than in Latin America, where financial loan transactions were the primary means for securing US financial and political leverage.[215]

Implicit loan guarantees, help explain, in part, both the rapid rise of large scale international banking during the 1970s, as well as the irresponsible nature that characterized it. Kapstein gives an account of how banks were induced by their national governments to recycle their petrodollars in the developing world, mainly in Latin America.[216] In other words, the private banks of industrial countries that were lending to Latin America were not guided by effective risk assessment. Rather, their incentives to lend, and indeed, over lend and take excessive risk, were a direct result of the implicit guarantee offered by their national governments that they would pick up

---

[214] Tomz 2007, 25

[215] See Pérez and Weissman 2007

[216] See Kapstein 1994

the bill in case of default by the debtor.[217] International bank lending, then, was serving an important policy goal from the perspective of government officials, especially in the United States, who were pursuing a liberal world economy and wanted to avoid balance of payment problems in the developing world.

Against this background, banks are not all equally susceptible to hegemonic influences and the degree could depend, in part, on their size and the nature and history of the relationship that they have with their home governments. It is worth noting that bank lending which is subject to home government hegemonic influences lies somewhere in between private and official lending. This chapter distinguishes between bank lending which is subject to indirect official influences and 'arm twisting' and official lending which can take the form of direct, formal guarantees to banks and is equivalent to insurance.

Regulation

As in all contracts, regulation (or the lack of regulation) is an important influence which can determine the amount of risk that parties can take and the types of activities that they can engage in. Commercial banks are regulated entities. When they operate domestically, they are required to meet certain capital adequacy requirements, or reserves, which limit their exposure to risky borrowers. These requirements both enhance the safety of the domestic banking system and give public authorities a means to control the money supply. Tomz notes that during the 1970s, the international activities of banks were much less regulated and as a result, banks were allowed to open offshore branches to escape the reach of domestic regulators.[218]

In the 1980's, following the Latin American debt crisis, regulations tightened and the United States passed the U.S. International Lending Supervisions Act of 1983. It required banks to increase their ratio of capital to total assets and establish loan loss reserves from problem debt.[219]

Ultimately, the management of banks has incentives to undertake overly risky activities, even without hegemonic influences pushing them to do so. Bankers in the

---

[217] In 1974, central bankers from the G-10 nations issued a public statement that many interpreted as a promise to supply lender of last resort facilities not only to resident parent banks, but also to overseas branches. See Tomz 2007, 204

By doing so, the G-10 "provided the financial marketplace with the safety net that it needed before (petrodollar) recylcling could proceed." Kapstein 1994, 66 (In contrast, the bondmarket had not been included in this implicit insurance scheme See Edwards 1986, 569)

[218] This became known as the Euromarket. During much of the 1970s, surveillance and control of the euromarkets was so light that the U.S. Federal Reserve did not even have reliable data on the foreign claims and liabilities of international banks. See Tomz 2007, 204

[219] Other developed countries have similar regulation. For example, Germany's Banking Act dates back to 1961 (Gesetz über das Kreditwesen) and United Kingdom passed the The Banking Act of 1979. For a review of comparative banking regulation SeeFriesen 1985

1970s sought profitable investments and were attracted by the generous fees and large spreads of the syndicated bank loans to the developing world. Their incentives to take excessive risk when attracted by the prospects of profit leads to a need for regulation. This is because most banks are corporations whose shares trade on the stock market and whose management is remunerated according to stock price movements, which usually reflect short term profit performance figures.[220] The financial crisis has brought to light the need for better regulation to address the incentive structure of investment managers. Rajan argues that the way compensation relates to returns implies there is typically less downside and more upside from generating investment returns and this results in managers having greater incentives to take risk. Furthermore, their performance relative to other peer managers matters, and, because risk and return are related, a manager looks as if he outperforms peers given the risk he takes.[221]

3.3.1.3 Official Creditors

Official sovereign debt relations are characterized by the political nature of the borrower and the policy interests that it brings to the transaction. Because official lenders often want to stay as long as possible in the debtor country, their policy interests can change during the time frame of the relation. The outside influences to the relation are the same external factors that influence the broad range of policy interests that an official creditor has.

For example, an official creditor's interests to lend can involve, at first, humanitarian concerns in the borrowing country and this, in turn, may be a result of public choice concerns domestically. This could be the case if humanitarian causes abroad are important for the domestic voting population.[222] If the global economic climate deteriorates and the financial resources in creditor countries come under pressure, foreign humanitarian causes may no longer be a domestic priority for governments in the short term and this will affect the nature of the relationship.

3.3.2 Number of Different Transactions with Debtor Country

3.3.2.1 Private Creditors: Bondholders

A sovereign debt contract can be influenced by other relations that a creditor has with the debtor. The relation that a bondholder has with a sovereign debtor is usually limited to the credit transaction. Unlike other types of creditors, bondholders do not have other simultaneous interests at stake in the debtor country. Consequently, if their interests in getting repaid are harmed, their incentives to employ reputation sanctions and "punish" the debtor are not obstructed by concerns about how their other relations

---

[220] For an overview of the often perverse incentives of bank managers and how the way banks manage risk is changing see The Economist May 14th, 2009

[221] Rajan 2005

[222] For example, domestic interest groups in countries such as Norway have managed to put debt and humanitarian issues high in the political agenda see Callaghy 2004

in the country could be affected. Investors will take their resources out of the debtor country and refrain from lending to it until they have been adequately compensated. Indeed, private credit which responds quickly to changes in reputation is an effective disciplining device for debtors. At the same time, this makes funds from these players more volatile and harder to manage.[223]

3.3.2.2 Private Creditors: Banks

The difference lies in the amount of transactions that a bank is engaged in with a particular debtor country. Some banks lend to sovereigns and do not have any other business relations with the debtor. Much like bondholders, then, their interests vis-à-vis the sovereign are concentrated with the particular debt relation itself and are only interested in recovering their funds. Other banks will likely be engaged in other various profit maximizing relations with the sovereign besides the debt transaction. For example, banks often invest in the domestic sector of the debtor country, have branches there and are engaged in multiple, ongoing activities which provide them with a steady flow of income. They want to be able to gain as much profit from all of their multiple relations with the debtor country. They have the long term interest of their relations to protect, and by the same token may be concerned with the long run economic condition of the debtor country. These banks will be less likely to opt for a complete exit option from the country when one individual relation breaks down, such as when a country defaults on one of its credits. Their desire to recover on the defaulted debt, or to punish the debtor for non repayment, is set against not wanting to jeopardize their other businesses in the country. The disciplining function of reputation, is therefore diluted with regards to the individual sovereign debt relationship. Nevertheless, reputation remains contingent on the portfolio of the different business relationships of the bank with the debtor country.

3.3.2.3 Official Creditors

Official creditors only lend to their 'friends' with whom they are likely to engage in a wide range of different types of relations. An official creditor will not be able, therefore, to limit its cost-benefit analysis to a particular debt transaction, but may treat all of its relations as a portfolio of sort. Like some banks, official creditors' desire to recover on the defaulted debt (or whatever interest underlies the relationship), will be set against how it will affect its other relations with the debtor country. These can include other business relations, such as trade and investment. They can also be cultural relations with former colonies that creditor countries do not want to disrupt. Conversely, a creditor country may want to avoid some of the externalities of taking its resources out of the country or exiting the credit relationship. This could be the case if these actions would lead to a deteriorated economic situation in the borrowing country and lead to higher illegal immigration or refuges to the lending country, for example.

---

[223] See UNITAR 2007

3.3.3 Form and Substance

The first two factors; outside influence and the different types of relationships, affect the third factor: the gap between the form and substance of the debt agreement. In response to the current financial and economic crisis, many experts have highlighted the importance of regulating financial activities according to their economic substance, as opposed to their legal form.[224] They are referring to the lack of regulation of institutions and financial devices which were performing bank-like functions but were not regulated as banks. This discussion is related to the long standing debate in the legal literature over formal and substantive approaches to the interpretation of contracts, and it pertains to sovereign debt.[225] Indeed, most types of sovereign lending contracts fall underneath the umbrella form of debt, and are considered as such from a formalistic legal perspective. However, the nature of the relationship and type of exchange between the parties, the substance, can vary greatly. This leads to uncertainty and a lack of transparency that can obstruct reputation and the efficiency of sovereign debt relations.

The form of a debt contract includes, most importantly, the promise to repay. The terms of the contract, such as the interest rate and maturity, should reflect the risk of non repayment and may also control it. The substance of a debt contract is the inherent exchange and nature of the relationship between the creditor and the debtor. In private sovereign debt contracts the economic substance of the relationship (in general) reflects the form. Conversely, in official sovereign debt relations, the gap between the form and substance of an agreement can be significant, especially when repayment is inessential to the relationship between the parties. In U.S. domestic law, the doctrine of re-characterization of claims in bankruptcy directly addresses the gap between the form and substance of an obligation and prescribes remedies.[226] There is no similar mechanism which exists in the context of sovereign debt. More attention needs to be devoted to this discussion. If something walks like a duck and talks like a duck, it should be called a duck and treated as a duck.

3.3.3.1 Private Creditors: Bondholders

Bonds are market based contracts whose purpose and substance generally reflect their debt form. The sovereign bond relation is centered around the promise to repay. Bondholders allocate credit based on their beliefs about a sovereign's reputation. They respond to reputations in several ways, which are reflected in the terms of the contracts. First, they charge for risk and increase the expected return to compensate for the danger of default. There is an inverse relationship between a bond's price and its yield. U.S. Treasury securities, which are considered to be free of default risk, trade in the market at a price that is higher than bonds which bear default risk and offer a

---

[224] See for example Turner 2009

[225] See for example Katz March 2004 and Atiyah 2001 93 - 120

[226] See Penn 1996

relatively low return. Developing country debt is generally characterized by higher yields offered to creditors in return for bearing a greater risk of default. Likewise, long-term debt is riskier that short-term debt, due to its higher price volatility and consequently investors will require a premium to hold it.

Bondholders also respond to reputation by seeking to control risk. For example, until quite recently, investors considered foreign currency denominated debt as safer than domestic debt, especially with regards to developing countries. This is because domestic currency debt is subject to moral hazard problems, since a country that cannot commit to low inflation can avoid repayment by inflating away its debt, or by generating depreciation.[227] Traditionally, emerging markets have had a reputation which has been good enough to be able to issue bonds, but not good enough to be able to have access to the same structure and terms of debt as that which is available to the mature markets.[228] This is a result of both lower creditworthiness relative to developed countries and poor institutional quality which prevents them from making long term commitments, as well as domestic politics which led to dubious borrowing and default. Consequently, for the most part, they have had to rely on foreign currency denominated debt, which is riskier, more expensive and harder to manage, but protects creditors from exchange rate and inflation policies that would decrease the value of their bonds. The short term maturity and foreign currency denomination that characterizes developing country bond financing has been referred to as "dangerous forms of debt", because they make developing countries more prone to contagion and risks such as foreign exchange risk, making crises more likely. The literature refers to this debt structure and problems that originate from it as the 'original sin.'[229]

As of the late 1990s, and more prominently after a series crises in the early 2000's, after which developing countries began to focus on saving money,[230] emerging countries have been able to improve their reputations and continually have an increased and more successful participation in the global financial landscape. Their improved reputation came as a result of several push and pull factors.

The "pull" factors, were a result of the actions taken by some developing countries which sent positive signals to investors and included reduced fiscal and current account deficits as well as reduction in their debt levels, sometimes brought about by countries buying back their external debt.[231] Furthermore, public debt management in emerging markets has become much more sophisticated by adopting leading practices

---

[227] Bohn 1990

[228] Mature markets are able to sell local currency debt to foreign investors. At the end of 2007, foreign resident held over 2 trillion in dollar denominated U.S. Treasury securities. See Gelpern and Gulati 2007, 8

[229] See Eichengreen, Hausmann et al. 2003; Rogoff January 22nd, 2003

[230] Gelpern 2008, 107

[231] See Bloomstein and Santiso April 2007

from OECD countries.[232] As a result, investors have begun to have a greater appetite for local currency debt in these countries and in turn, emerging economies have had increased access to non dollar denominated debt credit which reduces their exposure to foreign exchange shocks. The Bank for International Settlements states that the outstanding stock of domestic bonds in these countries has gone from one trillion dollars in 1995 to over four trillion dollars in 2006.[233]

The "push" factors came from the increased importance of institutional investors.[234] Furthermore, financial innovations, such as credit derivatives,[235] allow investors to insure against losses on their debt, thereby diversifying the risk and allowing for increased funding to emerging economies.[236] However, despite the enormous upsides of financial innovation, some scholars warn of new risks and uncertainty that can result from both an increased exposure to volatile markets as well innovation in the market surpassing regulation.[237] There is an increased lack of transparency as a result of financial innovations which lump together different products of different risks, and with regards to the increasingly complex terms of products, including governing law, residence of creditor and currency denomination among others.[238] These new products are particularly difficult to put a price on and some have argued that they allow for the uncertainty regarding the underlying value of the original asset to be spread.[239] Greater and more sophisticated access to new markets is certainly a positive development for developing countries. The caveat lies in giving attention to the increased uncertainty that new products can bring about, particularly with regards to the difference between their form and their substance.

---

[232] Ibid.

[233] BIS 2007, 31 In response to this development, J.P. Morgan has developed a new index of local emerging market debt, the GBI-EM See J.P. Morgan, Emerging Markets – Local Debt Package available at: http://www.jpmorgan.com/pages/jpmorgan/investbk/research/indexresearch/vendor/packages#lm

[234] Cali, Massa et al. 2008, 3

[235] An example of a credit derivative is a credit default swap (CDS) which is an agreement between two counterparties, in which one makes periodic payments to the other and gets the promise of a payoff if a third party defaults. The second party gives credit protection, a kind of insurance, and is called the "buyer." The second party gives credit protection and is called the "seller." The third party is referred to as the "reference entity" and is the one that might go bankrupt or default. See Hughes-Verdier 2004; Goderis and Wagner October 2006

[236] The terms of sovereign credit derivative, like bonds, are market based contracts and reflect reputation sanctions by creditors in the same way that bonds do. For example, the market for CDSs, mostly composed of emerging economies, is characterized by short term maturities and higher premia which is consistent with the market being less sure about returns in the event of default. See Packer and Suthiphongchai 2003

[237] Rajan 2005

[238] See Gelpern 2008

[239] Buffet March 8, 2003

Finally, countries with reputations that are very low are unable to borrow in the bond markets at all. This is evidenced by the vast majority of low-income countries which are excluded from the bond markets.[240] Investors cannot compensate the risk of lending to these countries with a higher yield because the interest rate needed may be so high as to perversely reduce the expected return. The heightened probability of default overwhelms the gains from charging a steeper price. Investors therefore avoid risk by refusing to lend.

3.3.3.2 Private Creditors: Banks

As private creditors generally, banks are motivated by profit and rely on reputation. This gives them incentives, like bondholders, to allocate credit according to how they perceive a debtor's reputation. When this is the case, the debt form of bank loans reflects their economic substance. However, when banks rely on means of enforcement, other than reputation, such as government guarantees for example, the terms of the loan may differ from the substance. In other words, when the risk of non repayment is independent from a debtor's reputation, the terms of the contract will no longer reflect a debtor's risk of defaulting.

Another source of discrepancy between form and substance lies in the balance sheet of banks. This is because banks have incentives to avoid recording losses on their books. They therefore have an interest in engaging in defensive lending to governments that have already defaulted. In the short term, new loans could help the debtor pay interest on previous debts, thereby sparing the banks from having to declare defaults and record losses on their balance sheets. Over the long term, new loans could help the debtor revitalize its economy and increase the chance of eventual repayment. Defensive lending can be efficient if the sovereign borrower is suffering from a liquidity problem. However, solvency problems can be difficult to distinguish from liquidity problems.[241] Defensive lending in times of solvency crises, aside from creating a gap between the nominal values in their books and the real losses that they incur, also leads to moral hazard on the part of the sovereign debtor. As a result of the rapid rise of the secondary market, banks are able to use it as an effective tool to manage credit exposure, thereby closing the form-substance gap.

3.3.3.3 Official Creditors

The gap between form and substance is most prominent in official sovereign debt relations. Official debt agreements can vary widely. By and large, however, the terms of the agreements are not designed to control the risk of default or maximize the prospects of repayment. While they all include a promise to repay by the borrower, in terms of substance, they fall within a range of types of transactions with different

[240] As an indication, J.P. Morgan's various emerging market bond index, which are traditionally referenced to obtain the value of emerging markets as an asset class, only include 19 developing countries.

[241] See for example, Kapstein 1994 describing how banks misinterpreted Latin America's solvency problems as liquidity problems in the 1970s

expectations of repayment. On the one end lie transactions that resemble debt in the traditional sense and are centered around repayment. On the other end, lie transactions that resemble grants, and do not involve any expectation of repayment. Official credits usually lie somewhere in between. They are not arm's length transactions such as in the private market, but they do not resemble altruistic gifts either.

The Functions of Debt Form

One obvious question to begin with is why the official sector bothers to document these transactions as debt, if the purpose of the transaction is not primarily, if at all, to get repaid and make a profit. In other words, why not call these transactions "money in exchange for raw materials" for example. Why is the duck not called a duck? The literature official debt, which has mostly centered on debt relief, has not addressed this question.[242] One notable exception is a recent contribution by Anna Gelpern, which specifically addressed the significance and purpose of the debt form in official debt, and examines the extent to which official debt is really debt.[243]

Gelpern argues that the debt form has both a domestic political and a foreign policy function for creditor states. The domestic political function stems from the assurance provided to the tax payers in creditor countries that their government is not giving away their tax money. The promise to repay reduces the appearance of a subsidy and suggests that creditors have a means to monitor the use of the loan proceeds over time and get the money back if anything goes awry.[244] Indeed, it is interesting that the principal agent problem has often been analyzed in the context of a borrowing state's responsibility towards its population, but seldom in the context of a creditor state's responsibility to its population, whose taxes finance the credit that it extends. The foreign policy function implicit in the debt form, in turn, lies in its capacity to entrench the relationship and reinforces a long term relational element in official transfers.[245]

Mutual Exchange and Reputation

Hence, there is a significant gap between form and substance in official debt. This does not mean, however, that official debt relations are not sustained by reputation. Furthermore, it also does not mean that there is no mutual exchange present in the creditor-debtor relation. What it does mean is that reputation is not entirely based on whether a debtor repays or defaults, but whether it delivers on the policy interest that motivated the creditor to lend in the first place. The more transparent and fungible the

---

[242] The debt relief literature addresses issues which include debt sustainability and debt overhang and conditionality.

[243] See Gelpern 2007

[244] Gelpern 2007, 99

[245] Ibid , 100

policy interest, the easier it is for the relation to be sustained by reputation. This could be the case if loans are extended in return for preferential access to raw materials. As long as the borrower delivers on its promise to grant access to its raw materials, it will continue to receive loans from the creditor.

Due to the reasons explained by Gelpern, however, it is politically difficult to make such a transparent contract. It would likely also be subject to scrutiny by the international community. Furthermore, in practice, creditors often go out of their way to formally disassociate their loans to a debtor country from their policy interests, reducing transparency. In effect, they go out of the way to disassociate the form of the relation from its strategic political substance.[246] For example, in Angola, which exported roughly 465,000 barrels of oil per day to China in the first months of 2007, Beijing secured a major stake in future oil production in 2004 with a U.S. $ 2 billion package of loans and aid that includes funds for Chinese companies to build railroads, schools, hospitals and bridges.[247] Interestingly, there is no formal link between the loans and the access to future oil production. China argues that its loans are characterized by "non intervention" and "have no strings attached."[248]

Transparency and the reputation mechanism are further compromised when the policy interest is not liquid. For example, a creditor can lend in return for political clout. Similarly, creditors also lend to maintain political allies. The examples are endless. Such interests are difficult to quantify. These types of loans can also be extended in return for a policy interest to be delivered and defined at a later date, such as a future political favour, possibly after the debt is due.

All of these types of opaque official debt relations are ultimately sustained by reputation as a result of the long term relations between sovereign creditors and debtors, mutual exchange and repeat play. However, there is no obvious relation between the terms of the contract and how it reflects the debtor's reputation, defined as the probability of delivering on the policy interest.

Lack of Mutual Exchange

As time elapses, it is possible that the debt form of the relation remains, but that the mutual exchange between parties diminishes. This is more likely in the case of a borrowing country that has no alternate means of finance. Unlike private creditors which can withdraw their funds once they refrain from gaining from the lending relationship, once again, official creditors have conflicting considerations. A creditor country may find itself in a situation where the benefits from the debt relationship in terms of policy interest have ended, but it is politically difficult for it to take its

---

[246] Interestingly, states also go out of their way to separate the form of debt forgiveness to its political strategic substance, such as the role of the United States in Iraq's debt forgiveness process, See Gelpern 2005

[247] Hanson June 6, 2008 available at: http.//www.cfr.org/publication/9557/#6

[248] Hanson June 6, 2008

resources out of a poor developing country or refrain from providing more credit, if the consequences would be devastating. This would resemble something like defensive lending of banks, but rather than lending to prevent losses in the balance sheets, it could involve lending to prevent any negative political and economic externalities from default or exit. The relationship is then sustained, not due to reputation, but because the costs of ending the relationship may be too large for both the borrowing country and the lending country.

Likewise, middle income countries that have a mix of commercial and official debt can always repay their official debt back and regain policy independence when they refrain from gaining from the relationship. However, many of the poorest developing countries rely on a few sources of official credit for external finance and rarely have the option to exit the relationship. They face a monopolistic or oligopolistic market for credit. In such markets, the monopolist is able to charge a higher price than would be the case if the market were competitive, and consequently can extract consumer surplus. While most of the official loans that poor countries receive are concessional, (below market rate), creditors may extract a borrower's surplus from the transaction through policy interests. Many of the conditionalities attached to official debt agreements are, in effect, the *purpose* of the contract.[249] Like in any monopoly market, the power and ability of the official creditor to extract surplus from the debt relation is a function of the number of creditors in the market. The borrower's leverage lies in its ability to mobilize credit from other sources, be it private sources or one of the major new players in official debt, such as Venezuela, China or Russia, for example.[250]

Just as globalisation and financial development has led to new players and in the private sovereign debt market, traditional (western) players in the official sovereign debt market are increasingly facing competition in some countries.[251] An interesting

---

[249] As opposed to the role of conditionalities and clauses in corporate and private debt for example, whose purpose is to control risk and maximize the propects of repayment.

[250]

[251] For example, although Chinese relations, including debt relations, with Africa have surged, Western states still make the vast majority of investments in Africa and remain highly influential, but new players like China represent competition in the region. See Hanson June 6, 2008

While competition can exist between creditor states, it can also exist between creditor states and IFIs. Indeed, prior to the current financial crisis, multilateral lending through international financial institutions, such as the World Bank and the International Monetary Fund (IMF), had been losing both trust and business across the world since 1997. Disbursements by the IMF have fallen by 90% since 1995, when it disbursed twenty seven billion U.S. dollars globally, to only two billion in 2007. See Mitra-Kahn 2008 available at www.livemint.com

As described by Bello and Guttal, "In 1985, the International Monetary Fund and the World Bank...stood at the pinnacle of their power." A decade later, in Argentina decided to "get emancipated" by repaying a big portion of its IMF back ahead of schedule. In the same month, Brazil, the IMF's biggest debtor, repaid in full its entire debt owed to the IMF two years in advance. The balance of power is shifting and is evident by the fact that some emerging country creditors, such as China, have equal or multiple times the financial power of the IMF. The financial crisis has renewed the role of international financial institutions as

question is whether competition will lead to a 'race to the bottom' or a 'race to the top.' This, in turn, will depend on how both debtors and creditors adapt to competition. Some debtors may be tempted by 'easy' forms of credit. An example could be Argentina, who decided to "get emancipated"[252] from the IMF by repaying a big portion of its IMF back ahead of schedule with the help of Venezuela, who bought a substantial amount of Argentina bonds to "help Argentina end its dependence with the IMF."[253] Traditional western official creditors can either position themselves in competition by providing similarly 'easy' forms of credit, or conversely, attempt to regain their relevance by improving the quality of their credit and restoring mutual exchange in sovereign debt relations. Indeed, the IMF may be trying to do both. Its new and more flexible approach to lending to emerging countries with strong track records, such as Mexico, by easing policy conditions is an example of the IMF responding to competition.[254]

In summary, official sovereign debt credit is characterized by a larger gap between form and substance relative to private sovereign debt. Reputation, therefore, may be based on the underlying mutual exchange in the relationship, other than repayment. However, it may be more difficult for parties to exit official sovereign debt relations, when the mutual exchange is diluted, possibly due to dependency on the part of the debtor. This further increases the gap between form and substance as well as the relationships between the reputation mechanism and the underlying exchange.

3.3.4 Information

The fourth factor that distinguishes different types of creditors and affects reputation in sovereign debt relations, is information. This section draws, in part, from the corporate finance literature on a firm's choice between bank lending and bond finance which focuses on the different types of information that are available to banks and bondholders.[255] The literature has referred to these two types of financing as arm's length lending and relationship lending and are both primarily motivated by profit. The literature highlights the distinction between the role of banks or other private lenders versus the public bond market, which is driven in part by the superiority of banks to collect and process information. While the public debt market, through rating agencies, also has this ability, the difference lies in the type of information that each specializes in collecting and understanding. Some scholars have referred as this as the difference

'lenders of last resort' but the IMF is nevertheless attempting to regain relevance by easing the policy conditions attached to its loans to emerging economies with strong track records.

[252] Subramanian January 27, 2006

[253] Baribeau December 21st, 2005 available at: www.venezuelaanalysis.com/news/1537 See also, The Economist August 9th, 2007 (dealing with the continued support that Venezuela has offered Argentina in the form of debt, in return for political support for President Chavez).

[254] . See IMF Website : http://www.imf.org/external/pubs/ft/survey/so/2008/POL102908A.htm "The IMF said it will create a new short term lending facility to channel funds quickly to emerging markets hat have a strong track record, but that need help during the current financial crisis to get them through temporary liquidity problems."

[255] See Diamond 1991; Rajan 1992

between "soft" and "hard" information.[256] The public bond markets collect "hard" information, which includes financial disclosure and accounting reports as well as default histories, which can all be reduced to a series of numbers. Banks also rely on this type of information, but also engage in costly additional information which is not available in hard numbers and is often a byproduct of the bank-borrower relationship, such as the perceived honesty of the firm manager for example.[257]

The aim of this section is to apply some of the insights from this branch of literature to the sovereign debt context and to look at how different creditors gather information about a sovereign.

3.3.4.1 Private Creditors: Bondholders

Petersen explains that the evolution of financial markets has been in part a replacement of soft information with hard information as the basis for financial transactions.[258] He argues that one of the advantages of using hard information is greater standardization and hence lower transaction costs, which can expand the size of the market. Hard information is difficult to contain and is therefore available to the public. Soft information is acquired as a byproduct of the creditor-debtor relationship and is not easily communicated to third parties.

This analysis is not perfectly applied to the market for sovereign debt, because the information that is available for a sovereign is not of the same type and quality as that which is available about a firm or a business project. Nevertheless, bondholders, because of their anonymous, small and dispersed nature, have to rely on the hard information about sovereigns that is publicly available, including, for example information that is provided by rating agencies.[259] Intermediaries, such as investment banks, also conduct 'buy side research.'

Although emerging market economies are increasingly hiring professional agencies such as Moody's and Standard and Poor's to monitor and rate them,[260] ratings only constitute one factor in an investor's analysis and information is still costly to convey for many developing countries. This limits the depth of the emerging market

---

[256] Petersen 2004

[257] Petersen 2004, 3

[258] Petersen 2004, 9

[259] See for example, Tanaka 2006 (arguing that the use of public information and public monitoring by bondholders makes them more easily transferable and therefore cheaper than other sources of credit)

[260] The number of emerging market economies rated by Moody's rose from 8 to 65 and by Standard and Poor's from 11 to 68 between 1990 and 2002. See Tanaka 2006, 11

bond market, and in turn, the market for derivative products which broadens the investor base by allowing bondholders to trade and diversify risk. [261]

This analysis suggests that bondholders employ reputation sanctions according to the hard information that they obtain in the market. As Petersen explains, one of the reasons that hard information involves less transaction costs, is that it is standardized. It follows, that through standardization, some information may be lost. For instance, it is widely known that investors tend to lump together developing countries in a region as a class, despite the fact that they may be substantially different in terms of the state of their economy and their creditworthiness at any given point in time. Paul Krugman's recent account of Asia's crash in the late 1990's concurs. He argues that, "The appetite of investors for the region has been fed by the perception of a shared "Asian miracle." When one country's economy (Thailand) turned out not to be miraculous after all, it shook faith in all the others."[262] In this case, countries in good economic health at the time, such as Indonesia[263], were nonetheless vulnerable to investors' self fulfilling panic, which is a result of their uncertainty and their lack of information about distinct developing countries.

The consequence is that bondholders only invest in countries on which they can obtain reliable public information and for which there is a secondary market in which they can trade and diversify their risk. This excludes a lot of the poorest, low income countries. Conversely, they invest in emerging economies at very expensive terms to compensate for the uncertainty and informational asymmetry in the market. If this is the case, then sovereign debt is too expensive and there is sub-optimal financing to developing countries due to informational constraints.

3.3.4.2 Private Creditors-Banks

Banks are able to engage in costly monitoring and information gathering which may allow them to have access to sovereign markets for debt that bondholders do not. Furthermore, many have been present and doing business in developing countries for many decades and this historical relationship allows them to develop personal ties within the borrowing country as well as local expertise and knowledge about specific challenges and risks. They may resemble most closely, "relationship banking" as described by the literature in the domestic banking context.[264] Rajan explains that a bank lending to a firm for a project can obtain information about the firm in the course of lending which the firm cannot easily communicate to others.[265] This suggests that

[261] See for example Dages, Palmer et al. May 2005

[262] Krugman 2009, 94

[263] Krugman 2009, 92-94

[264] Rajan 1992; Agarwal and Hauswald 2007

[265] Rajan 1992, 1368

they will have access to 'soft' information as byproduct of their local presence and personal relationships with government officials in the debtor country.

Their superior knowledge should make the reputation mechanism more accurate all else equal and less volatile than with bondholders. However, their close relationships and local presence within the debtor countries also interferes with their incentives to employ reputation sanctions strictly and disrupt any other relations or interests in the country.

3.3.4.3 Official Creditors

Like banks, official creditors have continued relations with the debtor country and have a local presence in the country which can allow them to have access to certain types of soft information. However, unlike in "relationship banking" where creditors rely on soft information but their ultimate goal is repayment and profit, official creditors rely on soft information, but their ultimate goal is not always, or entirely, profit. Consequently, the information that they will gather will not pertain to increasing the prospects of repayment, but will be relevant to their policy interests in the country.

Indeed, the information which is produced in a market guided by political incentives is different to that which is produced in a market guided by profit incentives.[266] Insights from Austrian economics argue that the market is conducive to an entrepreneurial process which reveals information such as unexploited profit opportunities. In the political context, information is also produced but only that which is relevant to political actors.[267] This is consistent with the reputation mechanism being dependent on whether the debtor delivers on the policy interests of the official creditor, as opposed to repayment.

3.3.5 Sovereign Debt Restructuring

An analysis of sovereign debt relations is not complete without an analysis of sovereign debt restructuring. When the stakes are high, both creditors and debtors have incentives to find manageable solutions. By and large, upon a debtor's default or imminent default, parties turn to debt restructuring.[268] For creditors that are motivated by profit, the incentives pertain to maximizing recovery, or minimizing losses. For creditors with profit incentives but a number of different relations with the debtor country, they will also have an incentive to restructure to preserve their other businesses in the country. Finally, restructuring can also be a means for creditors to further entrench the creditor-debtor relationship. The ability of different creditors to

---

[266] The branch of Austrian economics has highlighted this point, See for example Ebeling 2003

[267] Boettke, Coyne et al., 8

[268] Indeed, the prevalence of debt restructuring has been argued to have halted the development of law pertaining to international debt. See for example, King 2007, 58

engage in restructurings with the sovereign borrower will be a function of their nature and incentives.

It is clear that the incentives of debtors and creditors are very different at the time of restructuring; creditors want to cut their losses and recover as much as they can, while a debtor wants to offer them the lowest amount possible. A debtor, however, is constrained by reputation concerns. It knows that how much creditors are ultimately left with and how long they have to wait for it, will implicate its reputation.

3.3.5.1 Private Creditors: Bondholders

Conventional wisdom in the economic literature assumes that a debtor's decision to default is based on a comparison of the costs and benefits of default, but that default is always costly for creditors. However, for sovereign debt to exist, this cost must be made up by positive returns during normal times. In other words, creditors have a diversified portfolio and expect to win on average as opposed to gaining from every bond transaction. This means that lenders expect that they will not always be paid back in full. They seek to earn a target portfolio yield and try to recoup as much as possible in pre or post default restructurings of individual bonds. As Vincent Crawford explains, it is "not optimal to structure a loan agreement so that default…will not occur under any foreseeable circumstance, because risk sharing is an important source of potential gain for both borrowers and lenders."[269] Investors lend to governments that might default, provided that that the probability of default is not too high and the expected amount that investors would recover after a breach of contract, would still make the loan profitable.

Bondholders' profit maximizing incentives are present at the time that they extend credit, as well as at the time of renegotiation if a debtor defaults. Because loan contracts are not "renegotiation proof", following a default or a threat of non repayment, creditors have an incentive ex post to renegotiate the terms of the loan contracts, as they will be better off accepting something rather than nothing. Their incentives and willingness to restructure will depend, in part, on the value that the bonds are being traded at in the secondary market. After a debtor's announcement of default, the bonds lose trading value.[270] As in the context of lending, investors have different risk appetites. While some may prefer accepting a restructuring offer quickly, in order to get some money back now, others prefer the risk of waiting longer in hopes of getting more money back later. By waiting, investor may be able to successfully holdout on a debtor's restructuring efforts. The longer they wait, however, the higher the risk that the debtor's economy deteriorates and the lower their bonds will be worth in the secondary market which can affect their bargaining power in negotiations. Their satisfaction with their compensation received will depend on the relative compensation

[269] Crawford 1987, 2

[270] Speculative investors, such as hedge funds, are specialized in buying distressed debt in the secondary market at a discount, and they often agree to harsh restructuring terms because they hope to make large profits relative to the discounted price. See Gelpern 2005a, 7-8

of other creditors and the other relative options in the market. Finally, bondholders have no incentive to offer full debt forgiveness. It will only forgive part of the debt if it increases the prospects for repayment of the remaining obligation.[271]

Despite the fact that engaging in restructurings avoids deadweight losses for both a debtor and its creditors, and therefore is mutually beneficial, creditor coordination failures can delay debt restructuring, resulting in the problem of collective action. Collective action describes the circumstance where individuals acting rationally to maximize self interest generate an outcome detrimental to their interests as a group. The characteristics of bondholders which make them less susceptible to outside influences also make them particularly prone to collective action problems. These include the fact that they are many in numbers and widely dispersed, they cannot easily communicate with each other, and they have no relations between each other that would give them the incentives to cooperate and coordinate with each other. They are guided by their individual self interests in profit maximization. These collective action problems can involve a "rush to exit,"[272] where bondholders hurry to sell the debt, as well as the hold out problem, where a minority off bondholders hold out or free ride on a restructuring agreement.

Furthermore, the increased formalization of the private market for sovereign debt has led to the emergence of a new collective action problem; that of "rush to the courthouse" whereby bondholders hurry to sue the debtor.[273] Bondholders increasingly have greater individual enforcement rights, in part as a result of the demise of sovereign immunity in commercial contracts, making it possible for them to sue sovereign debtors in national courts, such as New York and London. Given that reputation is an alternate, second-best form of enforcement to the formal legal enforcement which exists at the domestic level, this increased formalization should be in the benefit of both the sovereign and its creditors. However, as the insights from the field of law-and-economics convey, this is not the case if investors use their increased enforcement rights against each other, in order to obtain relative advantages vis-à-vis each other.[274]

---

[271] This is explained by the Laffer Curve

[272] See Buchheit and Gulati 2000

[273] This problem, although it has received a lot of attention by academics, appears to have not substantiated in practice. For a discussion See Gelpern and Gulati 2007

[274] Sovereign bonds governed by New York law are uniquely prone to this problem because until recently, they contained no contractual mechanism to bind the potential holdout. By custom, documentation for such bonds required unanimous approval of the holders to amend financial terms. See Gulati and Choi 2004 .

Although restructuring could be accomplished effectively through the debt exchange (instead of amending the old bond, participating holders exchange it for a new one), creditors refusing to exchange retained the full original claim. In contrast, English law sovereign bonds could be amended by majority vote.

Although collective actions problems have been widely documented in the literature[275] and it is generally accepted that they interfere with bondholders' ability to enforce their debt claims, their specific effect on the reputation mechanism has not been directly highlighted. Coordination problems between bondholders undermine and obstruct the reputation mechanism. They delay restructuring, ultimately reducing the amount that creditors as a whole can recover. At the same time, because creditors are worse off as a result and receive less from a restructuring, the debtor will suffer reputation sanctions as a result. The negative effect on the sovereign debtor's reputation may then not be a result of its unwillingness to compensate investors, but rather a consequence of the coordination problems between creditors that prevent it from reaching an agreement with it. This increases the costs of default for debtors.

3.3.5.2 Private Creditors: Banks

In the 1980s, restructuring sovereign debt was a generally ordered process. The major creditors were typically commercial banks and they negotiated through a steering committee. Such a steering committee would be composed of around 15 people holding a large percentage of the debt, perhaps 85%. Banks have several incentives to cooperate. One reason has to do with the fact, mentioned earlier, that banks may have multiple ongoing activities within the debtor country. Consequently, they have an interest in restructuring their debt upon default to maintain good relations with the debtor and thereby safeguard any current and future business. Secondly, there are less creditors involved in a syndicate than in a bond issue and this makes it easier to communicate with each other and put pressure on individual banks that do not want to participate in a restructuring. Finally, syndicated bank loans benefit from a lead bank, which acts as delegated monitor, coordinates restructurings and represents the banks in negotiations. Banks abided by a sharing clause which required to share any proceeds recovered with their fellow creditors.

3.3.5.3 Official Creditors

The literature on official debt relief is vast. The incentives for official creditors to restructure may be as wide as their original incentives to lend. While profit maximizing creditors have no incentives to provide full debt forgiveness, official creditors, on the other hand, do. Their incentives to engage in restructurings are not primarily profit driven. Rather, incentives to forgive debt can arise out of humanitarian

Many have argued that the rush to the courthouse problem has been overstated and has failed to materialize in practice. By the same toke, some scholars have argues that collective action clauses (CACs)have had no significant effect in the markets, despite the vast attention that was devoted to them. These scholars argue that the main purpose of CACs has been a communicative one. CACs officially signal to private creditors that the official sector will not interfere with their restructurings. Consequently, private creditors should opt out the official sector from their boilerplate contracts. See Gelpern 2004, 20.

In any case, a solution to the problem has been found, maked by Mexico's SEC-registered twelve year global note issued in February 2003. In contrast to the unanimity convention under New York law, the notes allow 75% of the bondholders to change key financial terms. See Gelpern and Gulati 2007

[275] Gelpern and Gulati 2007; Dixon June 2000

and development concerns in the debtor country (which could be a result of domestic pressure in the creditor country).[276] Conversely, forgiveness can stem from less benevolent interests, such as political stakes involved in further entrenching the creditor-debtor relationship.[277]

The official sovereign debt restructuring process has become increasingly formalized, in the sense that vast amounts of debt are traditionally restructured under the auspices of one institution, using its guidelines and practices, and through the participation of its regular members. The institution is called the Paris Club and it has existed since 1956, grouping together the major western official creditor and providing a venue for them to find solutions to the payment difficulties of debtor countries. When a debtor to one or many of the member creditors finds itself in a situation of imminent default, it recurs to the Paris Club for restructuring. There is regular communication, information sharing and negotiation between the debtor and its creditors as well as frequent meetings. This makes the reputation mechanism particularly strong, all else equal. Information about a debtor's default is shared amongst creditors and implicates a debtor's reputation in the eyes of all of the member creditors. Having said that, the rise of new non-Paris Club official creditors such as China and Venezuela, for instance, is shifting the balance of power away from the Paris Club and its western creditor members, and has resulted in much more complex and less smooth restructuring procedures.

3.3.5.4 A Note on Inter-Creditor Equity

The relatively new and problematic issue of inter creditor equity in sovereign debt relations reflects the increasingly complex debt composition of borrowing countries. Restructuring becomes more complex when a debtor has to negotiate with different types and classes of creditors. Coordination problems are exacerbated across different types of creditors with different incentives and relationships with the sovereign as well as across different types of credit with different structures and maturities. The absence of explicit, enforceable priorities in sovereign debt has received virtually no policy or academic attention until recently.[278] The complexity of the debt composition may not be evident until after default. This in turn complicates risk assessment at the time of borrowing and creates poor management incentives.

Inter creditor issues are indicative of the limitations of separating creditor types and sovereign debt relations into clear cut, distinct and separate categories. Indeed, providing a taxonomy of different sovereign credito°rs is an increasingly complex task, especially taking into account the secondary market for sovereign debt. Nevertheless, this section has attempted to do just that. Although the three categories are simplified, they highlight the different incentives between bondholders, banks and official

[276] See for example Callaghy 2004

[277] Gelpern 2007

[278] Gelpern 2004, 21

creditors, and how different factors affect the dynamics of their relationships with sovereigns. This sets the stage for the following section, which analyzes how reputation is affected in each type of sovereign debt relationship and, in turn, how odious debt can stem from it.

3.4 Reputation and Odious Debt

3.4.1 Private Creditors: Bonds

3.4.1.1 Reputation

The analysis of the five factors affecting reputation indicates that, despite informational and coordination constraints, the strength of the reputation mechanism for bondholders is high relative to other investor types. This is due mainly to their pure profit maximizing incentives and their anonymous and dispersed nature which makes them relatively immune to outside influences. Investors have a primary interest in making as much money as possible from their lending transactions and rely primarily on the reputation mechanism as a means to that end. They have strong incentives to allocate credit according to how they interpret a debtor's reputation. Borrowers, in turn, have strong incentives to repay their debts in order to maintain or acquire a good reputation.

While on the one hand, there may a sub-optimal amount bond financing due to coordination and informational problems, on the other hand there may be too much financing of certain types of debt. This is the case when bond contracts do not take into account externalities generated by the creditor-debtor relationship. The relationship and the reputation mechanism is primarily based on repayment, and external factors, such as the use of the loan, do not enter the relation. Indeed, this is the crucial differences between 'debt' and 'equity.'

3.4.1.2 Odious Debt

What are the implications of this for odious debt and how does odious debt stem from sovereign bond relations? Because bondholders care primarily about how their expected profit is affected, if the odious use of proceeds from loans affects their repayment, this information will be reflected in the value of the bonds and will have an effect on a debtor's reputation. Indeed, many odious activities, such as financing genocide, repression of the population or the gross looting of funds, directly affect credit risk and the prospects of repayment. Investors, then, generally stay away from governments engaged in such activities as they are poor risks. Some of the most repressive or 'odious' governments, such as North Korea for example, have no private debt. Consequently, to the extent that the majority of odious activities are risky and non profitable, governments that engage in a lot of odious activities will not primarily attract bond financing. Conversely, bond financing will only be available at very expensive terms. Furthermore, because the reputation mechanism in bond lending is relatively strong, the enforcement mechanism acts as an effective disciplining device and gives strong incentives for debtors to refrain from engaging in activities, including odious activities, that negatively affect their repayment prospects.

On the other hand, because the reputation mechanism is primarily based on repayment and how much creditors ultimately gain from a transaction, any odious externalities that do not affect the private costs and benefits of the parties will not be taken into consideration. This is the case if the odious use of loan proceeds by a borrowing government does not affect repayment expectations. Investors will lend to governments with a good reputation in paying back their loans, even if they may have a less than perfect reputation in the human rights arena or other arenas associated with odious activities. Sudan sovereign bonds, backed by commodities such as oil, may be a case in point.[279] Some analysts have argued that while banks currently undergo increasing scrutiny with regards to financing sensitive projects which may harm local people or cause environmental concerns, the bond issues that they underwrite are not subject to the same restrictions. Hence, investors are free to purchase bonds and finance dubious projects in countries such as Sudan and Burma.[280] Odious debt then comes about upon a regime change, when the successor government and its population inherits any unpaid debt. Even in the case where odious debt is paid back by the predecessor government and is consequently not inherited by the successor regime, any odious externalities from the use of the loans proceeds may still be inherited and may be significant. This dimension of the odious debt problem has not been emphasized by the literature.

3.4.2 Private Creditors: Banks

3.4.2.1 Reputation

All else equal, the profit maximizing incentives of banks should make the reputation mechanism between them and the borrowing countries high. At the same time, all else equal, their superior information gathering and monitoring abilities as well as their local presence in many borrowing countries should make their assessments of borrowers' reputations relatively accurate. However, all else is seldom equal. The multiple types of ongoing relations that banks can have within a debtor country, their incentives to engage in defensive lending and their susceptibility to outside influences disrupt the reputation mechanism.

Reputation and the creditor debtor relationship is conditional, not purely on repayment, but on the extent of the relationships between the two parties in its entirety,

---

[279] Sudan's first issuance of securities took place in 2008 in the form of Islamic bonds. "An Islamic-compliant issue, backed by oil in some way, would appeal to an emerging Middle Eastern investor base." Reported Stuart Culverhouse, chief economist at Exotix Ltd. Cited in the Sudan Tribune available at: http://www.sudantribune.com/spip.php?article25506 For a discussion on Sudanese Islamic finance See "Country Focus: Sudan - Forgotten centre of Islamic finance" April 1st, 2009

[280] Rowling August 9th, 2005 available at : http://news.bbc.co.uk/2/hi/business/4134922.stm

including the different number and types of relations that exist in addition to debt.[281] When reputation is not based entirely on a debtor's performance in the debt relationship itself, the disciplining mechanism which gives incentives to borrowers to maximize repayment is diluted.

Furthermore, because banks do not always allocate credit according to a borrower's repayment reputation, but instead may be guided by hegemonic influences, implicit guarantees or short term profit performance figures, this results in both over-lending and over-borrowing.

3.4.2.2 Odious Debt

Odious debt can stem from sovereign bank lending in various ways which depend on the nature of the bank's relationship with the sovereign borrower. Banks who have incentives in getting repaid and lend to a sovereign with whom they do not have many other types of relations within the debtor country will have incentives to allocate credit according to their perception of a debtor's reputation. Like bondholders, they will be more inclined to employ reputation sanctions and take their resources out of the country in the case of non repayment. The interests of these banks vis-à-vis the borrower is to make a profit from the debt relationship itself. Any odious activities that negatively affect repayment will have a negative effect on a borrower's reputation and on their access to credit. Consequently, these types of banks will not finance non profitable odious activities. Arguably, however, whether odious debt will affect the prospects of repayment, will often be a question of time. Consequently, whether banks have short or long term interests in the debtor country will play a role in whether they finance activities that may turn out to be odious in the future.

Conversely, sovereigns that borrow from banks with multiple relations and business in their country know that if they use the loan proceeds for non profitable odious purposes that negatively affect their ability to repay, they will be able to either roll over their loans in the short term and then may be able to repay in the form of alternate business. In this way, odious debt can stem from the close bank-borrower relationship. A sovereign borrower, however, is still disciplined by the multiple relationships with the bank as a whole. If they engage in odious activities which negatively affect a bank's expected profit from all of its businesses combined, the bank will then prefer to exit.

To the extent that many odious activities are not profitable and are therefore discouraged by the disciplining mechanism of private creditors on sovereign

[281] A statement by the General Manager of the South Africa Reserve Bank shows how South Africa's relationships with banks involve multiple businesses. "The Reserve Bank has capitalized on this trust and developed it further by offering the banks reciprocity. Whereas previously reciprocity included gold business, today banks who lend money to the Reserve Bank can expect reciprocal business, such as clearing accounts, eposits, foreign exchange turnover or even an opportunity to manage some of the Reserve Banks foreign reserves. The banks know that we are strong on reciprocity and that we honour any undertakings and commitments." See Van Zyl 2001, 5

borrowers, it is important that banks bear the full costs and benefits of the transactions, and conduct risk assessment accordingly. This is not always the case, as a bank's incentives to lend may not always be based on a risk assessment of the expected repayment prospects or the expected return from the portfolio of different relations in the country. Instead, they can be guided by short term profit figures, hegemonic influences or implicit guarantees. This creates moral hazard and can result in over-lending. Odious debt, in turn, can stem from overly irresponsible lending and borrowing.

Finally, as in the case of sovereign bonds, odiousness can also be a result of externalities from the creditor-debtor relationship that do not affect the mutual exchange between the parties. The classic example, often cited the odious debt literature, is that of extensive bank lending to South Africa that took place during the apartheid era. The successor government inherited all of the unpaid, odious debt.

3.4.3 Official Creditors

3.4.3.1 Reputation

Official sovereign debt relations are not entirely sustained on a debtor's repayment reputation. By the same token, official credit is not always allocated to sovereigns on the basis of a creditor's assessment of its repayment prospects. Relative to private debt, official debt does not invoke the same disciplining mechanism and does not give borrowers strong incentives to repay their debt. Instead, the reputation mechanism is generally, in some way, contingent on the creditor's policy interest in the debtor country.

3.4.3.2 Odious Debt

When there is fungible mutual exchange, it is possible to structure a relationship based on reputation where the creditor lends in return for privileged access to raw materials, for example. In such relationships then, a borrower has incentives to perform and maintain a good reputation with regards to delivering on the policy interest. Repayment of the loan, however, will have no, or less of an effect on the relationship. Borrowers therefore, will not develop incentives to improve their debt management skills, pay back their debt and improve their repayment reputation. Odious debt can stem from such a relationship because the government borrower is free to use the proceeds from the loans for whatever purposes it desires, odious or not, as long as they don't affect the policy interest of the creditor. In very low income countries with poor institutions and weak checks on governments, government officials benefiting from huge inflows of money have strong incentives to appropriate funds or spend them in a way to retain power. In this way, official credit is in effect indirectly sustaining the current government in power.

Official creditors can also be guided by humanitarian and development concerns when lending to a poor country at heavily subsidized rates. The policy interests of the creditor country of IFI may be related to allocating resources to poverty reduction and development and liberalization among others. In this type of relationship, the reputation mechanism is much weaker. This is because creditors understand that a debtor may not be capable of fully or immediately delivering on the policy interests and will be content with obtaining a promise to deliver. This means that borrowers will have weak incentives to develop debt management capacity and repay the debt because reputation is not based on repayment. At the same time, they will also have weak incentives to deliver on the policy interests because the reputation mechanism in this exchange is weak. Consequently, this leads to moral hazard and over borrowing. Having said that, these arguments are not very useful to official creditors who are guided by short term purposes such as humanitarian needs in the borrowing country. Just as official creditors accept a certain degree of moral hazard and over lending, they accept a certain degree of irresponsible use of loan proceeds.

In general, official loan relationships are rarely very transparent. This is due to the dynamic and wide range of policy interests that can motivate a creditor to lend as well as the often significant gap between the debt form and the substance of the debt relation. Maintaining the debt form, through the rolling over of loans for example, further entrenches the relationship. Odious debt is created when the debt form is inherited from government to government in the debtor country. For debtors to regain policy independence, they are obliged to repay their official debt. In this way, they repay their debt twice, once in policy interests and then again by paying back their credit.

3.5 Conclusion

This chapter has highlighted the incentives that guide different creditors to lend to sovereigns. It analyzed several factors that affect the strength of reputation as an enforcement mechanism in sovereign relations as well as the underlying exchange which implicates reputation. Odious debt stems from these relations in different ways.

In general, when odiousness arises as an externality of a private sovereign debt relationship, but does not affect repayment, it is difficult to restrict the incentives of profit maximizing creditors from lending. However, the adoption of best practices by private creditors, such as the Ecuador Principles,[282] is an encouraging development. There is increasing international pressure and interest in exploiting the abilities of banks to monitor and control activities as well as disclose and report information. For example, many major banks have already agreed to a set of ethical principles in their own lending. The major English banks abide by the EIRIS Guide to Responsible Banking, which includes reports of lending policies adopted by banks. Among these are policies in relation to, "operating or dealing with countries with oppressive regimes."[283] Indeed, the monitoring, communication and information gathering abilities

[282] See Ecuador Principles at _

[283] EIRIS Guide to Responsible Banking 2003

of banks may indicate that they are the 'least cost avoiders' of odious risk. Aside from greater transparency, better regulation is also needed. Caution must be given to regulatory gaps in the shadow financial system. If greater scrutiny is given to the direct lending activities of banks, but not to the underwriting of bond issues and bond finance, sensitive projects by governments will be financed through these channels.

Official debt is motivated by a wide range of policy interests, some odious and some not. The gap between form and substance that characterizes official sovereign debt means that reputation is not always entirely contingent on repayment. The relationship between reputation and the underlying policy interest, other than repayment, is unclear. This, combined with a lack of transparency, weakens the disciplining mechanism for debtors which gives them incentives to develop policy and debt management capacity. Consequently, official credit which is motivated by development concerns, such as poverty reduction, should be accompanied with training and capacity development. The major IFIs continue to take steps in this direction but acknowledge that there is a lot of room for improvement. For example, the World Bank argues that it has yet to complete its shift from individual lending to capacity building. Furthermore, it seeks to improve capacity building in regions such as Africa, for example, by extending its traditional focus beyond developing individual skills to strengthening institutions.[284]

Official creditors are more willing to engage in costly measures such as training programs, to extend concessional credit to developing countries and may be more willing to addressing odious debt in the context of development and humanitarian concerns. While the divergent interests of official creditors may be more susceptible to contributing to a solution to odious debt, they are also the most prone to contribute to the creation of odious debt in the first place. On the one hand, odious debt may negatively affect their benevolent interests to address poverty and development, on the other hand, it may be a direct by product of a profitable official sovereign debt relationship. Even worse, odiousness may be embodied in the mutually beneficial exchange of the relationship, such as when official loans sustain a repressive government which provides the creditor in return with access to key policy interests.

What is true, however, is that the consequences of odious debt are no longer limited to the borrowing country, but are increasingly felt by the international community as a whole, as a result of greater interdependence between countries due to globalisation. To the extent that the odious use of loans and odious debt increases the risk of failed and rogue states, the stakes of not addressing odious debt are high. Furthermore, the threat of new forms of easy official credit from authoritarian regimes increases competition in the sovereign credit markets. Competition can lead to either a race to the bottom or a race to the top. For western official creditors and IFIs to regain their relevance and power, they may need to improve the quality of their lending

[284] http://www.worldbank.org/oed/africa_capacity_building/

practices as well as find ways to work together and be more inclusive of the new emerging economic powers.

4 An International Solution to Odious Debt: An Ex Ante Ex Post Analysis

The aim of this Chapter is to determine whether an ex ante approach or an ex post approach would be more suitable to tackle the international problem of odious debt. This chapter does not comment on whether it is actually desirable to have a solution which deals specifically with odious debt. Rather, assuming that such a solution is desired, it addresses the trade offs involved in each approach. Although a wide variety of proposals have been brought forth by the literature, none has specifically addressed the relative advantages and disadvantages of ex ante and ex post approaches in their entirety.[285]

The analysis draws from Shavell's well known analysis of ex ante regulation versus ex post liability in the context of tort.[286] It applies the four determinants Shavell derives to assess the relative desirability of an ex ante versus an ex post mechanism to the international sovereign lending context in order to see which would be more desirable to minimize the risk of odious debt. These determinants are: 1. the difference in knowledge about risky activities 2.the incapability of private parties paying for the harm done 3. parties would not face the threat of suit for harm done and 4. administrative costs. This analysis reveals the complexity of the nature of the problem of odious debt and its many dimensions and players.

Finally, one of the first and most ambitious proposals for odious debts from the economic literature by Jayachandran and Kremer, is analyzed.[287] They propose a mechanism of loan sanctions targeted at odious regimes. Their approach, in effect, lies somewhere in between the ex post and ex ante approaches and is therefore interesting to examine in this respect. Furthermore, in 2009, when the Obama-Biden campaign expressed interest in addressing the issue of odious debt, it specifically referred to the

---

[285] Ben-Shahar and Gulati 2007 discuss some of the advantages of an ex post liability approach to address odious debt.

[286] Shavell 1984; Shavell 2004

[287] Jayachandran and Kremer 2006

possibility of adopting loan sanctions, thereby introducing the proposal into the political realm.[288]

In conclusion, this chapter argues that neither an ex ante nor an ex post approach can completely eliminate the risk of odious debt. Different approaches will prioritize different aspects of the odious debt problem. Efficient ex ante incentives are needed to prevent perverse incentives of both creditors and lenders and encourage responsible lending and debt management. Ex post mechanisms are needed when odious debt does occur. The approaches are not mutually exclusive and can be used in combination. The nature of the combination should reflect the relative importance of ex ante and ex post advantages and disadvantages that are particular to the type of odious debt case being addressed.

This chapter is structured as follows; following this introduction Shavell's approach is briefly discussed and the differences between the domestic tort context which he analyses and the international sovereign debt context are highlighted. Shavell's analysis is then applied to the odious debt problem. Some of the costs and benefits of Jayachandran and Kremer's loan sanctions proposal from an ex ante – ex post perspective are analyzed. Finally, after Shavell's analysis has been applied to the context of odious debt and used to evaluate loan sanctions, some implications for addressing different cases of odious debt are drawn.

4.1 Applying Shavell's Analysis to the Odious Debt Context

Tort liability is private in nature and works not by social command but rather indirectly, through the deterrent effects of damage actions that may be brought once harm occurs. Standards, prohibitions and other forms of safety regulation, in contrast, are public in character and modify behaviour in an immediate way through requirements that are imposed before, or at least independently of the actual occurrence of harm.[289] Using economic analysis, Shavell compares the effects of liability rules and direct regulation and evaluates them on a utilitarian basis, given the assumption that individual actors can normally be expected to act in their own interests.[290] He sets out a measure of social welfare that is equal to the benefits parties derive from engaging in their activities, minus the sum of the costs of precautions, the harms done, and the administrative expenses associated with the means of social

---

[288] See www.barackobama.com 2007; www.politifact.com 2009

[289] Shavell 1984 358

[290] Shavell 1984 358

control.[291] The formal problem is to derive the means of control to maximize the measure of welfare.

Shavell looks at the relative desirability of regulation versus liability and brings forth some determinants to establish what the socially desirable way of employing these two means of alleviating risk is. Before continuing to analyze these four determinants in the context of odious debt, this section will look at how the domestic tort context which Shavell addresses differs from the international lending context. One crucial difference is the fact that there is no third party enforcement in international law. That is, there is no state police power ensuring that parties abide by regulation and there is no equivalent to a domestic court which enforces the rule of law. Many of the proposals in the odious debt literature implicate the involvement of international organizations such as the United Nations or the International Court of Justice. International bodies such as these enforce international law through reputation and can emphasize either forward looking regulation or backward looking resolve mechanisms. There are examples of both approaches adopted by international organizations in international finance and debt. For example, the Bank for International Settlements engages in ex ante approaches such as the development of best practices in banking supervision, credit disclosure and the regulation of minimum capital requirements for banks. The Paris Club, on the other hand, essentially adopts an ex post approach; it engages in ex post debt restructuring negotiations between a debtor and its official creditors. Interestingly, the Paris Club has recently also adopted ex ante best practices and guidelines, in conjunction with the private sector, in its efforts to promote more sustainable lending practices.[292]

Consequently, in the absence of a global Leviathan, the international community, via its international institutions, can address risks using either ex ante or ex post mechanisms, or a combination of both. This chapter aims at answering Shavell's question, "what is the socially desirable way to employ the two means of alleviating risks?" as it applies to the risk of odious debt.

4.2 Examination of Shavell's 4 Determinants

4.2.1 Difference in Knowledge about Risky Activities

4.2.1.1 Shavell's Analysis

The first determinant Shavell looks at when assessing whether ex ante regulation or ex post liability is more appropriate has to do with information and the difference in knowledge about risky activities as between private parties and a regulatory authority. This difference could relate to the benefits of activities, the costs of reducing risks, or

---

[291] Shavell 1984 358

[292] Paris Club Annual Report 2007 30

the probability or severity of the risks.[293] He argues that where private parties have superior knowledge of these elements, it would be better for them to decide about the control of risks, indicating an advantage of ex post liability rules, other things being equal.[294] An ex post mechanism like strict liability would be the most efficient given that it motivates the parties to balance the true costs of reducing risks against the expected savings in losses caused. He gives the example of an activity where private parties possess perfect information about risky activities and the regulator has poor knowledge. In this case, if the regulator were vested with the power of control, this would create a great chance of error as its standard would either be too stringent if it overestimated the potential for harm, or too lax if it underestimated the risk.[295] Under a system where parties are held liable for harm caused by the activity, they would be motivated to balance the true costs of reducing risks against the expected savings in losses caused and this would be efficient.[296] If, however, the regulator possesses superior information to private parties then direct regulation would be more attractive than liability.[297]

Shavell then goes on to address the question of when we can expect significant differences in information between private parties and regulators to exist. He argues that private parties should generally enjoy an advantage in knowledge as they are the ones who are engaging in and deriving benefits from their activities and therefore should be in a naturally superior position to estimate the nature of the risks created and the costs of their reduction.[298] In certain contexts, however, information about risk will not be an obvious by-product of engaging in risky activities but rather will require effort to develop or special expertise to evaluate. Consequently, there are contexts where the informational advantage of private parties is not evident and regulators might possess relatively better information.[299]

4.2.1.2 The Odious Debt Context

The first determinant applied to the context of odious debt asks whether the parties to the sovereign debt contract, namely the borrowing government and its creditor(s), possess superior information regarding the risk of odious debt than does the international community via its international organizations.

---

[293] Shavell 1984 359

[294] Shavell 1984 359

[295] Shavell 1984 359

[296] Shavell 1984 359

[297] Shavell 1984 359

[298] Shavell 1984 360

[299] Shavell 1984 360

A borrowing government has very good information about what it intends to use the proceeds of a loan for. It is in a naturally superior position to estimate the benefits, the nature of risks of harm from its activities as well as the costs of prevention. This is because the information is an ordinary byproduct of the government's activities. For an outside party to obtain comparable information would be a practical impossibility. This is in part to due to the difficulty in verifying such information which can be very costly.

The case for creditors is less clear. The amount of information that a creditor has about odious risk and whether it is in a good position to prevent it depends, in part, on whether the information is observable, and whether it can be obtained at low cost.

The literature has also discussed whether information about odious regimes can be a good indicator for information about odious debt activities. Bank loans to South Africa after United Nations Security Council sanctions were imposed on the apartheid regime are regularly cited in the odious debt literature as an example of creditors actively contributing to blatant violations of human rights.[300] It is clear that banks were or should have been reasonably aware that the loans that they were making would contribute to human rights violations in that country. More recently, China has been subject to a lot of scrutiny and criticism for its lending activities in Africa, including Sudan. Some argue that the loans have helped finance human rights violations and civil war in the country.

The issue is more complex, however. The odiousness of a regime is a subjective concept and difficult to define. Indeed, scholars have argued that one of the reasons that the doctrine of odious debt, formalized by Alexander Sack,[301] is unworkable in practice, is that it requires for debt to be incurred by a non democratic regime as one of the criteria for identifying public inherited debts. It involves, essentially, being able to observe and define when a state acts undemocratically, without the consent of the people. Determining whether a particular regime's structure of government is sufficiently democratic to form a basis for popular consent to government policies is challenging. Shafter points out the difficulties posed by contemporary political structures.[302]

Therefore, it is not self evident that creditors would best equipped to judge regimes in terms of their odiousness, not least because a clear definition of an odious regime does not exist, but because the exercise of judging regimes in general is a

---

[300] Hanlon 2002; Hanlon 2006; Abrahams August 2000

[301] Sack 1927, 157-63; Adams 1991

[302] " Iran holds popular elections, but candidates for office are strictly screened by unelected religious authorities who circumscribe the scope of the elected officials' power. The United States holds elections, but the authority of elected officials is limited by lifetime appointed judges whose decisions in some areas can only be overwritten by a process (constitutional amendment) so difficult and rare as to render it almost impossible" See Shafter 2007, 283

delicate and controversial one. Given the uncertainty and high stakes involved in judging regimes, it would not be efficient to put the burden on creditors. This would have perverse consequences in the market for international debt, such as a decreased access to credit for developing countries as a whole.

Even "bad" regimes can make. "good" use of their loans. Taking Chinese-Sudanese credit relations as an example, China has lent significant amounts to Sudan for infrastructure projects, including schools. The question the becomes whether all loans to a despotic regime are considered as an active contribution to odious risk, given that they help finance the regime and are fungible, thereby freeing up resources for other odious activities even if they are destined for "good" purposes. . At the same time, "good" regimes, which may not be blatantly odious, can use loan proceeds for odious purposes. Therefore, the odious or non odious nature of a regime, is not necessarily a good proxy for the odious debts of a regime. Consequently, it may be more efficient to focus on the information of parties with regards to the odiousness of individual loans, as opposed to regimes.

A more adequate mechanism is to give creditors incentives to take steps to avoid contributing to the odious risk of individual loans. As argued by some scholars, the problem of odious debt is similar to that of allocating liability among secondary contributors.[303] Creditors can have a secondary, yet active role in some instances of odious debt and therefore would be in a good position to take steps to reduce the risk of odiousness of the loans that they issue. The degree of a creditor's implication will depend on the amount of information that they have and whether they can obtain it at low cost.

There are cases when the odiousness of a loan will be a direct by-product of the creditor's activities and therefore they will have good information regarding odious risk by being a party to the contract. An example may be the case of a bank which is actively aiding and embedding odious rulers to deposit money into personal Swiss bank accounts.[304] One case which is often cited in support of the argument that "creditors should have known" about the odious nature of a transaction and are therefore partly responsible, is the 1923 arbitration case involving Great Britain and Costa Rica.[305] Mr. Tinoco overthrew the Costa Rican government in 1917 and became a dictator. Towards the end of his dictatorship, Mr. Tinoco borrowed money from the Royal Bank of Canada. The entire proceeds of the loan left the country at the same time as Mr. Tinoco did. The subsequent arbitration involved William Howard Taft of the United States as the sole arbitrator. While he adhered to the rule of state succession, Justice Taft refused to order Costa Rica to repay the Tinoco loans on the

---

303 Ben-Shahar and Gulati 2007

304 Ramasastry 2007

305 Arbitration between Great Britain and Costa Rica 1923 For a discussion of the Arbitration between Great Britain and Costa Rica See Ben-Shahar and Gulati 2007; Ludington, Mitu et al. Draft March, 17th, 2009 2009 #97

basis that the transactions were not of "an ordinary nature" but were "full of irregularities."[306] He added that the bank knew that this money was to be used by the retiring president, Mr. Tinoco.

What is particular about this case is the fact that Mr. Tinoco appropriated the entire amount of the debts for his personal use. For this reason, information about the odiousness of the loan was readily available at low cost and the creditors should have known. This rationale would be in line with several domestic legal tools which are used to deal with what can be viewed as domestic counterparts of the odious debt problem, such as the defenses of fraud and unclean hands.[307] These doctrines aim at not only deterring an undesirable activity, but also at deterring parties' incentives to contribute to it.[308]

However, in contrast to the Tinoco case, most cases of odiousness are not so blatantly obvious today, as the money that governments borrow is not entirely used for odious purposes. There is typically some effort, however marginal, for social benefit. Because money is fungible and the international financial system more complex, the odiousness of a loan may not be easily detectable or traceable. Nevertheless, it remains the case that there are instances when creditors are directly implicated in cases of odious debt and consequently have good information about odious risk.

Other times, although creditors may not actively be contributing to odious risk, they may be in a particularly good position to obtain information about odious risk at low cost. For example, some scholars have noted that most major private banks have branches or representative offices in the debtor countries and are thus in a favorable position to assess first hand certain types of information.[309] Furthermore, if banks have long term interests, and conduct different businesses in the debtor country, they may be concerned with the country's long term sustainability and development and may invest in information precisely to prevent any harmful odious activity which will harm their long term interests. Likewise, official creditors who may have long term relations

---

[306] Arbitration between Great Britain and Costa Rica 1923

[307] Ben-Shahar and Gulati 2007

[308] McClintock 1948

A creditor that colludes with a corrupt government in concealing the circumstance of a transaction, such as by paying a bribe to place a loan, can be argued to have committed fraud. Furthermore, contracts that are tainted with bribery or any other illegal activity can be subject to the defense of unclean hands. This doctrine can limit the ability of a lender to enforce a debt contracted under irregular circumstances. The doctrine was applied in Adler v Federal Republic of Nigeria, which denied the plaintiff who paid more than 5 million dollars in bribed to Nigerian officials, from recovering from them once the proceeds from their corrupt deal never substantiated. See 219 F. 3d 9th Cir. 2000, 869-873

[309] Buchheit 1995, 48

on many levels with the debtor country, may also have access to certain types of "soft information" that is not reflected directly in markets.[310]

Conversely, creditors with more short term profit maximization interests will rely primarily on hard information reflected in the market. Bond based lending currently dominates the supply market for private credit to sovereign states. Bonds are liquid instruments and the individual holders are atomistic, constituting many individual parties to the sovereign loan contract. Investors may not know what bond they are holding in their portfolios at any given point in time. The number of bondholders can be in the hundreds or thousands and very dispersed. These creditors are unlikely to know about the behavior of the governments they are lending to and rely solely on information which is transmitted in the market. The market can often be shortsighted and the information that private bondholders are concerned with may not include odious risk. For example, the repercussions from odious looting activities may only be reflected in the long run. Second, if odiousness is manifested in the form of externalities, it may not be immediately reflected in the information in the market.

Odiousness can be tied to the risk of non repayment, as is often the case when dictators drive their country into the ground. In these instances, creditors will not lend to a country, not because it is odious, but because the risk of non repayment is too big. Conversely, if odiousness is not directly reflected in the risk of non repayment, at least in the short run or because odiousness is an externality of the loan contract, then this information may not be reflected in the market and creditors do not necessarily have access to low cost information about odious risk alone.

The question is not whether private parties have complete and perfect information regarding the risk of odious debt, but whether they enjoy a relative advantage over a potential international regulator of odious risk which could include, for example, the United Nations, or an International Financial Institution such as the International Monetary Fund or the World Bank.

Definitional issues with regards to odiousness make it difficult to have sufficient information to come up with clear international guidelines that address the risk of odious debt specifically. Furthermore, as the sovereign debt market is increasingly complex, due to a broadening investor base and a developing secondary market, the ex ante informational and monitoring requirements to regulate it are high.

Shavell argues that, in some instances, a regulatory body may have better access to special expertise necessary to evaluate information.[311] International organizations and international financial institutions have many specialized agencies and have the ability to develop working groups on specific subjects. One possible implication may be that ex ante initiatives by an international regulator should be limited to those debt

[310] For a discussion of soft and hard information See Petersen 2004

[311] Shavell 1984

areas where it would have an informational advantage in terms of expertise, such as debt management or responsible lending practices. These would make the sovereign debt market more efficient and may tackle odious debt indirectly.

Overall, Shavell's first determinant applied to the context of odious debt points towards an ex post solution. The ex post informational advantage is twofold. First, parties to the sovereign loan contract have better information about the risk of odiously looting the proceeds of the loan. This is clear with regards to the debtor government, who has first hand information about what it intends to use the loan for. It is also true for creditors who have actively contributed to the odious activities of the debtor or who are in a position to obtain information about odious risk at low cost. Secondly, while judging regimes is a difficult and subjective task both ex ante and ex post, judging debts is arguably more feasible ex post. By definition, there is more information ex post regarding the uses of a particular loan and the degree of implication of different parties.[312]

4.2.2 Incapability of paying for full magnitude of harm done

4.2.2.1 Shavell's Analysis

The second of the determinants of the relative desirability of liability and regulation is that private parties might be incapable of paying for the full magnitude of the harm done.[313] Shavell argues that when this is the case, an ex post system such as liability would not furnish adequate incentives to control risk because private parties would treat losses caused that exceed their assets as imposing liabilities only equal to their assets. In contrast, under ex ante regulation, the inability to pay for harm done would be irrelevant, assuming that parties would be made to take steps to reduce risk as a precondition for engaging in their activities.[314] Shavell identifies the size of the parties' assets in relation to the probability distribution of the magnitude of harm as an important factor in this context: the greater the likelihood of harm much larger than assets, the greater the appeal of regulation.[315]

4.2.2.2 The Odious Debt Context

There are many reasons why sovereigns tend to over borrow. Indeed, Shavell's second determinant is particularly relevant as it highlights the inherent principal agent problem that contributes to odious debt. Public choice theory explains that the head of state is the agent of the population. Because all individuals are rational, utility maximizers, the incentives of the head of state may not always be perfectly aligned with those of the population. Consequently, the head of state may be inclined to over

[312] Ben-Shahar and Gulati 2007; Ludington, Mitu et al. Draft March, 17th, 2009 2009 #97

[313] Shavell 1984 360

[314] Shavell 1984 361

[315] Shavell 1984 361

borrow, often more than is socially desirable and will not always have incentives to use the proceeds of the loan in a way that most benefits the population of the country, the principal. Political economy problems as well as the short horizons of governments and institutional weaknesses in the country will typically generate a tendency to over borrow and assume excessive risks. Furthermore, incentives to over borrow also come about as a result of externalities. The sovereign debt contract only deals with the borrower's promise to repay and does not take into account any externalities generated by the contract such as negative effects borne by the population due to the reckless use of the proceeds from the loan. Finally, international financial institutions (IFIs) such as the World Bank and the IMF can create expectations of bailing out debtor countries and this leads to moral hazard on the part of borrowing governments. Finally, the fact that it is the state as a legal fiction that is responsible for the debts makes the despot further prone to over lend.

Perverse incentives also exist in the supply side of the sovereign credit market. Lax lending policies can come about for many of the same reasons that induce governments to over borrow, such as a failure to take into account any negative externalities of sovereign loan contracts, political economy problems and the expectation that IFIs will bail debtors out. Indeed the belief that "governments never go bankrupt" induces creditors to take more risk and lend more than they would, would they not be subject to moral hazard.

Incentives to over borrow and over lend exacerbate the problem of odious debt and negatively affect the successor government and the population of the country who inherits more debt than is socially desirable. Furthermore, an individual head of state will be unable to pay for the amount of odious harm caused by his looting activities. This will be due to several reasons: the harm may not be quantifiable if it is in the form of repression of the population, human rights violations or environmental harm. It may only become observable after a long period of time. Finally, even if the individual head of state's assets could be seized ex post, not only may they be difficult to trace but they will likely be less than the amount of harm caused.

4.2.3 Parties would not face the threat of suit for harm done

4.2.3.1 Shavell's Analysis

In the same way as the second determinant of incapability to pay for harm, the possibility that parties would not face the threat of suit for harm done dilutes the incentives to reduce risk created by ex post liability.[316] Shavell argues that the weight to be attached to this factor depends in part upon the reasons why suit might not be brought. He identifies three reasons why a defendant may be able to escape ex post liability. First, it might be that the harms created are widely dispersed, making it unattractive for any individual victim to initiate action. A second cause of failure to sue is the passage of a long period of time before harm manifests itself. He argues that

[316] Shavell 1984

this raises the possibility that by the time the harm manifests itself, the evidence may be stale or the responsible parties out of business.[317] Finally, a third reason for failure to sue is the difficulty in attributing harm to the parties who are responsible for producing it.

4.2.3.2 The Odious Debt Context

The problem of odious debt is characterized by the absence of the main culprit. A successor government and its people inherit public debt that was used against their general interest by a previous regime who is out of the picture. As some scholars have argued, there is a paradox in punishing either the creditor or the populace for the odious debt, since both are innately victims of the despot who stole from them.[318]

A head of state, current or former, has never been held specifically liable for creating odious debt. It could be possible, however, for a former despot to be wanted for human rights violations and other egrerious counts which are related to the looting of international funds and odious debt directly or indirectly. Taking action against a former head of state, however, is subject to significant collective action problems. While the international community as a whole is better of if past despots are held liable and future despots are deterred from misusing public power for private gain, it is costly for an individual state to initiate action. Large opportunity costs are involved in terms of the resources that a state could use for other purposes nationally, and all other states are better of if someone else handles the problem. Furthermore, judicial barriers to holding heads of state individually liable exist.[319]

Another reason why despots would be able to escape responsibility is related to the difficulty in determining correlation between the odious harm and the looting activities of the despot. This could be due to a large passage of time before odious harm is manifested. Furthermore, international funds may be more easily looted than funds form other sources, as they are less visible and correlation therefore more difficult to establish.

Shavell's third determinant therefore points towards an ex ante mechanism due to collective action problems at the international level, a difficulty in establishing correlation and an ability of the borrowing regime responsible for odious debt to escape suit.

---

[317] Shavell 1984

[318] Ben-Shahar and Gulati 2007, 15

[319] Kofele -Kale 2005

4.2.4 Administrative costs

4.2.4.1 Shavell's Analysis

The last of the determinants identified by Shavell is the magnitude of the administrative costs incurred by private parties and by the public in using the tort system or direct regulation.[320] When defining the costs of the tort system, he includes the time, effort and legal expenses borne by private parties in the course of litigation or in coming to settlements, as well as the public expenses of conducting trials, employing judges etc. Similarly, he includes the public expense of maintaining the regulatory establishment and the private costs of compliance in the administrative costs of regulation.

Shavell goes on to argue that with respect to these costs, there is an underlying advantage in favor of liability because most of its administrative costs are incurred only if harm occurs. As this will usually be infrequent, administrative costs will be low. He states that in the extreme case where the prospect of liability induces parties to take proper care and this happens to remove all possibility of harm, there would be no suits and thus no administrative costs. Another advantage of ex post liability is that under it resources are naturally focused on controlling the behavior of the subgroup of parties most likely to cause harm.

On the other hand, administrative costs are incurred whether or not harm occurs under regulation, and even if the risk of harm is eliminated by regulation, administrative costs will have been borne in the process. Furthermore, if there is no special knowledge about the parties' categories of risk, there is no tendency for administrative costs to be focused on those most likely to cause harm, because costs are incurred before harm occurs.

4.2.4.2 The Odious Debt Context

Many of the relevant costs associated with either an ex post or ex ante solution to odious debt depend on whether the institution in charge is already in place. Administrative costs would be minimized if an existing institution is used, as opposed to setting up a new institution. The literature has suggested using the United Nations or the International Court of Justice, among others.[321] It would arguably be more cost efficient to choose an international body and setting which already deals with sovereign debt issues. An example could be a body such as the Paris Club, which currently deals with debt issues between debtor countries and their official creditors. This would be less costly than attempting to introduce debt related issues, such as the problem of odious debt, in an international setting which currently does not deal with sovereign debt and which parties to international contracts are not accustomed to recurring to. This might also prevent duplicative costs of dealing with odious debt in

[320] Shavell 1984

[321] Khalfan, King et al. 2003

one setting, and other debt issues in another. Furthermore, even if odious debt could be treated in a legal setting such as arbitration or the International Court of Justice, the interests of creditors would have to be reckoned with through negotiation regardless. Dealing with all interested parties in one setting can also avoid duplicative costs and time. Efforts, therefore, could be devoted to improving the existing institutions which currently deal with debt and attempt to introduce odious debt within these efforts.

Furthermore, costs in terms of proportionality will be relevant both ex ante and ex post. These will vary depending on whether administrative and institutional costs are incurred specifically to address odious debt independently or within the context of other debt issues or wider goals such as a more efficient and equitable sovereign debt market.

Overall, Shavell argues that this determinant points towards an ex post mechanism as costs are then only incurred when cases of odious debt actually occur and resources are naturally focused on the parties most likely to cause harm. Ex post mechanisms are also generally seen as being less intrusive and disruptive. However, it is difficult to draw general conclusions with regards to administrative costs in the context of odious debt, as these will vary significantly depending on the nature of the individual approach, not only in terms of administrative costs but also political feasibility, collective action, coordination as well as any potential disruptive costs to financial markets that can be associated with some proposals.

4.3 General Advantages and Disadvantages of Ex Ante v Ex Post Approach to Odious Debt

After having evaluated Shavell's four determinants in the context of odious debt, we can see that the first determinant regarding information generally points towards an ex post mechanism. Two other determinants generally favor an ex ante mechanism, namely an inability to pay for harm done by the main culprit and the small probability of being held liable. The last determinant regarding administrative costs is largely dependent on the nature of the individual proposal adopted. Figure 1 shows the general advantages and disadvantages of an ex ante and ex post approach to odious debt. Essentially, what matters is the weight that is attached to each factor, and this will in turn depend on the cases of odious debt being addressed by a specific proposal. Different proposals will prioritize different aspects of the odious debt problem and focus on different advantages of ex ante or ex post approaches.

Neither an ex ante nor an ex post approach alone can deal entirely with the risk of odious debt, both are needed. Furthermore, the approaches are not mutually exclusive. Rather, they can be adopted in combination. The combination should reflect the relative importance of each of Shavell's four determinants in the cases of odious debt being addressed.

In light of this, the next section will look at one of the most ambitious proposals for odious debts from the economic literature by Jayachandran and Kremer which has both ex ante and ex post characteristics. The proposal will be analyzed in terms of its ex ante and ex post advantages and disadvantages as well as its feasibility and the cases of odious debt that it addresses.

Figure 1. General Advantages and Disadvantages of an Ex Ante v. Ex Post Approach to Odious Debt

	Advantages	Disadvantages
Ex Ante	Sets forward looking expectations Seeks to avoid odious debt by anticipating and preventing it. Can provide certainty for market participants by setting out clear rules in advance.	Can be over or under inclusive High definitional, informational requirements
Ex Post	More information about odious debt is available ex post, including its use, any benefits or costs for the population and any contributory role of creditors or other parties. Parties to the sovereign debt contract have an informational advantage.	Deals with odious debt once it has already been created. High probability that main culprit is out of the picture. Difficult to bring suit against culprit. Harm may not be quantifiable, dispersed and observable only after a long passage of time. Assets of culprit may be less than harm.

4.4 Loan sanctions from an ex ante v. ex post perspective

One of the first and main economic contributions to the literature on odious debt is offered by Jayachandran and Kremer.[322] They seek to address the problem of odious debt by introducing loan sanctions to the toolkit available to the international community. They propose a single large country acting unilaterally, or an on-going international institution, such as the United Nations Security Council, which would have the power to designate particular regimes as odious and impose loan sanctions on it, similar to trade sanctions.[323] The authors envisage an odious label being applied only

[322] Jayachandran and Kremer 2002; Jayachandran and Kremer 2006 They were the first to introduce the concept of odious debt to international financial organizations at an IMF conference in 2002

[323] Jayachandran and Kremer 2006, 19

to "the most egrerious violators of legitimate conduct."[324] How legal sanctions would work is that any future debt incurred by a particular dictator would be considered illegitimate and nontransferable to successor regimes.

The proposal involves some of the major powers, such as the United States and the European Union, implementing legal changes to prevent assets of the successor regime from being seized to enforce repayment of the dictator's debts. They argue that this would create incentives for lenders in third countries to avoid lending to the dictator, and could potentially eliminate equilibria with illegitimate lending. In essence, loan sanctions would prevent creditors from seizing the foreign assets of a debtor country which are located in the creditors' countries. The loan sanction eliminates the penalty to a country from repudiating odious debt, and anticipating this, most creditors would presumably avoid lending to sanctioned regimes, or at least charge a much higher interest rate to do so.[325]

The authors emphasize why they think that loan sanctions should only apply to debts which are incurred after the specific regime is designated as odious, as opposed to all the debts of the regime. They assume that an ex-ante mechanism is most efficient. They argue that the current movement to nullify some debts on the grounds of odiousness is hindered by the inability of creditors to anticipate which loans will be considered odious in the future. If odiousness is declared in advance, creditors will have to find alternative borrowers, but would not risk large losses from a successful ex post campaign that nullifies some of their existing outstanding loans. Also, they assume that the risk of bias by the international institution would be smaller than if the declaration of odiousness would be ex post, when interested parties have redistribution at stake.[326]

Under their assumptions, Kremer and Jayachandran's model improves the welfare of the affected population in mainly two ways. It relieves the successor government and its people from repaying any inherited debt that was incurred after the previous regime was targeted as odious. Secondly, the mechanism leads to separate equilibria where creditors lend to non-odious regimes but do not lend to odious regimes. The borrowing restrictions reduce the utility a dictator would obtain from being in power and therefore lower the probability of a dictator taking power in the first.[327] On the potential of their proposal Gelpern notes that it would, "remove some reputational

[324] Jayachandran and Kremer 2006, 19

[325] Jayachandran and Kremer 2006, 19

[326] Shafter 2007, 282

[327] Jayachandran and Kremer 2006

damage to a country from repudiating odious debt, would shield the country from lawsuits and would enable meaningful risk assessment by creditors."[328]

This section takes a closer look at Jayachandran and Kremer's proposal. It is a particularly interesting case to analyze for several reasons. First, it lies somewhere in between an ex ante and an ex post approach. Although its proponents highlight its ex ante advantages, it is partially ex post in nature, as a regime can only be deemed odious and be imposed with loan sanctions after it has acted "egreriously". However, the proposal has one major characteristic which is ex ante. Loan sanctions apply only to future debt contracted by the debtor country, after it has been labeled as odious. Given the lack of definition about odiousness in the market and the inability of parties to anticipate how and when odious debt will occur, the proposal deals with the problem of uncertainty and time inconsistency.[329] The odious declaration, in effect, acts as ex ante regulation, thereby regulating the obligation of debtors after the declaration has been made and consequently affecting creditors' incentives to lend. This approach is, in effect, a combination of both methods of alleviating risk. This section will evaluate loan sanctions in terms of their ex ante and ex post advantages and disadvantages.

4.4.1 Trade off between Information and Deterrence

Designating a regime as odious necessitates an ex post approach. Ex ante, a regulatory body is unable to anticipate which future regimes will be odious. Ex post, once the regime is in power, more information is available. The amount of information in terms of odiousness of a particular regime that a country or an institution such as the Security Council (UNSC) has to impose loan sanctions would differ depending on the timing of the sanctions. In fact, designating a regime as odious can have different consequences at different times throughout the period in which the regime is in power.

The earlier a regime is labeled as odious, the less information is available about it to justify the odious label. Jayachandran and Kremer have identified that a potential peril in their proposal is the risk of applying sanctions to a non-odious government.[330] The probability of this is greater the earlier a regime is labeled as odious. They seek to circumvent this informational problem by suggesting that loan sanctions should only be applied to 'egrerious' cases of odiousness, in other words, when there is sufficient and evident information to declare a regime as odious. Arguably, a regime needs some time to become 'egrerious' and more time will reduce the risk of mislabeling a regime as more information on it becomes available.

The chances of obtaining multilateral agreement by the members of the UNSC on labeling a regime as odious may increase as more time is elapsed by the regime. The

[328] Gelpern 2005, 21

[329] Jayachandran and Kremer 2006, 83

[330] Jayachandran and Kremer 2006, 89

more time a despotic government has been in power, the easier it may be to come to a consensus on its odiousness at the multilateral level. Information may become more observable to outside parties as well, including NGO's, the media and other bodies, which can exert pressure on the empowered institution to take action.

Lower informational, coordination and transaction costs will come at the expense of a decreased impact of the odious label and any imposed loan sanctions. Indeed, the longer the time frame before the odious label is applied to a debtor, the more ex post the loan sanction mechanism is and the smaller the ex ante benefits are. In terms of minimizing the amount of odious debt that is created by a regime and subsequently inherited by successor governments and their citizens, it is more efficient to declare an odious regime as such as soon as possible. The earlier the declaration is made, the earlier creditors will be aware that a loan sanction has been imposed against the regime and their incentives to lend to it will be curtailed. The sooner the odious ruler's access to international credit is diminished, the less proceeds from loans he has to loot. Preventing future odious debt benefits the population in two ways; it avoids the direct costs of having to pay back the debt as well as the indirect costs from odious externalities of the debt, such as human rights violations and repression. Furthermore, because the probability of a dictator taking power is endogenous to the spoils from office, and a decreased ability to borrow would decrease these, he will be deterred from taking power in the first place.[331] The timing of loan sanctions will affect their potential deterrence for future despots. The earlier they are imposed, the lower are the expected spoils from office and the larger is the impact of the sanction relative to the harm caused by the regime.

4.4.2 Definitional Issues

A trade off also exists with regards to the definition and criteria for odiousness that an institution with the power to impose loan sanctions adopts. Judging regimes is a difficult and delicate exercise. The stakes are high, as are the potential impacts on the functioning of international finance. Some scholars argue that if the loan sanction mechanism were to substantiate, it would likely develop a very clear definition of odious regimes because the institution would be significantly scrutinized on having a clear and consistent application.[332] The higher the threshold of the criteria and the stricter the definition, the easier it will be for states to agree on imposing loan sanctions on it since only specific extreme cases of odious regimes would be subject to them. At the same time, if the threshold is too high, the impact of the proposal will be under inclusive. Even 'egrerious' cases may find it easy to avoid the criteria if they are too strict.

On the other hand, it is not necessarily true that loan sanctions would be accompanied by a strict definition for odiousness. Institutions in the context of international lending

---

[331] Jayachandran and Kremer 2006, 87

[332] Feibelman 2007, 36

often intervene in an ad hoc way, while maintaining a certain degree of discretion and control. The fact that loan sanctions are partially ex post, allow for the regulatory body to react ex post to the different types of odious regimes that may come into power on a case by case basis. The danger with such discretion, of course, involves loan sanctions being applied at will.

Finally, judging regimes can also prove to be an over inclusive approach. This is due to the fact that the odiousness of the regime is used as a proxy for the odiousness of the debts it incurs. Even odious regimes can use the proceeds of loans for 'good' purposes. However, because loan sanctions reduce the incentives of creditors to lend, they deter lending of all types, including 'good' loans.

4.4.3 Ex Ante Certainty

The odious debt debate resurfaced after Saddam Hussein was ousted from Iraq and the question emerged regarding what should be done with the debt that he left behind. This led to the more general debate about how debt which has been used against the interest of the people should be dealt with ex post. Many argued that the debt should be declared as void by an adjudicating body ex post.[333]

There are two main disadvantages to such an ex post approach: first, it would create uncertainty for creditors who would be unable to anticipate whether the loans that they make today will be declared void tomorrow. In the face of this lack of clarity, the credit market would shut down. Without sufficient information to differentiate between loans that will be declared void in the future and those which will not, creditors will become risk averse and may be over inclusive in their response. Indeed, the risks exists that they will withdraw from all developing country debt as a whole, or substantially increase interest rates on sovereign lending to compensate for the risk of uncertainty. As the current and past financial crises have shown, in the face of uncertainty, creditors tend to clump the developing world together as a group and it will be the poorer countries who will suffer disproportionately from a lack of credit.[334] Indeed, one of the main reasons a mechanism to address odious debt has not substantiated in practice has to do with the rational fear that the cure may be worse than the disease.

As a response, the proponents of loan sanctions highlight that one of their main advantages has to do with their ex ante nature and the certainty that this provides to creditors.[335] Loan sanctions apply only to future debt contracted by a country, not existing debt. This avoids any time inconsistency problems and provides clarity to creditors. Creditors need to have clear guidelines regarding to whom they can lend to and there should be no uncertainty regarding their ability to enforce the loans that they

---

[333] Khalfan, King et al. 2003

[334] Krugman 2009

[335] Jayachandran and Kremer 2006, 281; Shafter 2007

make. Loan sanctions are designed to be used only in exceptional, 'egrerious' cases and the sovereign lending market as whole would remain unaffected. In theory, loan sanctions would provide ex ante certainty while minimizing any perverse disruptive impacts on open credit lines and the sovereign debt market as a whole.

4.4.4 Expectations from Ex Post Designation

While loan sanctions function essentially as ex ante regulation for creditors, they function as an ex post mechanism for debtor governments, that have expectations about being labeled as odious as a result. With any proposal, is it important to analyze the impact that it will have on the incentives of all parties involved. Loan sanctions provide ex ante certainty for creditors, but they fail to take into account some of the perverse incentives that they may have on despotic debtor governments. Their incentives will also be affected by loan sanctions, both before and after they are applied.

There is an uncertainty with regards to when a despotic government can expect to be targeted with loan sanctions. In the face of this uncertainty, a despotic government may react in different ways. The mere existence of loan sanctions as one of the actions available to the international community may have a deterrence effect on despots. Ideally, the threat of loan sanctions improves the behavior of a government in power.[336]

On the other hand, loan sanctions may also have perverse effects on the incentives of a despot once they have been imposed. Some argue that loan sanctions can have opposite effects with some regimes, making them more extreme and despotic as a result. This has been argued to be the case with North Korea.[337] Furthermore, if one of the effects of loan sanctions is that they may hasten the fall of the regime, it could make despots more shortsighted while they are still in power. Sudan's decision to expel humanitarian organizations from the country after an arrest warrant was issued against its president by the International Criminal Court is an example of extreme measures taken up by governments in the face of international action against them.

If indeed only egrerious cases of odious regimes are targeted by loan sanctions, a despot may need to only invest in the public a little bit, or invest more in concealing his looting activities and transactions, to escape the risk of a loan sanction.

Finally, if a decreased access to international credit is a consequence of loan sanctions, incentives would be created for dictators to search for funds from sources that may harm the economic resources, natural environment and population as much as, if not more than odious debt.[338] A more comprehensive view of the financing

---

[336] Jayachandran and Kremer 2006, 87

[337] Franck 2006

[338] Ochoa 2007, 5

mechanisms of despots must be taken.[339] By the same token, a more comprehensive view of the different types of international currency that states have to pay back loans needs to be considered.

4.4.5 Risk of Bias

Many of the proposals in the odious debt literature involve the presence of an international body. Jayachandran and Kremer identify that there is a higher risk of bias when an international body has the power to designate loans or regimes as odious ex post as opposed to ex ante. This is, in effect, a corollary of their argument that an ex ante mechanism provides more certainty for creditors, since one of the sources of uncertainty of an ex post mechanism is the inability of creditors to predict which loans will be declared void and why. They argue that if an adjudicating body places a high value on the welfare of a debtor country, it may have a bias towards relieving it entirely of its past debt and consequently labeling all its debt as odious, including legitimate debt.[340] Again, if creditors anticipate being able to collect on legitimate loans, then the debt market would shut down. Conversely, ex post, the creditors have already lent to the regime being targeted and are interested in getting repaid for their past loans. Given the redistributive stakes involved, creditors will therefore be inclined to influence the international body. Jayachandran and Kremer argue that loan sanctions minimize this risk of bias. This is because ex ante, creditors will be indifferent to who they lend to. If one regime is imposed with loans sanctions, they will lend to another one. They will therefore have no stakes in the decision of the international body to designate a particular regime as odious and will not attempt to influence it.

Nevertheless, because the consequences of being labeled as odious are so great, the political pressure will be present despite the ex ante nature of loans sanctions. Official creditors have many non static, long term interests when lending to developing countries, not all of which have to do with getting their loans directly paid back. Consequently, some creditors will not be indifferent as to who they lend to. Many will not be willing to disrupt relations with a debtor country with whom they have many long term relationships from which they benefit continuously, as opposed to on a one shot, loan by loan basis.

4.4.6 Action while Despot is Still in Power

Two of Shavell's determinants in the context of odious weighed heavily against an ex post mechanism. These were namely the inability of the despot to pay for the harm caused by the creation of odious debt as well as the low probability of him ever facing suit. Both of these factors are related to the fact that, ex post, the despot is essentially out of the picture. One of the benefits of loan sanctions is that they restrain the power of a despot and impose costs on him while he is still in power. Furthermore, by

---

[339] Ochoa 2007

[340] Jayachandran and Kremer 2006, 83

increasing awareness of an egrerious odious regime and its odious activities, loan sanctions may increase the probability of a particular despot being sued or targeted for former activities.

4.4.7 Failure to Deal with Odious Debt already Created

Loan sanctions emphasize deterrence and avoidance of future odious debt after they have been imposed. The certainty provided by their ex ante nature comes from the fact that the past debts of the despot are left unaffected and still need to be paid back. This forward looking mechanism will be weaker the later loan sanctions are imposed and if they come into effect once substantial odious harm and looting has already taken place. In such cases, the lack of a backward looking dimension to effectively respond to past odious debt will become more important. Loan sanctions would then benefit the successor government and its population less. If the despot was near the end of his reign at the time loan sanctions were imposed, the marginal benefit they provide to the successor government may be small.

4.4.8 Costs associated with the UNSC

Some of the costs associated with loan sanctions will involve obtaining political support for the proposal and addressing the collective action problems that may arise with regards to leading a multilateral effort to introduce them in practice. Some steps have already been taken in this respect. In 2009, Jayachandran and Kremer organized a conference at Harvard University to discuss the possibility of obtaining American political acceptance for a loan sanctions proposal to address odious debt.[341] This followed an expression of interest by President Barack Obama in playing a leading role in addressing odious debt and considering the possibility of loan sanctions in a white paper on economic development during his campaign in 2008.[342]

Other costs will depend on the multilateral setting and institution that is chosen to introduce the proposal. One of the cost advantages of choosing the UNSC as a venue has to do with the fact that it already possesses the experience and the power to issue trade sanctions. Furthermore, the UN has the advantage of preeminent global legitimacy and a preexisting institutional architecture.[343] Finally, costs would also have to be incurred nationally by creditor countries who would have to implement legal changes to prevent assets of the successor regime from being seized to enforce repayment of the targeted despot's debts.

However, the costs of introducing and setting up loan sanctions within the UNSC will be small relative in comparison to the costs of its implementation. There are large expected coordination and information costs as well as lengthy proceedings associated

---

[341] www.eurodad.org 2009

[342] www.barackobama.com 2007

[343] Shafter 2007, 291

with obtaining a consensus at the Security Council level to issue loan sanctions on a particular country. Indeed, not all of the permanent or rotating Security Council members have similar worldviews or interests.[344] Jayachandran and Kremer argue that coordination costs would be minimized and difference in interests reconciled in the face of cases such as apartheid-era South Africa or Tudjman-era Croatia, which they argue may have been able to obtain the necessary consensus for action at the Security Council level.[345] Although the UN should not be viewed as a wholly impossible implementation venue, the difficulties in obtaining a consensus on judging regimes should not be underestimated. Indeed, the case of present day Sudan under President Al-Bashir may be a case in point. On the 4th of March of 2009, the International Criminal Court (ICC) issued an arrest warrant against the President of Sudan on five counts of "crimes against humanity" and two counts of "war crimes."[346] This followed years of attention devoted to the situation in the country, particularly in Darfur, by the media, NGO's and politicians worldwide. On the one hand, Sudan is an example of the international community coming together and calling for action against such an egrerious regime. Indeed, Sudan may be just the egrerious case that Jayachandran and Kremer envisaged loan sanctions being applied to as a "potent addition to the international community's toolkit of sanctions"[347] alongside action by the ICC, for example.

On the other hand, the case of Sudan is also indicative of the limitations of the Security Council. The UNSC initially directed the ICC to take on the Darfur case in the first place. It is relevant to point out that, strikingly, the United States had been the only country at the Security Council that refused to support the criminal court's investigation of the Darfur atrocities.[348] After the criminal court has taken up the case and issued an arrest warrant, President Al-Bashir responded to the indictment by revoking the licenses of at least 10 aid organizations working the country, thereby scorning the court and victimized Darfuris desperate for humanitarian assistance. The Security Council then failed to agree on a joint response when China refused to sign a text which called on Sudan to reverse its decision.

In the face of such potential transaction costs associated with the implementation of loan sanctions via the Security Council, a question of proportionality arises. If disagreement at the Security Council level with regards to egrerious cases of odiousness would prevent loan sanctions from ever being applied, this would mean that a lot of costs would be borne ex ante, but the proposal would have no effect on

---

[344] Shafter 2007, 291

[345] Jayachandran and Kremer 2006, 83

[346] The Hague Justice Portal. http://www.haguejusticeportal.net/eCache/DEF/9/502.html Last retrived on May 9, 2011

[347] Jayachandran and Kremer 2006, 83

[348] Laurenti 2009

odious debt. This raises the question of proportionality regarding the amount of costs involved with the proposal compared to the amount of times, if any, when it would be used.

4.4.9 Risk of Collision by "Rogue" States and Globalisation

Other venues or settings may prove to be less costly in terms of obtaining a majority to implement loan sanctions. For example, Shafter has argued that a more practical alternative to the UN might be implementation among the advanced industrial democracies that comprise the G-7 or the OECD. He argues that, while the interests and worldviews of the member countries are not identical, there remains enough of a shared fundamental outlook that implementing an odious debt outlook would be more feasible at this level than at the level of the UN.[349]

Again, a trade off exists. Introducing loan sanctions via a group of the G-7 countries may reduce coordination and transactions costs associated with implementation and would maximize its effects if these countries encompass a sufficient mass of the world's credit pools. However, it may also have perverse consequences, in the form of strengthened ties between the targeted debtor and precisely those creditors, such as China, who would not have agreed to loan sanctions at the Security Council level. Ginsburg et al. have argued of the danger of a mechanism that addressed odious debt perversely strengthening autocracies and contributing to their economic integration.[350] Examples of this occurring exist in practice. Countries that the West associates as "rogue" collaborate together on many levels. For example, North Korea does business with Syria, Iran and Iraq among other countries that the West traditionally views as "dangerous" from a security perspective.

Furthermore, in an increasingly globalised world, it is difficult to isolate countries, especially those which are rich in resources for which the international community has a highly inelastic demand. Point source exports are a source of international currency for states. The emergence of new players with deep pockets has made the political and economic power in the international realm more dispersed. There are more creditors and more types of credit transactions.

Sanctions, therefore, may not only be disruptive and have perverse effects such as inducing more extreme action by the targeted regime and strengthen rogue ties, but they may also be weaker in the context of globalisation. While the costs of exclusion are greater, there are more players.

---

[349] Shafter 2007, 292

[350] Ginsburg and Ulen 2007, 18

4.5 Summary of trade offs and conclusion

Figure 2 illustrates some of the ex ante and ex post trade offs involved in loan sanctions, which will particularly depend on their timing. The earlier a regime is targeted as odious and loan sanctions are imposed on it, the more the ex ante advantages of the proposal are maximized. At the same time, however, there is less information and evidence about the regime and its odious activities at an early stage and hence less ground to justify loan sanctions. Conversely, the later loan sanctions are imposed on a regime, the more they involve the inherent advantages and disadvantages of ex post approaches. Later in the regime, there is more information about blatant odious activities of a regime and this will make coordination and agreement in the international community relatively easier. There is also a lower risk of mislabeling a regime. The main disadvantages, in turn, are that the impact of loan sanctions and the deterrence effects derived from them are lower the later they are imposed.

Perhaps the biggest costs associated with loan sanctions are in the form of opportunity costs. Assuming that a mechanism to deal with odious debt is desired at the international level, and given that a single proposal cannot address all odious debt in its entirety, it is important to look at which subset of odious debt cases is being addressed by any proposal and which is subsequently left out.

Loan sanctions would address cases of odious debt that are characterized by despotic governments who have already caused significant and observable harm to their populations and who are able to continue to finance their odious activities via international loans. While the proposal entails significant costs and can have perverse consequences, it has the potential of preventing the accumulation of odious debt that the successor population will inherit and will significantly limit the ease and ability with which despots will be able to behave freely. It focuses on deterrence and preventing a sitting despot from incurring more odious debt than he has already done so.

Figure 2: Trade Offs Regarding the Timing of Loan Sanctions

Regime comes into power	Time Frame of Targeted Regime ⟷ **End of term**
Advantages	
▪Minimizes future odious debt incurred by regime. ▪Maximizes deterrence for future potential odious leaders.	▪More information available to base loan sanction on. ▪Lower risk of false positive : labeling a non odious regime as odious. ▪Lower coordination costs: easier to obtain consensus with more information and evidence, more international & political support.
Disadvantages	
▪Less information available to base loan sanction on. ▪Higher risk of false positive: labeling a non odious regime as odious.	▪Lower impact/benefit of loan sanction for successor government and population.

The size of the benefits derived from loan sanctions will vary depending on their timing and other practical considerations but, theoretically, a successor population will always be better of with sanctions than without.

The opportunity costs of loan sanctions are therefore those cases of odious debt which are not addressed by them. They have no effect on past odious debt of a targeted despot, which is higher the later loan sanctions are imposed. Further, loan sanctions leave many types of odious debt un-addressed. While certain cases of despotic looting are addressed, the many cases and forms of odious debt which can be widespread in both democratic and undemocratic regimes are not. Loan sanctions are designed to be used only seldom. They do not seek to substantially change the sovereign debt market as a whole or seek to alter the status quo of indiscriminate lending, where debtors generally pay back regardless of the nature of the loans, who incurred them or what they were used for. Indeed, their limited impact is both a main advantage and a main disadvantage of loan sanctions.

An implication of this may be that loan sanctions would be suitable as a means of last resort for intervention in extreme cases. Their interventionist nature makes them suitable in those cases when a priority has been outlined by the international community to restrain a particular despot who is still in power. However, besides having a quasi ex ante /ex approach designed as a method of last resort, traditional ex ante and ex post mechanisms are also needed to address a wider subset of odious debt.

More mainstreamed approaches could take the form of improving existing ex initiatives such as responsible lending practices to promote more efficient and transparent incentives in the sovereign debt market. Ex post mechanisms are also needed as a response to deal with odious debt once it has already been incurred. Introducing odious debt within existing ex post settings such as debt restructurings could be one option.

Of course, these suggestions require further detailed analysis. The main trade off relates to the point that one approach will not be able to address all cases of odious debt and that questions of proportionality and opportunity costs need to be considered when weighing the costs of an individual proposal.

The aim of this chapter was to address the many ex ante and ex post considerations involved in an international approach to deal with odious debt. This highlighted the complexity of the task and the different trade offs involved. The current financial crisis has shown that ex ante regulation to prevent irresponsible behaviour and effective ex post mechanisms to respond to critical situations when they do occur, are both necessary for a sustainable and efficient financial market. The crisis has opened the possibility to address and question the status quo of international finance and its regulation. The debate on odious debt is sure to continue within this context.

5 Odious Debt: Driving Change in Sovereign Debt Governance

Many solutions to the problem of odious debt have been proposed by the literature, yet none have made the transition into practice. This is due, in part, to the fact that many proposals are brought forth without first considering the environment in which they aim to be introduced. Accordingly, this chapter first analyses the web of international economic governance that surrounds sovereign debt and looks at its role in shaping the current discourse on odious debt. Whether the debt regime as it stands will move towards addressing the problem of odious debt will largely depend on the actors that are capable to drive change within it. Past experience has shown that the evolution of the official governance framework with regards to debt stems from synergies between various forms of power over key institutions, evolving knowledge and understanding as well an evolving discourse on key issues of debt.

The major players in the international community which have been active in the odious debt movement will be analyzed. These have been namely; the official sector (states and international organizations), NGOs devoted to odious debt, and the epistemic community which is mainly composed of academics from the legal and economic fields. Indeed, these are the same three categories of players which have been instrumental in bringing about change in debt governance in the past. Callaghy refers to them as the three branches of governance, which together make up a "triple helix."[351] Whether this governance framework will move towards addressing odious debt will depend on the interests at stake of the actors within each branch, as well as their willingness and ability to bring about change.

These actors drive change in sovereign debt governance, and influence the processes of the international debt regime. The second part of the chapter considers the relationship between these processes, such as debt restructuring, and international law. It goes on to analyze the possibility of introducing the issue of odious debt into the negotiations which take place under the auspices of the Paris Club.

---

[351] Callaghy 2004

5.1 International Economic Governance: Odious Debt

Addressing equitable considerations in international finance, such as odious debt, may seem impossible or too costly to many. Indeed as much as the odious debt cause has many proponents, it has many more sceptics. Nevertheless, prominent legal scholars such as Robert Howse remind us that not only have notions of equity been present in contractual relations for a long time, but also that transitional contexts have historically taken into account a range of equitable considerations, some of which may be regrouped under the concept of odiousness.[352] Furthermore, one need only look at other causes in the context of international debt which, not long ago, were dismissed as "unthinkable"[353] and are now being addressed by the international community through the established norms and practices of its institutions. A notable example is that of comprehensive treatment of poor country debt through the Heavily Indebted Poor Countries Initiative in which the Paris Club, the IMF and the World Bank take part.[354]

The analysis of the triple helix governance framework as it pertains to international debt issues highlights the structural, institutional and political environment needed to bring about change in the debt regime. Indeed, the environment needs to be just right; collective action problems at the international level need to be overcome. This can occur if one of the major actors in the governance environment has significant interests at stake in taking action, either via direct benefits or the avoidance of direct threats. The political climate, both internationally and domestically needs to be suitable to address change. One issue area, such as odious debt, will be in competition with many other issue areas. Both the NGO and the epistemic community can play a role in making an issue area politically saliable. This was the case with debt relief in many developed countries. For NGOs to have influence and power, the institutional environment in which they operate needs to be democratic and accountable. Finally, the extent of the influence that the epistemic community has is a function of how fragmented its constituents are and the extent with which they work closely with decision makers either in public office or within international organizations.

The starting point of this chapter is the rational argument that a solution to odious debt will not come about as a result of the benevolent and moral concerns of parties in international finance. Instead, it must be in their self interest to do so. The analysis therefore assumes that the behaviour of actors in the debt regime, including states, is rational. The rationalist approach emphasizes the role of power and interests in determining outcomes in international relations and in driving change. As power is

---

[352] Howse 2007, 24

[353] Callaghy 2004, 1 (referring to the idea of providing favourable debt relief treatment to the poorest developing countries.)

[354] Callaghy 2004; Paris Club Annual Report 2007

becoming less concentrated in the international realm as a result of the emergence of new players, this has affected both the dynamics of relationships between players and the hegemonic power of some of them to bring about change unilaterally.

While this chapter does not deal with the complex question of how preferences change, it does allow for states to be influenced by public choice considerations. Particularly, it acknowledges that NGO's are capable of influencing a democratic state's interest in addressing certain international problems, such as debt.[355] Finally, drawing from the insights of Callaghy and Haas,[356] the chapter is also influenced by the constructivist approach which focuses on the role that knowledge, ideas and the process of learning have in governance. The work of epistemic communities is able to create linkages between different issue areas such as debt relief and development for example. In the context of globalisation, states face greater uncertainty coupled with a greater risk of trans-boundary externalities. This consequently creates a demand for expert knowledge and increases the linkages that are tied to any particular issue area. For example, the case of Iraq's debt demonstrates how debt forgiveness can be tied to national security interests of states.[357]

Accordingly, this section looks at the three main branches that together compose the triple helix of governance surrounding odious debt. The interplay between actors is uneven, inherently political and complex. The aim of this section is therefore to provide a general view of each branch and focus on the interests and capabilities of the actors within it to bring about change. Finally, it will look at how the different players in each branch are already actively involved in the odious debt cause.

5.1.1 The Official Sector

Official economic governance is composed primarily of states on the one hand, and the international organizations and financial institutions of which many are members and have influence over, on the other. States can have the size, power and political capital to drive change in the international community. Larger and more strategically important states have greater power and weight to push for change than do weaker and less economically important states. Nevertheless, as power in the international context becomes more decentralized with the emergence of new players, it is more difficult and costly for states to bring about change unilaterally. Pushing for change in the international context entails opportunity costs for a state which could devote the resources towards domestic priorities instead. Consequently, because driving change is costly, a rational state must have an interest and derive a benefit from pursuing it.

---

[355] For a discussion on the concept of the "disaggregated state" and how networks can influence international governance See Slaughter 2004 ; For a discussion on how a rational approach and public choice considerations can be combined See Guzman 2002; Guzman 2008, 129 See Also Tomz 2007

[356] Haas June 2003 and Haas Winter 1992

[357] Weiss 2007

The interests of the official sector are wide ranging. This section briefly considers three general reasons which have been relevant for the official sector in driving change in the context of international debt and considers how they can play a role in addressing odious debt. The first involves direct strategic interests that include linkages between addressing debt issues and national security, geopolitics or financial threats. The second type of interest derives from domestic pressure that developed governments face to address certain issues. The third interest considered regards the role of competition between different actors in the official sector and the role of new and emerging concentrations of power that can drive change. The last part of this section looks at the (lack of) role of developing countries in international economic governance and draws some implications for their role in the odious debt cause.

5.1.1.1 Strategic Interests – The Case of Iraqi Debt

Just as official lending is motivated in part by policy considerations, so is official debt relief and debt forgiveness.[358] Creditors can have a direct interest in promoting the debt relief of strategic debtor countries. Iraq is a case in point. The United States played a pro active role in the treatment of Iraq's debt burden, which it had inherited from the regime of Saddam Hussein. The United States first led an initiative to immunize Iraq from action by its creditors and subsequently was a key actor in achieving a high level of debt relief for the country. Upon the ousting of Saddam Hussein, Iraq found itself burdened with a debt of more than 125 billion US dollars.[359] Because of its substantial oil reserves, Iraq is considered a middle income country and not a least developed country (LDC). Iraq arguably would have been able to service its existing debts once its petroleum industry was functioning. Therefore, many analysts argued that Iraq should not be eligible for complete cancellation of its debts, but rather should have its debts rescheduled.[360] Others were concerned that if Iraq's future oil revenues were used to fund repayment of old debts, not enough would remain to fund its current and future economic needs.

One of the first developments following the end of the Saddam regime was a Resolution by the United Nations Security Council to grant a stay on the enforcement of any debt claims.[361] In effect, this Resolution prohibited any country from initiating debt claims against the proceeds of Iraq's petroleum or gas industries until December 31st of 2007. The intervention was justified by both the United Nations and the United States on grounds of international security.[362] The former described Iraq as "an

---

358 For a discussion on debt relief See Udombana 2005; Cheru 2006

359 Weiss 2007, 1

360 See for example Weiss 2006, 7

361 Security Council Resolution No 1483 UN Doc S/RES/1483 May 22, 2003

362 See The President Ex Order 13,303 Protecting the Developing Fund for Iraq and Certain Other Property in Which Iraq has an Interest May 28th, 2003; The President, Exec Order 13, 364 Modifying the Protection

international threat to peace and security", the latter, "an unusual and extraordinary threat to the national security and foreign policy of the United States."[363] Discussion of cancelling Iraq's debt ensued soon after the stay was granted on claims of Iraq's assets. Weiss explains that the Bush administration led the negotiation of a consensus which agreed to grant Iraq debt relief on terms that were unique for its economic resources, but not unprecedented given its political situation.[364] As a result of the strong support for Iraq debt relief by the Bush administration, the Paris Club, the international ad hoc "forum" which deals with official debt, decided to reshape its approach to debt relief and introduced the Evian Approach in the 2003 Evian G8 Summit.[365] While debt forgiveness was traditionally only granted by the Paris Club to the poorest countries on the basis of economic arguments, the Evian Approach now allows for debt forgiveness for those countries that do not qualify as LDCs on an ad hoc, case by case basis.[366] Essentially, what the Evian Approach does is introduce a new strategy for determining Paris Club debt relief levels that is more flexible and can provide debt cancellation to a greater number of countries that was available under prior Paris Club rules. The debt relief provided to Iraq by its official creditors (which was of 80%) set the stage for the terms of the renegotiations between Iraq and its non Paris Club official creditors and private creditors.[367]

Gelpern describes the solution to the Iraq debt as having a "Presto! Feel to it."[368] The pro active role of the Bush administration and the rapidity with which the international community was mobilized is illustrative of several points. First, it illustrates the rapidity and efficacy with which the international community shields a debtor which poses a political threat, as opposed to when a debtor suffers from misfortune or mismanagement.[369]

When the benefits a state derives from taking action are concentrated as opposed to widely dispersed, it will be more willing to bear the costs of taking action and the collective action problem at the international level is weakened. This will be the case if direct interests are involved, which can include an interest in protecting the valuable natural resources of a debtor country and by doing so gain strategic access to them. Cheng emphasizes the United States' call for debt cancellation was not merely for the

Granted to the Development Fund for Iraq and Certain Property in which Iraq has an Interest and Protecting the Central Bank of Iraq November 29th, 2004

363 Gelpern 2005, 400

364 Weiss 2006, 6

365 Weiss 2006, 7

366 Paris Club Annual Report 2007

367 Weiss 2006, 7

368 Gelpern 2005, 396

369 Indeed, the quick procedure in bringing about the Evian Approach at the Paris Club starkly contrasts with the difficult and long process that preceded the development of the Heavily Poor Countries Initiative See Haas June 2003 and Gelpern 2005, 400

benefit of the Iraqis. Rather, it was also a benefit to the U.S. government not only because on May of 2003, the U.N. Security Council charged the United States with the international obligations of an occupier in Iraq.[370]

Conversely, direct interests can stem from interest in avoiding costs associated with contagion or any other negative transboundary externalities or avoiding threats such as those that stem from terrorism. The U.S. government had made representations to its domestic constituencies that it would not withdraw forces from Iraq until it had established peace and democracy there. A stable economy is therefore in the interest of facilitating this process and minimizing the international and domestic costs of a prolonged occupation in Iraq.[371]

An important implication for addressing odious debt is the fact that the interests of the major powers in the official sector need to be taken into account. While the major can be potential enablers to change, they can also be the largest obstacles to it. Consequently, addressing the odious debt cause must implicate either a direct benefit to the primary governance actors, or conversely, implicate the avoidance of greater costs, such as negative trans-boundary externalities of odious debt. One scholar has posited that the confluence of factors that brings about change in the context of international debt governance is wrapped around the central structural dilemma of our times which consists of "the emergence of a group of weak states and economies that have not been able to benefit as easily or quickly from economic reform and democratisation as elsewhere in the world."[372] He argues that this dilemma poses important difficulties for the functioning and evolution of the international political economy and for international peace and conflict.[373] In other words, the persistent reality of the situation of many of the poorest debtor countries, and the implications that this has on the international community as a whole, underlies the drive for change in the international governance framework. While the question of whether odious debt is an independent issue, or one that is tied to development and debt relief remains,[374] it is the case that the odious debt discourse primarily stems from an inherent concern for the situation of developing countries. Consequently, assessing the potential to address odious debt implies looking at why the actors in international economic governance have an interest in caring about the developing world.

Secondly, the treatment of Iraqi debt is further illustrative of the general preference of the international community to deal with debt issues on an ad hoc and

---

370 Cheng 2007, 26

371 See Id. (arguing that economic stability would have been further delayed if Iraq remained saddled with $140 billion debt. "Under these circumstances, U.S. elected officials had a strong political interest in Iraq's debt cancellation.")

372 Callaghy 2004, v

373 Callaghy 2004, 7

374 For a discussion See Rasmussen 2007

case by case basis. The world economy functions within the political framework provided by nation states and is reflective of a balance between common international interests and competing national concerns.[375] This ex post, flexible and ad hoc approach to debt issues reflects this balance. States do not want to delegate their control over policy instruments related to lending and debt to a higher order. They further do not want to tie their hands in advance and prefer flexible tools, such as the Evian Approach. As one scholar has argued, the more flexibility states have for their decisions, the more political and strategic interests that they can incorporate.[376] Furthermore, the Evian Approach provided enough flexibility to address the immediate concerns of Iraq, while at the same time was framed as a sufficiently "exceptional" initiative, so as to not affect the incentives or expectations of the players in international finance and therefore did not majorly disrupt the well functioning of the market. Indeed, the UN Resolution to freeze Iraq's assets, together with the Evian Approach, occurred rather innocuously and without much scrutiny. The approaches did not address important issues such as creditor equity, a balance between creditor and debtor interests, a check on debtor abuses and any moral hazard consequences they may create.[377] This preference for exceptionalism[378] is evidenced by the acceptance of the international community of the 'exceptional' UN standstill on creditor rights in the case of Iraq, while it rejected it when it was proposed as part of a formal mechanism by the IMF via its Sovereign Debt Restructuring Mechanism proposal.[379]

Accordingly, any proposal to address odious debt that aims to be introduced into the international governance framework, must attempt to reconcile the different tensions that actors in the international community face. It must also address the stakes that the actors currently dominating the official branch of governance have in change.

5.1.1.2 Domestic Pressure – Norway as a Sympathetic Creditor

From a rational perspective, a state's "sympathy" for debt causes and the situation of poor developing countries will always stem from a direct or indirect self interest. As discussed in the previous section, such an interest can be derived from substantive linkages such as those in the case of Iraq, where debt forgiveness promulgated by the United States was tied to preserving national security, among other interests. A substantive linkage can also stem from a state's public choice concerns. Liberal theory posits that states channel and respond to the demands of domestic actors. Therefore,

[375] Kapstein 1994

[376] Damle 2007, 151

[377] Gelpern 2005, 397 (contrasting this with the carefully thought out, but ultimately rejected Sovereign Debt Restructuring Mechanism proposed by the IMF)

[378] For a discussion See Tarullo 2001

[379] Weiss 2006, 11

democratic governments seeking to be elected or re elected will be in part guided by the interests and priorities of the voting population. If debt causes are important for the population, then governments will have an interest in addressing them. The citizens of the countries which are home to international NGOs and in which issues such as developing country debt are politically saliable, will tend to push their governments to take action internationally. Indeed, official lenders, as a result of pressure from their shareholders, have increasingly engaged in initiatives to improve their international lending practices.[380] Furthermore, domestic interests groups, such as those in the socially democratic European countries, have played a major role in influencing their governments to push for an international approach to address the debt burden of the poorest countries.[381]

A related interest can stem from the desire of a state to develop a good reputation in a particular international field, such as being a leader in promoting equity in international relations and a more fair financial system. This argument is a derivative of the previous argument, as a good reputation may be important to the voting population. Again, several socially democratic European countries can be seen as being an example of countries which currently strive to be at the forefront of international social causes.

In the context of odious debt, Norway has received a lot of praise and attention for *ex gratia* cancelling over 80 million dollars of debt owed to it by five developing countries after determining that the loans were not granted in good faith and incurred illegitimately.[382] The debts date back to the period between 1976 and 1980, when the Norwegian ship building industry was in crisis and Norway sold 156 ships and accompanying equipment to poor countries. The original motivation for the loans was to bolster Norway's own economy. The projects lacked sustainability and failed, at which time Norway became the creditor. In its announcement, the Norwegian government publicly admitted it had made a "policy failure" and that it had played a role in adding to the "illegitimate debt" that those countries accumulated. What is significant and unprecedented is the claim made by Norway that the debt forgiveness would be without any attached conditionality and would also not be considered as part of Norway's official development assistance.

Besides the cancellation of debts, Norway has also been at the forefront of developing a discourse on odious debt in the international community by promoting research and discussion on the subject and by sponsoring academic papers and

[380] Nehru 2007, 26

[381] Haas June 2003

[382] See for examplewww.50years.org/cms/updates/story/346; Norway takes historic step 2006 A press release from October of 2006 by the Norwegian foreign ministry announced that the countries thaht would benefit were Ecuador, Egypt, Jamaica, Peru and Sierra Leone. Burma and Sudan would also be able to benefit from the plan in the future

studies.[383] It has played a role in fostering the dialogue on odious debt between the three branches of governance; the official sector, NGOs and the academic community.

5.1.1.3 The Role of Competition

Competition within the official sector can give incentives to the major actors in governance to support and drive change. Competition exists at the international level between states as well as between international bodies. The main actors in the international governance framework compete against each other primarily for power. As new players emerge in international finance and new centres of power develop, old and established players have to compete and adapt to retain their dominance in different fields. In the financial context, there are multiple examples of this. One scholar describes the Paris Club's continued fight for dominance against the World Bank and the International Monetary Fund (IMF) over "the battle over multilateral debt."[384]

Another example involves the IMF. Despite "continued success over the past three decades,"[385] there is an increased perception by the international community that it has lost relevance and legitimacy due to a greater role of the private sector in international capital flows, as well as the increasingly controversial fact that its governance continues to be dominated by the major industrial countries, in particular the United States and the European countries. The global financial crisis has provided an opportunity for the IMF to regain its legitimacy, relevance and consequently its dominant position in global economic governance. Following the G-20 Summit in London of March of 2009, the IMF committed to becoming more inclusive, provide a larger role for finance ministers in the daily running of the Fund to give it greater political legitimacy and has introduced a "Flexible Credit Line" which is credit without the Fund's characteristic controversial conditionalities.[386] The changes currently undergoing in the IMF illustrate the fact that times of crises are also times of opportunity to address new issues and drive change.

New concentrations of power between states can also foster competition and concerns for national security which may be a driving force behind change. For example, China has received a lot of scrutiny and criticism for its 'non interventionist' relationship, including its 'zero conditionality' lending activities, in Africa. While China has been present in the African continent for a long time, only now that it has

---

[383]The government of Norway sponsored papers such as that written by Robert Howse on the subject, in collaboration with UNCTAD See Howse 2007

[384] Callaghy 2004, 13, 35 (Discussing how the HIPC Initiative came to fruition after much resistance and bargaining and ultimately came about with the major actors striving to obtain a central role. The IMF was brought on board as decision makers within it "ultimately saw the wisdom of trying to steer the design of the mechanism rather than resist it."

[385] Truman January 22, 2009, 3

[386] Springing into action 2009

become an important economic and political power has its human rights record and the equity and sustainability of the debtor countries with whom it does business become a concern for the West.

Finally, previous experience has shown that collective action problems exist at the international level which make actors in the official sector reluctant to take the first concrete steps in addressing issues such as odious debt. However, as one scholar put it, when "the writing is on the wall"[387] that the international community is moving towards addressing a certain issue, actors that did not want to be the first to get involved may well be competing for a leadership role. This happened with regards to the HIPC Initiative and the issue of addressing unsustainable debt.[388]

5.1.1.4 A Note on Debtor States – Not at the Forefront of Change

It is debtor states who have the most at stake in driving change in the international regime that governs debt. Interestingly, however, they have been the relatively least active in promoting and pushing for change. Indeed, with regards to notable developments in the evolution of governance surrounding developing country debt, such as the HIPC, debtor states were not a driving force behind such innovation.[389] This lack of leadership and involvement may be due to a number of reasons.

One primary reason may stem from the fact that developing countries may face an ever greater collective action problem in driving change at the international level, than their developed counterparts. First, their marginal impact on the international community may be smaller than more powerful countries and therefore more costly for them to take action. The opportunity costs involved in devoting resources to driving change will also be larger, given the smaller size of their economies. Furthermore, they will be reluctant to take the first step to change or question the status quo in the debt regime for fear of exclusion from the financial markets, or fear that they will strain ties with the creditor countries from which many are dependent.[390]

In the context of odious debt, debtor states again have, by and large, been reluctant to address the topic. In fact, they have actively disassociated themselves from the odious debt discourse. For example, South Africa dismissed calls by NGOs to

---

[387] Callaghy 2004, 35

[388] Callaghy 2004

[389] Callaghy 2004, vi

[390] One exception was during the 1970s and the 1980s when a groupd of Southern states proposed the New International Economic Order (NIEO). This was a set of proposals put forward through the United Nations Conference on Trade and Development to promote the interests of developing countries and addressed a range of trade, financial, commodity and debt related issues. It was meant to be a revision of the international economic system in favour od developing countries, replacing the Bretton Woods system, which was perceived as having benefited the leading states that had created it. Neveretheless nothing substanties from this intense state to state bargaining.

repudiate its apartheid inherited debt.[391] Similarly, Daniel Ortega ultimately decided against repudiating the debts that his government inherited from the Somoza regime, who had reportedly looted between 100 million and U.S.$ 500 million.[392]

Ecuador has been an active exception to the rule, as it recently made good on its promise to forego scheduled interest payments on private bonds on grounds that the loans were illegitimate, as deemed by the country's debt audit commission. Responding to calls from Ecuadorian civil society and the international Jubilee Network, President Rafael Correa's government created an independent debt commission in 2007 which investigated all debt issued to the country from the period between 1970 to June 2006.[393] The audit of the debt took place with the participation of economists, lawyers and representatives of social organizations from Ecuador and other nations. Among other findings, the audit uncovered criminal violations by previous governments who sold debt to pension funds, hedge funds and other overseas investors.[394] Correa's strategy was to use default and the debt audit as leverage to renegotiate the debt with foreign creditors.[395] The Washington Post credited Ecuador's move and noted that it was rare for a developing country to cease payments, not because it can't afford to pay, but because it has made a political decision not to. It also stated that Ecuador was "playing a high stakes chicken game with investors."[396]

While some, notably NGOs and debt activists, praised the Correa regime for defaulting on the debt,[397] by and large the creditor community interpreted his actions as opportunistic.[398]

5.1.2 NGOs and Odious Debt

Debt governance is continuously changing as new players enter, existing players acquire more accountability and power and together interact with old and established players. The World Bank describes a shift in governance in the context of debt which has gone beyond what was once a "state and international financial institution –

[391] See for example: S. Africa Shuns Apartheid Lawsuits November 27, 2002

[392] Jayachandran and Kremer 2002; Somoza's Legacy: Plundered Economy November 30, 1979; Cuba's Debt Mistakes:A Lesson for Nicaragua October 5, 1980

[393] See hoy.mec.ec 2008

[394] See www.odiousdebt.org; "http://jubileeusa.typepad.com/blog_the_debt/2008/12/ecuador-defaults-on-illegitimate-debt.html)" 2008; www.hacer.org 2008

[395] Zeledon 2009

[396] Faiola December 13, 2008

[397] Outcome document 2008, 3

[398] For a discussion See Chapter 2 of this book, "Reputation and Odious Debt"

centric" international debt regime.[399] It argues that the result of this shift has been a much more complex web of international economic governance.

The active role of NGOs over the last two decades in the context of developing country debt is widely documented. There has been an impressive emergence of NGOs of different backgrounds, including religious, humanitarian, labour and environmental, which have focused on issues pertaining to developing country debt. Over this period of time, their role in international governance has evolved. They began working largely on the sidelines of the governance framework and played a marginal role, often dismissed as being overly normative, bias and lacking credibility and expertise. Today, some NGOs play a much more central role which has the potential to become increasingly powerful and relevant. Their discourse is based on normative considerations and a belief that the debt burden of the developing world is unfair. This discourse is a powerful one, questioning the status of quo of equity, justice, accountability, representation and transparency.[400] Their aims are wide ranging and ambitious and can include, for example, "a one-off cancellation of poor country debt by the year 2000 of the backlog of unpayable debt owed by the world's poorest countries, under a fair and transparent process."[401]

This section focuses on the factors that contributed to the evolution of the role of NGO networks in the debt regime. It draws some implications on where this role should be headed, based on their comparative advantage and disadvantages relative to the other branches of debt governance. Finally, it looks at the role that NGOs are playing in the odious debt discourse and its potential.

5.1.2.1 Improved Communication and Information

Technological innovation and improved communication channels have contributed to the more prominent role of NGOs in international economic governance. First, it has allowed NGOs to access and collect information more easily, both on the situation of developing countries and debt issues more generally. At the same time, they have better access to information from other expert sources, such as academics, and this allows them to increase their capabilities and the sophistication with which they approach the causes that they are championing. Secondly, transaction costs have been lowered with regards to communication and information sharing between different NGOs. Furthermore, better information channels have widely expanded the reach that NGOs have, as a result of greater exposure to the international community. The media has also played an informational role in increasing their exposure, through the active participation of celebrities and public figures who advocate the work and causes of debt NGOs, from U2's Bono, to the Pope.

---

[399] Callaghy 2004, 6

[400] See for example, Eurodad, www.cadtm.org, Probe International; www.odiousdebt.org, Jubilee movements

[401] Callaghy 2004, 18

5.1.2.2 Increased Pressure on Developed Country Governments

The vast majority of debt related NGOs are based in developed countries. This has been argued to be due in part to the fact that NGO campaigns on the ground are much easier, politically, in the North, where there is greater transparency of government decision making and where NGOs operate with less risk.[402] Increasingly, more NGOs have been able to capitalize on their unique position to pressure their governments to take action on international debt issues. This power stems from various sources. As a result of improved information channels which have increased public awareness about the existence, work and causes of NGOs, several debt issues have become politically saliable subjects in some developed countries. Improved information has also increased the credibility of NGOs, thereby increasing their sympathizers and supporters, who can in turn also play a role in pressing their governments to take action. Finally, NGOs are increasingly better able to obtain information about their government's activities and are able to monitor them and hold them accountable to their promises. Their ability to lobby and pressure is not limited to their respective home governments but has extended to other actors in the official sector such as multilateral bodies, including the IMF, the World Bank and former G7, now G8 summits.

5.1.2.3 Collaboration with the Global South

Increasingly, Northern NGOs have helped create, link up with and foster Southern NGOs interested in debt and other development issues.[403] Some even have a network of offices in poor countries through which they can gather information and work with local actors. Consequently, some NGOs may have a comparative advantage, relative to other governance actors, in their capacity to obtain hands on, grass roots information. Furthermore, it is possible that they may be perceived by local actors as working on a more equal footing with them, as opposed to the perceived imposed and more top down approach of other bodies present in developing countries, such as the IMF and the World Bank. This may increase their effectiveness in developing a discourse and the debt capacity of local actors.

5.1.2.4 NGOs and Odious Debt

Currently, NGO debt networks are actively advocating an odious debt campaign. Several have been notably active, including the bigger and more established NGOs which have previously played a role in advocating other debt issues such as debt relief. These include, for example, EURODAD[404] and Jubilee movements around the

---

[402] Haas June 2003, 20

[403] For a discussion See Haas June 2003

[404] See http://www.eurodad.org

globe.[405] Others emerged specifically in the context of odious debt such as Probe International's Chapter on Odious Debt, lead by Patricia Adams. Several church organizations have also been notably active. The Lutheran World Federation, the Church of Sweden and Norwegian Church Aid together organized an International Symposium on Illegitimate External Debt in Oslo, Norway in late 2008.[406]

The NGO discourse on odious debt is a derivative of the moral considerations that shaped NGO networks on debt and continues to be primarily normative. It distinguishes itself from previous discourses on debt by stressing the gross injustice involved in holding the population of debtor countries liable for debt which was incurred for odious purposes, against the general public interest, by despotic and irresponsible governments. At the same time, the discourse also highlights the enabling and often active role of creditors in odious debt.

5.1.2.5 Comparative Advantages and Limitations of NGOs

The comparative advantage of the NGO community role may lie in its ability to gather support and influence governments and states, through rewards or threats. In effect, their communication and information dissemination skills can provide carrots or sticks to governments. Carrots are provided in the form of favourable exposure. Norway has received a lot of praise in debt circles with regards to its active role in the international odious debt campaign. Sticks can come in the form of negative media exposure, such as the type which has been effective in the realm of international environmental governance, for example.

While the NGO community may enjoy an advantage in drawing public attention on issues such as odious debt, they may also have a relative disadvantage in expert fields such as economics and international law. This is reflected in their adamant defense of the odious debt doctrine by clinging to its purported benefits, without fully taking into account the costs that a developing country would bear if it recurs to it. Indeed, There is a lack of consequentialist perspective inherent in their discourse, which fails to take into account the real threat of exclusion from financial markets that developing debtors face.

Furthermore, while their persuasion and power stems in part from their alarmist, moral discourse, it also reduces their credibility and threatens their power in the international community. The worst case scenario would be for them to steer the debt regime towards a direction that is detrimental to the developing world. These concerns

---

[405] See Jubilee networks such as those in Germany, South Africa and Iraq which have been active in the odious debt debate.

[406] Outcome document 2008

are real.[407] Indeed, some of their proposals in the odious debt field would harm the very interests of the developing world that they are trying to help.

The influence of the NGO community on international economic governance will depend on their ability to gather support in policy circles. Whether their influence is a blessing or a curse for developing debtor countries will depend on whether they guide the international community in a direction that benefits them in the long run, as opposed to a one shot gain. Consequently, it is important that they work together with experts in other fields.

Increased sophistication and capacity building of NGOs has given them a bigger role, particularly in establishing partnerships with other governance actors, such as academics and international organizations. The rise of the Enhanced Heavily Indebted Poor Countries initiative, as described by Callaghy, is descriptive of the important role that they have when working together with such actors.[408]

Interestingly, the NGO discourse on odious debt seems to be moving towards a more collaborative direction, one which fosters research and discussion with actors in the other branches of governance, such as academics, international organizations and states. For example, the International Symposium on Illegitimate External Debt organized by several church organizations, invited government representatives, Parliaments, UN agencies and international financing institutions as well as academics.[409] Another example includes the Round Table organized by EURODAD, the World Bank and members of academia.[410] The next section looks at the complementary role that the epistemic and NGO communities can have.

5.1.3 The Epistemic/academic community

The epistemic community comprises the third branch of the triple helix.[411] It is defined by Haas as "a network of knowledge based experts or groups with an authoritative claim to policy-relevant knowledge within the domain of their expertise."[412] Their influential function stems from their expertise on the different policy issues that shape international economic governance. Their evolving knowledge and understanding about the nature and consequences of the different debt problems of developing countries has allowed for the concerns raised by NGOs to be translated into the

---

[407] See Haas June 2003 (providing examples of how the NGO community can steer international governance in a direction with perverse consequences that harm the very interest that they champion in the environmental field.)

[408] Callaghy 2004

[409] Outcome document 2008

[410] Nehru, Bank et al. 2008

[411] Callaghy 2004, 21

[412] Haas Winter 1992

discourse of policy circles, including governments and international organizations. This section will look at the factors that have been important in the evolving role of the epistemic community in international governance. Essentially, through knowledge and the learning mechanism which they enable, they have contributed to an endogenous source of change in international governance and have helped create substantive linkages between issues such as debt relief and development.

5.1.3.1 Informational Asymmetries

Globalisation has brought about an increased interconnectedness between nation states and has created trans-boundary and global externalities. With this, has come a deepened uncertainty faced by states with regards to their interactions in the international community.[413] Consequently, globalisation has increased the demand for expert knowledge at the policy level, as policymakers face ever larger asymmetries of information, particularly in technical areas. Haas argues that as a result, epistemic communities have been granted more deference in public policy circles.

Consequently, the role of the epistemic community is heightened in domains where large informational asymmetries exist. These domains are increasingly common throughout recent international politics. Policymakers require knowledgeable experts when they are faced with a decision about which they have little background knowledge. They may also have an increased role in times of failed policies, when their expertise may allow to determine why a certain policy failed and present alternatives to it.

In the context of debt, there is a large epistemic community composed mainly of economists working in various fields and sectors. They provide technical knowledge about the functioning of the global economy and complex inter-related issues such as development, debt overhang and debt crises.

5.1.3.2 "Insiders" and "Outsiders"

Members of the epistemic community are present in all of the institutions and processes of the international debt regime, such as the Paris Club, its member governments, the IMF and the World Bank. They have been referred to as the „insiders" of the international debt regime.[414] Callaghy has argued that an important factor in the evolution of the international debt regime has been the role played by some epistemic community members inside the major units of power who are sympathetic with parts of the NGO discourses on debt.[415] This implies that the influential power of the epistemic community is a function of its ability to acquire influential positions within national governments and international institutions.

---

[413] Haas June 2003, 4

[414] Callaghy 2004, 22

[415] Id.

At the same time, the "outsiders" who are members of the epistemic community which are not in major position of structural power, have also played an important role in the ongoing debates about debt.[416] Some have been active working with NGOs and providing independent analyses about the status of individual country cases for them. Other such "outsiders" include academic and think tank scholars and private consultants. Finally, some insiders have become outsiders and vice versa.[417]

Within this governance branch, the learning mechanism is allowed to develop and function more rapidly and efficiently. An example of how it has evolved in the context of debt can be evidenced by how the official sector debt treatment has shifted from pure debt collection to debt rescheduling. Indeed, creditors have learnt that in several instances, it is in their interest to reschedule debts, rather than insist on full repayment.

Accordingly, members of the epistemic community can act as hinges between NGOs and the official sector. One way that they can do this is by identifying substantive linkages between the causes championed by NGOs and the interests of the official sector. For example, they can help define the self interests of a state, in the context of debt forgiveness for example, and situate it within the evolving governance discourse. They can further help identify the different roles that a state can take on within such discourse.

5.1.3.3 The Epistemic Community on Odious Debt

The epistemic community on odious debt is composed primarily of lawyers and economists. Multiple academic conferences, notably in prominent law schools in the United States, have been devoted to the subject.[418] Furthermore, a rich academic literature on odious debt has developed.

The involvement of academics has extended beyond the academic field. Already at the beginning of the renewed discourse, which came about at the time following the Iraq war and the debate that ensued from Iraq's debt, two economists first introduced the subject of odious debt to the international financial organizations at a conference held at the IMF.[419] Since then, the collaboration between the international organizations, NGOs and academics has increased. For example, Robert Howse, a prominent legal scholar, wrote a paper on the topic for a 2007 UNCTAD conference

---

[416] Id.

[417] Id, 21

[418] See for example, Odious Debts and State Corruption conference held at Duke University on 26th of January, 2007. Papers were published in the Duke's Law School Journal; Law and Contemporary Problems Vol 70 See Also: Colloquim on Odious Debt at the University of Chapel Hill, Papers published in North Caroline Journal of International Law (June 2007)

[419] Jayachandran and Kremer 2002

which devoted a panel to odious debt.[420] An economic expert which could be described as an "insider" working at the World Bank, Vikram Nehru also made odious debt the focus of a recent paper[421] and subsequently organized a round table on the subject whose participants included NGOs, the World Bank and academia.[422] The World Bank has also sponsored other scientific papers and panels on the subject.[423] More recently, a conference was organized at Harvard University which aimed to discuss pragmatic possibilities fort the Obama administration to address odious debt via loan sanctions.[424] These ongoing partnerships are a relevant advancement in the governance discourse on odious debt.

5.2 A Comment on the Triple Helix and Odious Debt

Against the background of the triple helix, several implications and caveats can be drawn for addressing odious debt within the dynamic framework of international economic governance. The power of the triple helix lies in the collaboration, information sharing and partnerships, between the three branches. Each branch of governance is briefly considered in turn.

The current political climate may provide a window of opportunity to introduce the odious debt cause into the official sector. In the context of the financial crisis, concerns for equity in international finance, together with greater lender and borrower responsibility have increased. At the same time, the crisis provides for an opportunity for change and innovation. The crisis has illustrated the dangers of contagion and the greater stakes involved in the interconnection between countries brought about by globalisation. It is important to address the interests of the actors in the official sector who are able to drive change, and finding substantive linkages between odious debt and other relevant issue and policy areas may be one way to do so.

Currently, Norway has been the only developed country at the forefront of the odious debt campaign. Other creditor countries and the international organizations, although they have engaged in the discourse, have not yet taken any concrete steps. This could be due both to a collective action problem and the fear that taking action will inhibit uncertainty in international finance. The fact that the discourse on odious debt, although rapidly evolving in different circles, remains fragmented and vague is also a factor which increases uncertainty and consequently the reluctance that actors have in addressing it. Indeed, the uncertainty surrounding odious debt was one of the

---

[420] Howse 2007

[421] Nehru 2007

[422] Nehru, Bank et al. 2008

[423] Paulus 2007; Panel on New Expertise on Odious Debts 2008

[424] www.eurodad.org 2009

main reasons that the United States refrained from officially using it as an argument at the time that it was seeking arguments to relieve Iraq of its debt burden.

The NGO community has been largely responsible for bringing international attention to the issue of odious debt. Its role may be limited to just that, however. Whether it will be extended to bringing about a solution to address odious debt in practice will depend on several factors. Two important ones are credibility and legitimacy. This will depend, in part on the sophistication of their discourse which should steer away from an "all or nothing" tone and refrain from being overly biased. Moral arguments can be substantiated on positive facts and knowledge, which will be more effective and credible than anti creditor, anti capitalist preconceptions. Also, they can be backed up by important economic considerations. If the NGO debt networks wish not to be confined to the sidelines of international economic governance, they will have to work together with the actors in the system and contribute to finding sustainable and pragmatic solutions to the world's debt problems. Their comparative advantage is of value and will vary from NGO to NGO, but may include their ability to gather support and mobilize social networks, their monitoring activities and their ability to hold governments accountable to their promises as well as providing grass roots information on the situation of odious debt in different countries, working in partnership with NGO communities and governance actors in the South and continuing to increase awareness on the topic.

Finally, the epistemic community has played a powerful role in shaping and guiding the discourse on odious debt towards a more pragmatic and consequentialist direction. In this respect, insights from the field of law-and-economics will continue to have a prominent role in the academic discourse on odious debt. This will help in building a bridge between the considerations highlighted by the NGO community and the interests and capabilities of the official sector. Their influence and role in the odious debt debate will be a function of the number of "insiders" from the epistemic community in powerful positions in different policy circles. Furthermore, it will also be a function of how fragmented the epistemic community is. A certain degree of fragmentation is necessary to provide sophisticated analysis and debate, but too much fragmentation may increase uncertainty and limit the power of their voice.

A promising avenue could be that already adopted by American academia, which has recently organized academic conferences devoted to assessing how the current American administration could address the topic of odious debt through loan sanctions.[425] Other active academic circles on odious debt, such as Germany, could do the same. Conferences which bring together the different actors of the three governance branches, such as that of UNCTAD are also promising avenues to develop the odious discourse together and translate it into practice and policy circles.

Taking these factors into consideration, the following section will offer a modest proposal to address odious debts in the context of debt negotiations within the Paris

[425] See www.eurodad.org 2009

Club. It will look at the role of the players in each branch in bringing about the proposal.

5.3 Introducing Odious Debt into Debt Negotiations

A few articles in the literature have noted that odiousness may have played an "added argument" in the Paris Club negotiations and restructurings of countries like Iraq and Nigeria.[426] In a 2007 conference, Robert Howse considered that, "rather than repudiating debt, a debtor State might invoke concerns of odious debt in negotiations with its creditors in order to reach a compromise that promotes financial stability and future access to credit.[427] In a symposium organized on illegitimate debt organized by a council of churches, Germany and Norway proposed for a discussion in the Paris Club on the subject and working for support from other Paris Club members.[428] Recently, at a conference, Joseph Stiglitz expressed his interest in working towards including odious debt in restructurings.[429]

The rest of the chapter takes this idea as a starting point and pursues it further, taking into consideration the role of the different players in the debt governance framework. Specifically, it looks at the potential of introducing odious debt into the debt negotiations that take place under the auspices of the Paris Club. After addressing the relationship between odious debt and debt restructuring, it provides an overview of the Paris Club and analyses some of its key features that could make it particularly suitable to address odious debt. It then considers some potential obstacles.

5.3.1 Towards a Legal Solution to Odious Debt

The relationship between sovereign debt restructuring and international law governing debt issues is under-theorized. There is a widespread preference and acceptance of the international community to deal with sovereign debt issues via negotiation and restructuring agreements. This has led to some key negotiation forums and the mechanism of debt restructuring to become an inherent part of sovereign debt relations. At the same time, more formal international legal forums have had less relevance to sovereign debt and are rarely recurred to.

This status quo raises several important questions. On the one hand, one could argue that the preference for debt restructuring has been one of the main reasons why international law regarding issues of sovereign debt is relatively under-developed, as compared to other fields, such as international investment law. On the other hand, the

---

426 Damle 2007, 649; King 2007

427 Howse 2007, 11

428 Outcome document 2008, 3

429 Presentation at the International Labour Conference on the Financial Crisis, March 2009 Geneva, Switzerland

forums where negotiations and restructurings take place are realms where valuable precedents are created and where the discourse on sovereign debt issues is constantly changing and evolving.

The political realm and the international legal realm do not evolve in isolation from each other. Negotiations between states takes place in the shadow of reputation sanctions, or other sanctions, stemming from the legal obligation itself.[430] At the same time, the discourse that evolves in the political realm can enlighten the general understanding of international law in different issues areas. The implication is that odious debt can first be introduced in a negotiation forum, such as the Paris Club, in the context of sovereign debt restructuring discussions. This would allow it to be part of the evolving discourse of the international community with regards to sovereign debt and equitable considerations. This, in turn, could be the first step towards the development of more formal legal rules and norms.

5.3.2 Overview of the Paris Club

The Paris Club is one of the major players in the official debt governance regime. It is an informal group of 19 official bilateral creditors, representing the major industrialized countries, who voluntarily come together to renegotiate the sovereign debt of their borrowers. For over 50 years, their aim has been to find "...coordinated and sustainable solutions to the payment difficulties encountered by debtor nations."[431] Paris Club creditors agree to reschedule debts due to them. Rescheduling is a means of providing a country with temporary debt relief through a postponement and, in the case of concessional rescheduling, a reduction in debt service obligations.

Nineteen countries are members of the Paris Club and may participate in the negotiation sessions.[432] As these industrialized countries are the largest official creditors in the sovereign debt market, it is often the case that a sovereign default will involve at least some of the Paris Club members. Furthermore, because the majority of the debt structure of the least developed countries (LDCs.) is composed entirely of official debt, all of their debt is usually treated under the auspices of the Paris Club. The Paris Club is therefore an instrumental body in the sovereign debt market as a whole and the world of sovereign debt restructuring.

---

[430] Khalfan et al. Discuss political efforts and their relationship to international law. They further discuss how political means shaped the general understanding of international law in the area of international nuclear issues. See Khalfan, King et al. 2003 54-57

[431] Paris Club Annual Report 2007

[432] They include Austria, Australia, Belgium, Canada, Denmark, Finland, France, Germany, Ireland, Italy, Japan, Netherlands, Norway, Russian Federation, Spain, Sweden, Switzerland, United Kingdom and the United States of America.

Other official creditors can also take part in Paris Club debt negotiations, provided that the permanent members and the debtor agree.[433] International institution observers can also attend the negotiations. In particular, the International Monetary Fund and World Bank representative attend every single Paris Club meeting.

The first meeting with a debtor country was held on May 1956 when Argentina met its public creditors in Paris. Since then, the Paris Club has reached 403 agreements with 85 debtor countries. These agreements have covered a total of more than USD 500 billion in nominal value since 1956.[434]

The Paris Club has remained strictly informal and voluntary. Agreements are reached in accordance with a set of rules and principles agreed upon by its members to secure agreements efficiently both amongst creditors and between creditor and debtor countries.

The 5 key principles of the Paris Club are as follows:

1. Case by Case: The Paris Club makes decisions on a case-by-case basis in order to tailor its action to each debtor country's individual situation.

2. Consensus: Paris Club decisions cannot be taken without a consensus among the participating creditor countries.

3. Conditionality: Debt treatments are granted to countries that need debt relief and adopt appropriate reforms to solve their payment difficulties. In practice, conditionality is met when an appropriate program supported by the IMF demonstrates the need for debt relief.

4. Solidarity: All members of the Paris Club should act as a group in their dealing with a given debtor country and be sensitive to the effect that the management of their particular claims may have on the claims of other members.

5. Comparability of Treatment: The debtor country that signed an agreement with its Paris Club creditors should not accept from its non-Paris club creditors terms of treatment of its debt less favourable for the debtor that those agreed within the Paris Club.

Before a debtor country approaches the Paris Club for negotiation, it must first undergo an IMF debt sustainability analysis which determines whether the country is suffering from a liquidity problem, a sustainability problem, or both. It concludes an agreement with the IMF on a program that shows that the country is unable to meet its obligations and thus needs a new payment arrangement with its external creditors.

---

[433] Brazil, Israel, Portugal and South Korea are the creditor countries which have participated in the largest number of Paris Club negotiations.

[434] Paris Club Annual Report 2007, 5

Among the different types of debt, Paris Club agreements concern only public debts. Debts owed by private entities and guaranteed by the public sector are also considered to be part of public debts.[435] Furthermore, medium and long term debts are treated by the Paris Club. Short term debts (debt with maturity of one year or less) are usually excluded from the treatments, as their restructuring can significantly undermine the debtor country's capacity to participate in international trade. When a debtor country first meets with Paris club creditors, a "cut off date" is defined. Credits granted after this cut off date generally are not subject to future rescheduling. Finally, multilateral claims are not rescheduled and other claims have to be treated in terms comparable to those set in the Paris Club agreements

5.3.3 Key Characteristics of Official Debt Renegotiations

Addressing odious debt via the context of Paris Club debt negotiations puts the issues in the hands of the official sector and the political, ad hoc and responsive approach that characterizes it. This section makes a case for why this environment is better suited to address odious debt than other alternatives which have been brought forth by the literature.

5.3.3.1 Negotiation versus Litigation

Several proposals in the literature seek to address odious debt via formal, legal mechanisms. They aim to achieve strict legal rules and a level of predictability that is incompatible with the way international law works and the lack of third party enforcement that characterizes it. Legal recourse in the international context is perceived not only as an ineffective means of resolving disputes, but also as the most disruptive.[436] It is associated with ending the relationship, as opposed to resolving issues between parties. Secondly, the multiple goals of the official sector and the parameters within which it operates contrast with the dogmatic and strict legal responses to the problem that have been brought forth by the literature.

Conversely, the context of official debt negotiations is reflective of the complex dynamics between hegemony, power and a balance between shared interests and competing national concerns for states. Indeed, the Paris Club is a reflection of how international law functions. It refers to itself as a "non institution" and at the same time, as one scholar describes it is, "the closest the international community has come to submitting to binding decisions promulgated to an international authority."[437] It functions very differently from a legal institution as it exists in the domestic context. It is not a court and does not have an impartial and independent ruling body. With regards to standing, only interested parties have the capability to initiate proceedings and states control access to the process. It does not function via third party

[435] Paris Club Annual Report 2007, 42

[436] See Gottlieb Spring 1983

[437] Damle 2007, 153

enforcement, in the sense that it lacks the authority to impose sanctions directly and cannot force parties to follow its rules. It is entirely voluntary for its members as well as for the debtor who initially willingly approaches the Club for negotiations.

With regards to Paris Club agreements, they are not legally binding contracts. Rather, creditor countries taking part in the debt treatment sign the Agreed Minutes, also signed by the representative of the debtor country, which is a recommendation to their governments to negotiate and sign a binding bilateral agreement with the debtor country. Paris Club agreements can most adequately be described as "pledges" rather than contracts.[438] In the words of Raustalia, who speaks of form and substance in international agreements, they are an example of an endogenous cooperative strategy between states, as opposed to an externally imposed set of rules.[439] He argues that when there is a high degree of uncertainty and states value flexibility, discretion and confidentiality, they will tend to prefer such weak contracts, or "pledges."

Despite its informal, voluntary aspects and its lack of third party enforcement, Paris Club agreements have a high compliance rate. This is due to several characteristics which make the context of official sovereign debt restructuring particularly adequate to make informal enforcement via reputation and self enforcement effective. Members of the Club meet regularly on a monthly basis (*tours d'horizon*). The number of parties involved in Paris Club negotiations is small, therefore reducing transaction, coordination and communication costs between them. Parties are able to monitor each others' behaviour. This pertains to monitoring not only the debtor's behaviour with regards to abiding by Paris Club terms, but also the monitoring between creditors countries so that they effectively provide the amount of debt relief that they pledged at the Paris Club. Information is easily disseminated in such a context and it is also easy to detect if someone has defected from the agreement. Also, because states are not complete strangers to each other and they engage in a multitude of different and related relationships together at the international level, this increases the stakes of breaking agreements and disrupting their reputation vis-à-vis other states.

5.3.3.2 The Political Context versus the Legal Context

When looking at the institutional and governance context in which odious debt could be addressed, it is relevant to look at how sovereign debt issues in general are treated. Indeed, the general preference of the international community to deal with international debt issues in an ex post, ad hoc and political framework can be evidenced by the context of sovereign debt restructuring itself. Much of the debates in the odious debt literature regarding whether a formal legal approach is suitable to address odious debt parallel the same question in the context of sovereign debt

---

[438] Raustalia July 2005, 2

[439] Raustalia July 2005, 27

restructuring.[440] Despite calls for a comprehensive legal system for sovereign workouts, such a framework has not substantiated. Tarullo argues that this is due to several reasons, including the fact that the official sector prefers the policies of incrementalism and flexibility to a self contained system.[441]

Many who emphasize a formal and legal response to odious debt also explicitly seek to eliminate politics from the picture. For them, the cause for odious debt is political and the solution is politics-free. While political economy issues play a significant role in the causes of odious debt and influence debt relations generally, it is implausible/unrealistic to have a mechanism introduced in the sovereign debt context which does not take politics into consideration, much less attempt to relieve the international debt market from politics. To go to the other extreme, politics may not only be inevitable, they may also be desirable. Rasmussen suggests that political considerations can play a positive role in this area and argues that rather than crafting regimes to avoid political influence, we should endeavour to find systems that harness it.[442] One of the advantages of the political context is its ability to bring the divergent and dynamic interests of parties to the negotiating table on a case by case basis and its ability to reconcile the international community's interest in achieving common goals, while maintaining flexibility.[443]

Furthermore, not only is the context of sovereign debt inherently political, but, by definition, so is the context of political transitions. Reina has argued that the most direct path to the resolution of disputes concerning responsibility for contracts incurred by the predecessor state is the political arena.[444] Approaching successor state liability at the political and diplomatic levels offers a better solution to potential disputes than legal recourse.[445] Proscribing rules and norms in an attempt to regulate behaviour in a systemic manner is at odds with the idiosyncratic needs of all players in situations following state succession.

Finally, the aversion of a political solution to developing country debt by many is related to the inherent power relations present in political negotiations. Because power relations in essence make the political context biased towards the developed countries, many believe that the political context is therefore inappropriate to deal with odious debt. In the context of sovereign debt, creditor-debtor power relations become apparent once the debtor is unable to repay a loan and negotiations ensue. The system of debt rescheduling and the practices of debt reduction and debt forgiveness are

---

[440] See for example, Hughes-Verdier 2004

[441] Tarullo 2007, 9

[442] Raustalia July 2005, 260

[443] Gelpern 2005, 393

[444] Reina 2004, 584

[445] Id.

characterized by the affirmation of the financial obligation of the debtor state and a shared understanding of the debtor's moral responsibility and blame. Some scholars argue that what is missing in these practices is the acknowledgement of any responsibility of creditor states.[446]

This chapter acknowledges the existence of politics and power relations in sovereign debt and sovereign debt restructurings. It accepts these as inherent and inevitable characteristics of the international order and furthermore, as a necessary tool for creditors which require an effective enforcement mechanism. This chapter does not make a normative statement with regards to the desirability of such a system. Rather, it takes the point of view that politics and power relations are an inevitable part of the international regulatory order. When this is a taken as a given, the aim then becomes on improving the system, and adapting it to new needs and developments, taking into account its inherent characteristics. Efforts may be focused on improving the current framework. To misquote Audre Lorde, the master's tools should be used to dismantle the master's house.[447]

5.3.3.3 The Ex Post Nature of Debt Renegotiations

Proponents of addressing odious debt ultimately have two goals: they seek to prevent odious debt from occurring and/or seek to relieve debtor countries that are saddled with odious debt which has already occurred. Ideally, both goals are needed. The nature of the odious debt problem, however, forces approaches to emphasize one or the other. This is because the main culprit responsible for odious debt is no longer present ex post and this therefore limits the deterrence effects of an ex post approach.

Despite this limitation, an ex post approach is still needed. Introducing odious debt into the context of debt restructuring would emphasize the ex post necessity of dealing with the debt of debtor countries which has been used against the general interests of the population at large and which they are now responsible for. The financial crisis has shown the importance of adequate, efficient and quick responses to financial problems. Indeed, there is often a trade off between pursuing the aim of long run, first best solutions and the short term ex post urgency of many poor developing countries who become saddled with odious debt. This resembles the problem that many countries recently faced in the midst of the financial crisis, regarding the question of whether they should come to the rescue of their banks. While bank bailouts might lead to more moral hazard in the long term, the cost of not bailing them out in the immediate present may be even costlier. Indeed, bailouts are arguably pragmatic, not ideological. Likewise, odious debt exists in a decidedly second best world and implicates the development of many poor countries. While first best solutions are required and the sovereign debt market needs to become more efficient, responsive, ex

---

[446] Hattori July 2008, 17

[447] Aidre Lorde, American poet and activist famously stated, " The master's tools will never dismantle the master's house"

post and pragmatic responses are also required. These could be mainstreamed into the already existing mechanism of sovereign debt restructuring and be dealt with in conjunction with other debt issues.

Emphasizing the need for an ex post mechanism for odious debt does not imply that efforts which target deterrence should be ignored. Indeed, odious debt, as do other issues of sovereign debt including debt crises, require both a responsive and a preventative approach. This chapter focuses on how such an ex post responsive approach could look like, with an emphasis on feasibility and political acceptability. However, such an ex post approach which emphasizes treating the existing odious debt of debtors countries, could be combined with an *ex ante* approach which focuses on deterrence.

5.3.4 Key features of the Paris Club to address Odious Debt

Having made the case for the non legal, political and ex post context of official debt restructuring, this section now considers specific features of the Paris Club which are relevant for addressing odious debt within it.

5.3.4.1 Existing Institution

From a pragmatic and cost perspective, there are several reasons why addressing odious through the Paris Club would be efficient. Firstly, it has existed for over 50 years and has developed experience in issues of sovereign debt. It is generally recognized by the international community. The creation of a new, international debt forum or tribunal, as suggested by some in the literature, would be administratively costlier in comparison.[448] Furthermore, the process of sovereign debt restructuring, though complex and disorderly, is an established and accepted feature of sovereign debt relations.[449] It is embedded in the expectations of parties to sovereign debt contracts. Therefore, in terms of minimizing any disruption to parties' expectations and creating uncertainty, the context of negotiations would not constitute an institutional departure from the status quo. Finally it would arguably be more efficient to address all debt issues within one forum, in order to minimize conflicting agreements and duplicative costs.

5.3.4.2 Least Developed Countries

Although official credit does not dominate the sovereign debt market as a whole, it does dominate the supply of credit to the least developed countries. Therefore, introducing odious debt via Paris Club debt negotiations would implicitly introduce it into the context that the poorest countries recur to when they suffer from debt problems. These countries often do not have other alternatives to official debt and do not have other means to deal with their debt issues than the official sector. Out of

---

[448] See Khalfan, King et al. 2003; Adams 2004

[449] Buchheit, Gulati et al. 2007

dependency and competition, they will probably be reluctant to take drastic steps such as recurring to an international tribunal or take action that would compromise their relationship with their creditors, from whom they depend on. However, they may be more willing to bring up the argument in a setting such as debt negotiations.

The current political and regulatory framework with regards to sovereign debt emphasizes a responsive approach to the debt crises of debtor countries. Among other interests at the negotiating table ex post, one pertains to relieving the debtor country of debt and aiding it in dealing with issues such as debt overhang which can prevent a country from achieving a sustainable level of economic recovery.

One recurrent question in the literature pertains to whether odious debt should be addressed independently, or in conjunction with other issues such as poverty and economic development.[450] For some, addressing odious debt is a reflection of the perceived inadequacy with the current amount of debt relief provided to debtor countries, in particular poor countries. Others consider that debt relief and odiousness are separate issues. For the latter, rich countries who inherit debt which was used against their interests should also be addressed by the odious debt debate.[451]

Ideally, all morally repugnant debt which is the result of oppression of a population (or worse) should be addressed, regardless of whether the debtor country is rich or poor. However, a trade off may exist. The more ambitious and more inclusive an approach is, the more costly it will be. By the same token, there is an opportunity cost in making an approach more inclusive. This cost will be in the form of a less targeted approach to those countries that need it the most.

Gelpern argues that the public international law doctrine of odious debt has languished because it is an inefficient tool for securing quick debt relief.[452] She further notes that most debtor countries have sufficient means at their disposal to obtain debt relief or substantial debt restructuring without having to recur to the doctrine of odious debt. Unlike recurring to the odious debt doctrine, addressing odious debt via debt restructuring would not be a substitute to the current system of debt relief, but a complement. The aim would be for the odious debt argument to be mainstreamed in sovereign debt relations, and utilized when appropriate and ultimately lead to more debt relief for the poorest countries who bear the burden of odious debt.

Addressing odious debt via the context of debt restructuring explicitly links the issue of odious debt to that of economic development, debt relief and debt overhang and it also by and large focuses on the poorest developing countries whose debt is largely official. Arguably, the consequences of odious debt are gravest in the poorest countries. This is, in part, due to the fact that the opportunity costs of devoting limited

---

[450] Rasmussen 2007, 251

[451] Id.

[452] Gelpern 2005, 414

resources to service the debt are larger. Consequently, they have the most to lose from the lack of a fast, efficient and pragmatic mechanism ex post. Furthermore, odious debt is one of many other concerns that a country has to address when undergoing a political transition. Political transitions are complex and countries need to deal with debt in the context of economic reconstruction, sustainability and recovery as well preventing the recurrence of future debt crises. Addressing odious debt in the context of debt restructuring and in conjunction with debt relief would contribute to these goals.

5.3.4.3 Interests of the Official Sector

If odious debt were to be addressed in a context other than official debt negotiations, the interests of the members of the Paris Club, the major industrialized countries, would have to be reckoned with regardless. As one scholar argued, one of the main limitations of many odious debt proposals is their failure to demonstrate to lending nations that it would be in their interest to give up the political clout they currently have when a country seeks debt relief.[453] As the actors in the official sector constitute an important governance branch of the triple helix surrounding debt, any odious debt proposal must take their interests into account. The context of sovereign debt restructuring would face this issue head on, by throwing odious debt into the complex bargaining dynamics and the many interests considered in Paris Club negotiations.

As previously argued, the official sector has a wide range of interests and different factors can influence it to care about equitable considerations such as odious debt. These include direct interests, domestic political pressure or competition. Indeed, some have argued that the international community acts a sort of court and is used to assessing and interpreting case specific facts and considerations.[454] In contrast, private creditors have more strict profit maximization and shorter term incentives than their official counterparts. They are therefore generally seen as relatively less open to moral and non economic justifications for non repayment.[455]

5.3.4.4 Ability of the Paris Club to "bail in" other Creditors

Paris Club debt negotiations are generally "successful" in the sense that the debtor usually comes to some sort of agreement with the Paris Club members regarding the treatment of its debt. Negotiations that involve many different types of creditors, including private bondholders, are much more complex. Therefore, if a debtor and its Paris Club creditors agree on a level of debt relief, based on the debtor's economic situations and taking into consideration any past odiousness associated with the debt, the next step would involve convincing non Paris Club creditors, particularly private creditors, to provide rescheduling and debt relief on comparable terms.

---

[453] Rasmussen 2007, 17

[454] Howse 2007

[455] Gelpern 2007

One persistent issue in the international debt regime has to do with the question of how to reconcile the different interests of different creditors at the time of renegotiations. Any particular debtor may have a complex debt composition, including both private debt in its various forms and official debt from both Paris Club and non Paris Club creditors. The Paris Club has several tools and means at its disposal to "bail in" non Paris Club creditors. This ability to "coerce" other creditors to provide the debtor with similar terms as those agreed in the Paris Club is particularly useful if introducing odious debt into debt negotiations is to lead to a lower debt level for the debtor country. Without this ability, the official sector would be reluctant to step in and provide exceptional terms of refinancing and restructuring.

One of the primary tools that the Paris Club has to bail in outside creditors is the 'Comparability of Treatment' clause (the Clause) in all Paris Club agreements.[456] It aims to ensure a balanced treatment among all external creditors of the debtor country. According to the Clause, the debtor commits itself to seek from its non Paris Club creditors a rescheduling which is comparable from that negotiated with its Paris Club creditors in its Agreed Minutes.[457] Non Paris Club creditors comprise official bilateral creditors which are not members of the Paris Club as well as private creditors, namely banks, bondholders and suppliers. The purpose of the Clause is to ensure that debt relief provided by the Paris Club membership does not accrue to the debtor's other creditors and that all creditors share proportionately in the burden of helping the debtor resolve its payment problems. If the debtor fails to obtain comparable treatment from

[456] "http://www.clubdeparis.org/en/presentation.php?BATCH=B01WP06" 2006

[457] Id. Multilateral lending institutions such as the IMF and the World Bank are granted preferential status and are excluded from the Clause. Historically, the Paris Club has accepted that the debtor should continue to meet its obligations to these multilateral creditors in a timely manner and before servicing other creditors' claims. One of the reasons for this is that both the debtor and the Paris Club creditors are members of these institutions and therefore both benefit from this excemption. All of the official creditor members of the Paris Club, despite the differences in terms and purposes of the loans they make, are expected to contribute on a comparable basis to the debt relief of the debtor. All credits extended prior to a specific date should be rescheduled with the same grace and repayment periods. What may differ is the interest rate that the creditors charge on its rescheduled debt with certain parameters. For example, there is a general understanding that concessional credits will remain concessional and that penalty rates must be charged on non performing debts.

There are not specific guidelines to determine 'comparable treatment,' Rather, the Paris Club creditors have generally taken a broad approach in applying the Principle. The look at a range of factors including the types of creditors, the change in nominal debt service, the net present value of the debt and the terms of the restructured debt in determining whether the treatment provided by the non Paris club creditors is comparable to that offered by the Paris Club. The comparability regards not so much the form of restructuring but rather the effective debt relief provided in cash flow and present value terms, as well as the maturities of the restructured claims as measured by duration. At the same time, sometimes comparability is not demanded by the Paris Club when debt is short term or constitutes only a small amount (indeed this was the initial treatment for bondholder debt which used to comprise only a small portion of a debtor's composition, but increasingly comprises a majority – although the poorest countries still had a majority of official debt). Intuitively, comparability is easier to establish the more similar the loans are between creditors. Non Paris Club official creditors generally make the same type of medium long term loans that the Paris Club creditors provide. Experience is that non Paris Club official creditors often restructure on terms very similar to those agreed by the Paris Club. Conversely, it is more difficult to make a direct comparison between the loans and terms extended by private creditors which may differ substantially. For a discussion See Veer and Jong August 2006

non Paris Club creditors, it risks losing its renegotiation agreement with the Paris Club.

There are a number of rationales which justify instruments such as the Clause to intervene in the restructuring of international debt. Information asymmetries, coordination problems and complex bargaining dynamics can be effective barriers to restructurings. Coercive instruments to lower transaction costs of including an agreement may be warranted.

First, upon default of a sovereign debtor, although most creditors have incentives to engage in negotiations, they face a collective action problem. An individual creditor prefers to hold out while the others restructure. All creditors face this same incentive and restructuring is not possible. Although the transaction may make the group as a whole better off, opportunistic creditors have incentives to hold out and free rise on the restructuring efforts of other creditors. Because of its size and power, the Paris Club is able to take the first step and negotiate on behalf of the other creditors, in much the same way that syndicated banks did during the years that bank lending dominated the market. The case of Iraq's debt illustrates this role. Before the Paris Club stepped in, Iraq was not servicing its debt at all. The generous restructuring terms offered to Iraq via the Evian Approach were actually an improvement in terms for most creditors, including non Paris Club and private creditors. Indeed, due to the Paris Club, creditors had the choice between taking an 80 percent reduction or continuing not to get paid.[458]

The Paris Club, therefore, helps counter the collective action problem and can help outside creditors obtain better repayment prospects than they otherwise would. This is one of the reasons that outside creditors accept to be bailed in.[459] Another reason is that although creditors are unhappy with accepting large haircuts, they also prefer an expedient process that avoids prolonged uncertainty regarding the status of their debts.[460] Furthermore, as the Evian Approach illustrated, creditors will accede to political pressure and treat it as a one off "exceptional" event.[461]

The official sector, via the Paris Club, has significant stakes in the Clause. While official creditors are willing to provide exceptional financing to support members' adjustment efforts, they are not willing to provide new financing in a fashion that allows other creditor groups to unwind their exposure. This is intended to protect official bilateral creditors' interests. Furthermore, it is unlikely that practices that lead to costs of resolving crises being borne disproportionately by taxpayers would be politically tenable. Another problem is that of moral hazard for non Paris Club creditors, particularly private creditors. There is a concern that a willingness by the

---

[458] Damle 2007, 149

[459] See Veer and Jong August 2006

[460] Damle 2007, 147

[461] Rasmussen 2007, 6

official community to extend exceptional financing on a scale that would, in effect, shelter private creditors from market risk and give them a free pass on contributing to the resolution of crises could give rise to moral hazard. This could, in turn, increase the severity and frequency of future crises.

Besides the Clause, the Paris Club also employs other means to bail in non-Paris Club creditors, including the ability to buy commercial debt from private creditors through initiatives such as the Debt Reduction Facility.[462]

Consequently, one of the key advantages of the Paris Club, with regards to odious debt, is its ability to take equitable considerations into account in its debt negotiations and subsequently has means at its disposal to coerce other creditors to apply comparable terms of relief.[463]

5.3.4.5 Ad Hoc Nature and Increased Flexibility in the Paris Club

The ad hoc nature of sovereign debt restructuring allows the Paris Club to be particularly flexible in incorporating equitable, political or other factors into negotiations. Its ad hoc process allows for a case by case approach to address the specific debt situations of different countries. As the development of its working terms shows, this flexibility has allowed the Paris Club to adapt and address new issues and needs of the international community as well as having the ability to deal with countries as different in income and debt structure as Nicaragua and Iraq.

The trend towards flexibility has been increasing as the Paris Club has evolved. This is evident by looking at the development of its working practices. Paris Club treatments are defined individually, on a case by case basis, and agreed by consensus by all creditor countries. However, most treatments fall within pre defined categories.[464] These categories have been increasingly generous and amenable to the distinct situations of debtor countries. These developments include, among others, a change from a purely market rate loan restructuring to concessional (below market) rate restructuring, and subsequently the inclusion of the possibility to cancel debts with an initial ceiling of 33.3% of outstanding debts which was later increased to 50%, as well as longer repayment and grace periods.[465]

---

[462] See the World Bank's Debt Reduction Facility at the World Bank's Website www.worldbank.org, See Also the efforts by the Paris Club to collaborate with the Debt Reduction Facility in Paris Club 2007 Annual Report

[463] The ability to « bail in » private creditors is limited to the poorest countries which predominantly have official debt. Bailing in private creditors is much more complicated when a debtor's debt composition is more diverse and official debt does not constitute a majority. See Veer and Jong August 2006 However, with regards to this proposal that focuses on the poorest countries, it remains the case that they are ,by and large, primarily financed by official credit.

[464] Paris Club Annual Report 2007, 44

[465] Id.

One particular example of the amenability of Paris Club treatment is the Heavily Indebted Poor Countries Initiative (HIPC) which was a response by the international financial community to the recognition that the external debt situation of a number of low income countries had become extremely difficult. In effect, the economic development prospects of these countries were suffering despite full use of the traditional Paris Club rescheduling and debt reduction mechanisms alongside the continued provision of concessional financing and the implementation of sound economic policies.[466] The donors therefore identified 41 countries that qualified under the HIPC initiative and which would be eligible for exceptional assistance and reduction of their external debt burdens to sustainable levels. The final goal of the HIPC is to allow these countries to strongly increase their poverty reduction expenditures.

While the HIPC demonstrates the ability of the Paris Club to apply more generous terms to the poorest countries, the Evian Approach exemplifies the ad hoc and tailored approach that the Paris Club can adopt to strategically important middle income countries. Two countries which have benefited substantially from the Evian Approach are Iraq and Nigeria.[467] Some scholars have argued that the odious debt argument may have been taken into consideration during their negotiations with the Paris Club. Damle argues that the fact that Iraq framed the discussion of debt relief to include moral considerations as well as economic and international security have the new Iraqi regime far more leverage than it would otherwise have had, although it is difficult to separate the effects.[468]

5.3.4.6 Secrecy and Information

One of the main criticisms of the Paris Club pertains to its notorious lack of transparency regarding the content of its negotiations. Indeed, its restructuring process is notably opaque and it is extremely difficult to obtain information about how a successful agreement between a debtor and its creditors comes about. By extension, it is difficult to predict the treatment that a particular debtor will obtain under the Paris Club. Furthermore, the Club does not share information about it calculations such as those regarding a debtor's capacity for repayment.

Many view this secrecy as an excuse for the arbitrary treatment of different debtors and a sign that creditors have something to hide. While there is no doubt that the secrecy which characterizes Paris Club proceedings serves the interests of the creditor countries and allows them to take any case specific interests into consideration, secrecy also serves a distinct purpose which allows for the smooth functioning of the sovereign debt market. Specifically, it prevents two types of moral

---

[466] Id, 52

[467] Id.

[468] See Damle 2007

hazard, on the part of non Paris Club creditors on the one hand, and outside debtors on the other.

If outside creditors, such as commercial creditors, could predict under what conditions a debtor would be bailed out by the official sector, they would be tempted to over-lend as well as to lend more recklessly and engage in less risk assessment. On the part of outside debtors, if they know in advance under what conditions their debt will be rescheduled or forgiven, they will have incentives to over-borrow or behave recklessly. For example, a debtor country may take actions that would lead to deterioration of its economic situation or liquidity situation, in order to obtain more favourable or generous treatment in negotiations. While the sovereign debt market is second best and some degree of moral hazard is accepted, secrecy in the Paris Club aims to keep it at a minimum.

Secrecy would also serve a distinct purpose when addressing odious debt. One of the reasons that a solution to the odious debt problem has not been translated into practice yet is due to the rational fear that it would have a perverse effect on developing countries' access to credit. If creditors anticipate being unable to collect on their loans because they were deemed odious, they will be deterred from lending and may be over-inclusive in their reaction, such as refraining from lending to developing countries as a whole or charging them much higher interests rates. This over-inclusive response would be due to the fact that there is no useful definition of odious debt.

Against this background, secrecy in Paris Club negotiations would allow for the odious debt argument to be introduced in a way that would minimize uncertainty for outside parties. Of course, the first challenge involves convincing Paris Club creditors that odiousness is an excusable reason for non repayment and justifies debt relief. The ex post nature of Paris Club negotiations is able to capitulate on the informational advantage present when odious debt has already occurred. More information will be available with regards to the use of specific loans and the activities of the previous government ex post. In some cases, odiousness may be easily observable if, to take another odious debt scholars' adjective, it is "egrerious."[469] There may be strong evidence that the previous government used part of the funds from international loans to repress the population or finance human rights abuses. In other cases, there may be a lot of information on the uses of particular loans.

Although the ex post nature of Paris Club negotiations allows for more information to be available with regards to odious debt, it is not necessarily the case that this information should then be made public. While odiousness may be obvious in some cases and therefore Paris Club creditors may be sensitive to it during negotiations, it may nevertheless remain difficult to define and predict in future cases and there may not be an interest in setting an official precedent. Secrecy would do away with the problem of having to define odious debt and constrain its many forms to a definition.

---

[469] Jayachandran and Kremer 2006

Finally, it could also be the case that Paris Club creditors could have been implicated in blatant cases of odiousness and would therefore have an interest in such information being kept secret. In such cases, the bargaining power of the debtor country and the added value of the odious debt argument will be larger. Furthermore, there is an interest in secrecy when it comes to bailing in non- Paris Club creditors so as to maintain "constructive ambiguity." Consequently, the ex post nature of Paris Club negotiations would allow for the most amount of information on any odious debt to be available. At the same time, the notorious secrecy of the Paris Club would minimize the risk of moral hazard and uncertainty with regards to odious debt by outside parties. While there is a case for secrecy with regards to the content of Paris Club negotiations, there may be a case for increased transparency *ex ante*, such as more information about creditors' lending practices. Encouraging creditors to be more transparent and provide more information about their lending activities might by itself have a positive impact on odious debt and at the very least deter blatant contributions to odious activities. This is indeed already the approach that is being adopted and developed in the Paris Club. While remaining characteristically secret about its negotiations, the Paris Club is involved in efforts to increase transparency about the behaviour and lending activities of creditors.

5.3.5 Potential obstacles in addressing odious debt via the Paris Club

Having identified some of the key characteristics of the Paris Club that would enable it to include odious debt in its negotiations, this section now addresses some of the potential obstacles of such a proposal. In doing so, it analyses the role of the different branches of governance in the triple helix in circumventing these obstacles.

5.3.5.1 Different Amounts of Debt Relief

One relevant obstacle to including odious debt in debt renegotiations is getting all of the Paris Club creditors to agree on a level of debt relief. Some creditors may be more sensitive to the odious debt argument or have more political or financial interests in providing debt relief to countries suffering from odious debt than others. One possible solution to this could be for the Paris Club to provide an initial level of debt relief to which all of its members can agree on, (and which will be easy to get non Paris Club creditors to get on board), while allowing those countries who have a self interest in providing additional debt relief to do so on their own. Such an arrangement would not be a complete break with the past. Indeed, before the HIPC Initiative was adopted by the Paris Club, the multilateral debt of poor countries was not subject to rescheduling under the norms of the international debt regime. In the case of Uganda for example, debt rescheduling was provided under the Paris Club terms from 1985 to the late 1990s, with multilateral debt not included despite the fact that it accounted for a substantial resource problem for the country.[470] However, parallel to this rescheduling, the Ugandan Multilateral Debt Fund was being created as a result of the network connections that were created between a small group of socially democratic European

---

[470] Callaghy 2004, 22

countries active as both Paris Club members and aid providers.[471] Callanghy explains that this group of countries had norms of debt and structural development that were more flexible than that of other industrialized creditors and were more sympathetic to reforming poor countries. As a result, together with NGOs, consultants from the epistemic community and the Ugandan government, they created a special Multilateral Debt Fund into which sympathetic countries could contribute funds to service multilateral debt.[472]

The Multilateral Debt Fund (the Fund) demonstrates the ability of creditor countries to not only address issues in different contexts, but also the different interests that become prominent in these different venues. A similar mechanism could be envisaged for odious debt. The debtor country suffering from odious debt could first bring up the subject in the confines of Paris Club debt negotiations. If successful and credible, the odious debt argument would provide the debtor country with additional debt relief or more favourable terms than it otherwise may have obtained. If countries such as Norway, for which the humanitarian and debt concerns of developing countries play an important part in their domestic political agendas, had a self interest in providing additional debt relief, this could be done voluntarily either unilaterally or multilaterally through innovative efforts such as the Multilateral Debt Fund.

5.3.5.2 Crowing Out Private Creditors?

One concern with this proposal could be the risk that it is part of the "slippery slope" of debt. In other words, if odious debt can be introduced into the Paris Club and lead to more generous terms for debtor countries in negotiations, then other considerations will follow and the boundaries of the process of debt restructuring become grey. One consequence of this is that Paris Club involvement in debtor countries can crowd out private investment.[473]

These are legitimate concerns, yet they do not pertain specifically to introducing odious debt into the Paris Club, but rather to the process of Paris Club debt restructuring as a whole. The Paris Club needs to continue to improve its efforts to ensure that the debt treatment granted to debtor countries subsequently contributes to an improvement in their economic situation as well as their future repayment prospects, improve their policy and management capacity and gradually increase their access to more diverse, including private sources, of credit lines.

In the early stages of the economic recovery process, private investment can undermine the debt relief efforts of the official sector. This is because although debt relief improves the macroeconomic outlook of the poorest countries as well as their

---

[471] Id.

[472] Id., 24

[473] For a discussion See Veer and Jong August 2006

debt ratios, they often continue to have high debt distress risk ratings.[474] This makes them vulnerable to private investment. Indeed, a tension exists, poor debtor countries require to be sheltered from the private market initially, but ultimately need access to it to acquire sustainable growth levels, reduce dependency and regain policy capacity. Much like the dismissed "infant industry" argument in economics, there is the fear that countries which are sheltered from the markets and dependent on official loans and debt relief will never grow up. While there is an economic case for not protecting infant companies and letting them exit the market, rather than having the government protecting them *ad infinitum*, the cost of not helping countries and the risk that they fail are much too great for the international community. Instead, efforts should be focused on helping debtor countries make the transition by investing in initiatives to improve their policy capacity alongside with debt treatment. The Paris Club already engages in initiatives such as capacity building and training programs for debtor governments.[475] The NGO community in collaboration with members of the epistemic community can also play an important role in this regard.

5.4 Conclusion

This chapter first considered the actors that shape and drive change in sovereign debt governance. These include the official sector, civil society and the epistemic community. They influence the processes of the international debt regime, including the debt restructuring process of negotiation forums such as the Paris Club. The underlining legal obligations influence this process, and at the same time, law is responsive to the evolving discourse that stems from it. Against this background, the idea of introducing the issue of odious debt in the context of Paris Club debt restructuring negotiations was considered. If odious debt could be considered within this context, it could prove to be a valuable precedent.

---

[474] Nishio 11 June, 2008

[475] Paris Club Annual Report 2007

6 Summary and Outlook

The history of sovereign borrowing is often seen as a history of sovereign debt defaults and sovereign debt crises. As a consequence, sovereign debt has often found itself in the midst of highly emotive political and public debates. The recent financial and economic crisis has placed debt back at the heart of the problem of financial irresponsibility. Today, concerns about sovereign debt are widespread, and it is not only and no longer a purely developing country problem.

As the world economies slowly recover, many are dealing with high levels of public deficits. Indeed, debt remains a key issue in the post crisis context. Furthermore, the issues embodied in the odious debate, including the intersection between ethics and finance, remain ever-relevant. This book treats the problem of odious debt within the overarching policy and economic agenda to move towards a new, more sustainable, financial architecture. Analysis of the odious debt problem can shed light on the direction that policymakers should take and the opportunities that institutions have to reform themselves to become more inclusive and regain relevance in the field of international sovereign debt governance.

Beyond looking at the intriguing topic of odious debt, this book is part of an increasing movement which applies law-and-economics analysis to issues of cooperation in the international arena. It seeks to further the understanding of the mechanisms that sustain cooperation between states under anarchy and looks specifically at the role of the role of law and reputation in the field of sovereign debt. The sovereign borrower-creditor relation was treated from a rational, economic perspective. How odious debt stems from the different sovereign borrower - creditor relations was analyzed and the legal and economic aspects of the problem of odious debt were highlighted.

Sovereign debt is an important policy tool for states. Understanding how countries manage their public finances and the tools available provides a window to better understand their behaviour. Further, a full understanding of the nature of sovereign borrower-creditor relations and the mechanisms that sustain them is a pre requisite for any proposal to reform them. In order to build a more sustainable financial system, reformers must know what gives investors the confidence to lend and why governments decide to repay or default. Only with that knowledge can leaders build a system that plays to the incentives of key actors.

Reputation, although it is not a perfect substitute to third party enforcement as it exists in the domestic legal context, is the main force that sustains a sovereign borrower's relationship with its creditors. A sovereign borrower's reputation in the eyes of investors is a function of its behaviour, past and present, as well as the context of its behaviour. Creditors care about factors beyond repayment and default and seek to obtain contextual inferences about whether a state's decision is a reflection of its *ability to pay* or its *willingness to pay*. Investors have ways to learn about a particular borrower's ability to pay, such as economic indicators, but they ultimately lack information about its willingness to pay, which depends on a debtor's preferences. These preferences are unobservable to investors. Consequently, investors must make loans with only partial information about a key variable in the investment equation.

While traditional reputation models generally assume that the preferences of parties' are static, it was discussed that new reputation theories try to include political change and public choice considerations into their analysis, and hence allow for changes in preferences. The specific context of sovereign debt is indeed one where politics are extremely relevant and can therefore provide much explanatory power with regards to a state's decision to repay or default

A government's preferences about debt may shift from regime to regime due to various political factors which can determine how leaders balance debt repayment against other priorities and in turn, whether they are willing to elevate foreign debt above other policy concerns. Justifying default on odious debt grounds is interpreted by investors as a claim that the debtor cares more about redressing past grievances that it does about its future borrowing prospects. The reason for default is not in itself important, but the economic context at the time is. Putting odious debt, or any other policy concern, above repayment in good economic times, is considered graver than during bad economic times.

The reputation repercussions from repaying or defaulting on inherited public debt are one of many policy concerns that a new government or state has. When the benefits of maintaining a reputation in the sovereign debt market are larger than the benefits obtained from elevating other policy concerns above external debt, a state will repay its debt. Only states that value addressing odious debt more highly than their access to future credit in the international markets will default on their odious debt. Given the importance of access to finance for most new states and regimes, and given that they will have weaker priors with regards to how investors judge their behaviour, they will have greater incentives to repay any successor debts, whether odious or not. This is because their decision to repay of default will have a larger marginal effect on their reputation all else equal.

Against this background, the role of international law in sovereign debt relations was analyzed. Since the erosion of a sovereign's immunity from lawsuits, the commercial market for sovereign debt has continued to move towards a more formalist direction. The resources devoted to sovereign debt contracts, the increased recurrence of bondholders to domestic courts and the efforts of sovereign borrowers to justify their behaviour with legal arguments may appear puzzling at first. If reputation is the main enforcement mechanism, what then is the role of law? This question was addressed by taking a broader view of reputation, one which analyzes how the mere act of entering into an agreement and making a promise in the international context can have important consequences and will implicate a state's reputation. The reputation at stake is not only with regards to sovereign debt, but with regards to complying with international law more generally.

The implications from this discussion to the odious debt problem are numerous. Notably, one implication concerns the limitations of the legal proposals which have been brought forth by the literature to address odious debt. These propose that odious debt may be rendered unenforceable in national courts by recurring to legal doctrines such as fraud and unclean hands, agency principles and unjust enrichment among others. On the one hand, legal analysis highlights that the innate elements of the odious debt problem are neither intangible nor alien to the law. On the other hand, the limits of these proposals lie in the fact that they are assuming a third party enforcement mechanism, with the power of coercion as it exists in domestic law. To view international law through the lens of domestic law is not only inadequate, but the comparison often undermines its function, as it deems it ineffective in comparison.

A second implication concerns the effectiveness of the infamous doctrine of odious debt as a tool to address the issue. A reputation-led perspective of international law implies that a borrowing state will consider how its decision to repay or default will affect its reputation about complying with international law. Because, to date, the doctrine of odious debt is not recognized in international law, repudiating on the grounds of the doctrine not only negatively affects a state's reputation in the sovereign debt context, but also its reputation in the international law context.

International law on sovereign debt is relatively underdeveloped as compared to other areas such as international trade and international investment. The development of international law in this field would allow states to make firmer commitments and promises in the field of sovereign debt and further implicate their reputation.

Taking reputation at the centre of sovereign debt relations, the analysis then shifted towards addressing how it can be obstructed or weakened depending on the type of creditor-borrower exchange. The distinct relationships that fall under the umbrella heading of "sovereign debt" were outlined and the different incentives of creditors in each of them highlighted. Although they all have a common promise to repay, beyond that they differ substantially in form and substance. Some relationships are characterized by arm's length transactions sustained by a debtor's reputation to repay. In others, the reputation mechanism is obstructed by outside factors such as hegemonic interests and influences. Less transparent creditor-debtor exchanges also exist, where reputation is based not on whether a debtor repays, but on whether it cedes policy control, or provides access to strategic resources. Still others are based more on dependency and control than on reputation at all.

Five factors which have a direct effect on the reputation mechanism of these different relationships were identified, namely; outside influences, the number of different transactions that a creditor has in a borrowing country, the difference between the debt form of the relationship and the substance of the actual exchange, the information available to creditors and the prospects from sovereign debt restructuring.

How reputation is obstructed and what it is contingent on can determine whether and how odious debt stems from the sovereign borrower-creditor relationship. Odiousness can be the result of externalities from the sovereign debt contract. Other times, odiousness can directly affect the risk of the contract and therefore implicate a party's reputation. Odious activities can also be embodied in the mutual exchange between creditor and debtor.

One of the conclusions to be drawn from this analysis is that there are some types of exchanges between sovereign borrower and creditors which are more prone to produce odious debt. For example, despite informational and coordination constraints, the strength of the reputation mechanism in private sovereign bond contracts is relatively high. This is due to bondholders' pure profit maximizing incentives and their anonymous and dispersed nature which makes them relatively immune to outside influences. Reputation is contingent on repayment, and insofar as the odious use of funds does not affect the borrower's repayment prospects, it is left out of the equation.

In contrast, state to state lending is characterized by a large gap between form and substance. While official debt agreements very widely, by and large, the terms of the agreement are not designed to maximize the prospects of repayment. Official credits usually lie somewhere in between debt in the traditional sense - with full expectation of repayment - and grants - with no expectation of repayment. Relative to the arm's length transactions that characterize private sovereign debt, official debt does not invoke the same disciplining mechanism and does not give borrowers strong incentives to repay their debt and improve their debt management skills. Instead, the reputation mechanism is generally, in some way, contingent on the creditor's policy interest in the debtor country - whether humanitarian or odious.

One issue which was not fully developed within the analysis of reputation in this book is that of creditors' reputation, as opposed to the borrower's reputation. The recent financial and economic crisis has brought the issue of irresponsible lending back to the forefront, thereby implicating the reputation and complicit role of creditors into the debate.

There are several reasons which explain why creditors are increasingly under the spotlight. One has to do with increased information that is available about their lending activities abroad. This can affect their reputation in other fields such as human rights at the international level. The fact that China has received a lot of scrutiny from its "non conditionality" loans in Africa is a case in point. Interestingly, China has recently become involved in the policy debate surrounding debt and discussed the issue of responsible lending and borrowing for the first time at an international conference last year.[476]

Voters and civil society in creditor countries have also played an important role in elevating the issue of sovereign debt and creditor's responsibility at the policy level. In this light, the book discussed the case of Norway, which in 2006 cancelled over 80 million dollars of debt owed to it by five developing countries after determining that the loans were not granted in good faith and incurred illegitimately. This example has been repeatedly championed in the odious debt literature. It was analyzed in this book from a rational choice perspective. It highlighted the fact that a creditor state's interest in promoting a good reputation in a particular field can be linked to public choice considerations domestically. At the same time, it can be linked to strategic interests in being at the forefront of issues which will prove to be high on the global policy agenda for years to come.

Finally, the costs of reckless lending and the repercussions that it has on borrowing countries increasingly have cross border implications due to globalisation. In other words, creditors increasingly bear the costs of irresponsible lending behaviour. The role of creditors in the discussion of odious debt is key in order to find a sustainable solution and the fact that they increasingly have more at stake further ensures their involvement.

This discussion reflects the evolution of the topic of odious debt which has moved in the direction of achieving responsible lending and borrowing guidelines, within the broader context of building a more sustainable financial architecture and a fairer division of burden between creditors and debtors.[477]

The direction the discourse has taken is forward-looking, in the sense that it focuses on preventing future odious debt by providing guidelines to both creditors and debtors, ex ante. In essence, internationally agreed guidelines could take the form of a global regulatory mechanism. This is in stark contrast to many of the initial ex post litigation approaches brought forth by the literature which are more backward-looking, and seek to redress past cases of odious debt. The broader question of whether the problem of odious debt should be addressed through an ex ante or ex post mechanism and the trade-offs involved, was analyzed in the book, drawing from Steven Shavell's seminal treatment of the topic applied to the international realm.

---

[476] See UNCTAD High Level Conference on Guidelines for Responsible Lending and Borrowing within UNCTAD's World Investment Forum, 2010 in Xiamen, China: http://unctad-worldinvestmentforum.org/page/about_wif See also

[477] UNCTAD is developing Guidelines for Responsible Lending and Borrowing, See UNCTAD, 2010. See also AFRODAD's 2011 launch of a Borrowing Charter which contains principles and guidelines on sovereign financial borrowing: http://www.afrodad.org/index.php?option=com_docman&task=doc_details&Itemid=11&gid=138

One of the main advantages of internationally agreed ex ante lending and borrowing guidelines is that these can implicate the reputation of both creditors and debtors in the debt arena and would contribute towards the development of international law in this area. Ultimately, such guidelines could evolve into a multilateral treaty on responsible lending and borrowing.

At the same time, an ex post mechanism is necessary to address cases of odious debt when they occur. The current system of sovereign debt restructuring is a well established and accepted ex post mechanism of sovereign debt. On the one hand, precisely because the restructuring process is so well established, it has stalled the development of international sovereign debt law. On the other hand, it represents an important platform where precedent is set and the discourse on sovereign debt is evolving.

Some of the advantages of addressing odious debt within an already existing venue, such as the Paris Club, were discussed. These include the fact that other debt issues are already being treated there. The secrecy that characterizes sovereign debt restructuring also has the advantage that it can reduce the reputation sanctions of a borrowing country which uses the odious debt argument. Further, it allows for odious arguments to be introduced and considered in the restructuring negotiations, without having to define odiousness specifically. Having said that, there is ample room to make the process of sovereign debt restructuring more inclusive and relevant.

Finally, intermediate approaches, such as loan sanctions, as proposed by Kremer and Jayachandran, may be a useful policy tool in the case of "egrerious cases" of borrowing governments acting against the interest of the population. Upon analysis, loan sanctions posit themselves somewhere between an ex ante and an ex post approach with the trade offs from each respectively depending on their timing. The earlier a regime is targeted as odious and loan sanctions are imposed on it, the more the ex ante advantages of the proposal are maximized, but there is less information available about the regime and its odious activities at an early stage and hence less grounds to justify the sanctions. Conversely, the later sanctions are imposed, the lesser the risk to mislabel a regime but the deterrence effects from the sanctions are also lower.

Odious debt is only one of the many complex and intricate facets of sovereign debt. More work is necessary to understand how it relates to and implicates other sovereign debt issues and international finance in general. This book tried to set the groundwork for future research on odious debt, a topic that is surely to continue to be of legal, economic and policy relevance.

Bibliography

Abrahams, C. P. (August 2000). The Doctrine of Odious Debts: Does international law provide a remedy to instances where debts are contracted for purposes of committing recognized international wrongful acts? A contemporary case of the Apartheid Debts, Rijks Universitaet Leiden. LL.M. Public International Law: 96.

Adams, P. (1991). Odious Debts: Loose Lending, Corruption and the Third World Environmental Legacy.

—. Arbitration between Great Britain and Costa Rica (1923). 1 UN Rep. Int'l Arb. Awards 369.

—. "Arbitration Between Great Britain and Costa Rica." (1924). American Journal of International Law **18.**

—. 2004. Policy Analysis: Iraq's Odious Debts. Cato Policy Analysis No. 526, CATO Institute.

Agarwal, S. and R. Hauswald (2007). The Choice between Arm's Length and Relationship Debt: Evidence from eLoans.

—. Argentina's friendship with Venezuela (August 9th, 2007). The Economist.

Aggarwal, V. K. (1996). Debt Games: Strategic Interaction in International Debt Rescheduling. Cambridge, Cambridge University Press.

Alesina, A. (1988). The End of Large Public Debts. High Public Debt: The Italian Experience. F. Giavazzi and L. Spaventa. Cambridge, Cambridge University Press: 34-79.

Aristotle (1877). Aristotle's Politics.

Atiyah, P. S. (2001). Form and Substance in Contract Law. Essays on Contracts. Oxford, Oxford University Press: 93 - 120.

Baribeau, S. (December 21st, 2005). "Venezuela to Buy Argentine Bonds, Backs IMF Payoff." Venezuelaanalysis.com.

Bedjaoui, M. (1977). "Ninth Report on Succession of States in respect of matters other than Treaties, A/CN.4/301." Yearbook International Law Commission **2**(1).

Ben-Shahar, O. and M. Gulati (2007). "Partially Odious Debts? A Framework for an Optimal Liability Regime." Law and Contemporary Problems **70**.

Birdsall, N. and J. Williamson (2002). "Delivering on Debt Relief: From IMF Gold to a New Aid Architecture."

BIS (2003). "International banking and financial market developments." BIS Quarterly Review(September).

—. 2007. Financial stability and local currency bond markets. CGFS Papers, Committee on the Global Financial System.

Bloomstein, H. and J. Santiso (April 2007). "Successful Emerging Domestic Bond Markets in the Global Financial Landscape." OECD Development Centre, Policy Insights **No. 39**.

Boettke, P. J., C. J. Coyne, et al. "Saving Government Failure Theory from Itself: Recasting political Economy from an Austrian Perspective."

Bohn, H. (1990). "A Positive Theory of Foreign Currency Debt." Journal of International Economics **29** (November): 273-292.

Bolton, P. and D. Skeel (2007). "Odious Debts or Odious Regimes?" Law and Contemporary Problems **70**(4).

Bonilla, S. (February 7th, 2007). A Law and Economics Analysis of Odious Debts. Conference of the Graduate College of Law and Economics. Hamburg.

—. 2009. Reputation and Odious Debt. Institute of Law and Economics. Hamburg, University of Hamburg. **PhD**.

—. 2009b. Towards a Taxonomy of Sovereign Debt Relations: A Focus on Creditors and Odious Debt. Institute of Law and Economics. Hamburg, University of Hamburg. **PhD**.

Bratton, W., M. Gulati (2004). "Sovereign Debt Reform and the Best Interests of Creditors." Vanderbilt Law Review **57**(January): 1-79.

Brown, K. (2005). Market Discipline in Sovereign Debt: Reinforcing the Rights of Bondholders and Private Creditors. Program on International Financial Systems. Cambridge, MA, Harvard Law School. **LL.M.**

Buchheit, L. C. (1986). "Sovereign Immunity." Business Law Review(February): 63-64.

Buchheit, L. C. (1995). "Cross-Border Lending: What's Different This Time?" Northwestern Journal of International Law and Business 16: 48.

Buchheit, L. C. and M. Gulati (2000). "Exit Consents in Sovereign Bond Exchanges." UCLA Law Review **48**(59).

Buchheit, L. C., M. G. Gulati, et al. (2007). "The Dilemma of Odious Debts." Duke Law Journal 56(5).

Buffet, W. (March 8, 2003). Warren Buffet's Annual Letter to Shareholders of Berkshire Hathaway.

Bulow, J. I. and K. S. Rogoff (1989). "Sovereign Debt: Is to Forgive to Forget?" American Economic Review **79**(1): 43-50.

—. Can pay, might not (November 27th, 2008). The Economist.

Cali, M., I. Massa, et al. (2008). The Global Financial Crisis: financial flows to developing countries set to fall by one quarter, Overseas Development Institute.

Callaghy, T. M. (2004). "Innovation in the Sovereign Debt Regime: From the Paris Club to Enhanced HIPC and Beyond." The World Bank Operations Evaluation Department.

—. "Country Focus: Sudan - Forgotten centre of Islamic finance."(April 1st, 2009).

Carr, E. H. (1985). A History of Soviet Russia: The Bolshevik Revolution. New York, MacMillan.

Cheng, T.-H. (2006). State Succession and Commercial Obligations. Ardsley, NY, Transnational Publishers.

—. 2007. "Renegotiating the Odious Debt Doctrine." Law and Contemporary Problems **70**: 7-31.

Cheru, F. (2006). Playing games with African lives: the G7 debt relief strategyand the politics of indifference. Sovereign Debt at the Crossorads. C. Jochnik and A. P. Fraser, Oxford University Press: 35-54.

Choi, A. H. and E. A. Posner (2007). "A Critique of the Odious Debt Doctrine." Law and Contemporary Problems **70**: 33-51.

—. Choose Taft as Arbitrator (November 2nd, 1922). New York Times. New York.

—. "Compare Summary Records of the 1425th Meeting U.N. Doc A/CN.4/SER.A/1977." (1977). Yearbook International Law Commission **49**(1): 54.

Cole, H., J. Dow, et al. (1995). "Default, Settlement, and Signalling: Lending Resumption in a Reputational Model of Sovereign Debt." International Economic Review **36**(2): 365-85.

Conway, E. (August 22, 2006). "Reborn Russia clears Soviet Debt." Telegraph.co.uk.

Craven, M. (1998). The Problem of State Succession and the Identity of States under International Law

Crawford, V. P. (1987). "International Lending, Long Term Credit Relationships, and Dynamic Contract Theory." Princeton Studies in International Finance **No. 59**.

Cuba's Debt Mistakes: A Lesson for Nicaragua (October 5, 1980). The Washington Post.

Dages, G. B., D. Palmer, et al. (May 2005). An Overview of Emerging Market Credit Derivatives Market, Federal Reserve Bank of New York.

Damle, J. (2007). "The Odious Debt Doctrine After Iraq." Law and Contemporary Problems 70: 139-156.

DeMott, D. A. (2007). "Agency by Analogy: A Comment on Odious Debt " Law and Contemporary Problems **70**.

Diamond, D. D. (1991). "Monitoring and Reputation: The Choice between Bank Loans and Directly Placed Debt." The Journal of Political Economy **99**(4): 689-721.

Dixon, L., D. Wall, Ed. (June 2000). Collective Action Problems and Collective Action Clauses. Financial Stability Review.

Eaton, J. and M. Gersovitz (1981). "Debt with Potential Repudiation: Theoretical and Empirical Analysis." Review of Economic Studies **48**(April): 289-309.

—. Ecuador's winning strategy (June 17th, 2009). The Economist.

Ebeling, R. (2003). Austrian Economics and the Political Economy of Freedom. Cheltenham, UK, Edwards Elgar Publishing.

Edwards, S. (1986). "The Pricing of Bonds and Bank Loans in International Markets: An Empirical Analysis of Developing Countries' Foreign Borrowing." European Economic Review **30**(3): 565-89.

Eichengreen, B. (2001). "Whither IMF Reform?" Finanz und Wirtschaft.

Eichengreen, B., R. Hausmann, et al. (2003). "Debt Intolerance and Original Sin: Why They Are Not the Same and Why It Matters." National Bureau of Economic Research Working Paper **No. 10036 3**.

EIRIS Guide to Responsible Banking (2003). London, Ethical Investment Research Service.

Faiola, A. (December 13, 2008). Calling Foreign Debt 'Immoral,' Leader Allows Ecuador to Default. Washington Post.

Feibelman, A. (2007). "Contract, Priority and Odious Debt." Law and Contemporary Problems.

Feilchenfeld, E. (1931). Public Debts and State Succession.

Finn, P. (August 22nd, 2006). Oil Profits Help Russia Pay Off Soviet-Era Debt. Washington Post.

Foorman, J. L. and E. M. Jehle (1982). "Effects of State and Government Succession on Commercial Bank Loans to Foreign Sovereign Borrowers " University of Illinois Law Review **1**(9).

Frankenberg, G. and R. Knieper (1984). "Legal Problems of the Overindebtedness of Developing Countries: The Current Relevance of the Doctrine of Odious Debts." International Journal of the Sociology of Law **12:** 415.

Franck, R. (2006). "The Political Economy of Sanctions Against North Korea." Asian Perspective 30(3): 5-36.

Frieden, J. A. (1988). "Classes, Sectors, and Foreign Debt in Latin America." Comparative Politics **21**(1): 1-19.

—. 1989. Winner and Losers in the Latin American Debt Crisis: The Political Implications. Debt and Democracy in Latin America. B. Stallings and R. R. Kaufman. Boulder Co., Westview Press.

Frieden, J. A. (1991). Debt, Development and Democracy: Modern Political Economy and Latin America, 1965-1985. Princeton, NJ, Princeton University Press.

Friesen, C. M. (1985). "The Regulation and Supervision of International Lending: Part I." International Lawyer **19**(Fall).

Gelpern, A. (2004). "Building a Better Seating Chart for Sovereign Debt Restructurings." Emory Law Journal **53**.

—. 2005. "What Iraq and Argentina Might Learn From Each Other." Chicago Journal of International Law **6**(1): 390-414.

—. 2005a. After Argentina, Institute for International Economics.

—. 2007. "Odious, not Debt." Law and Contemporary Problems **70**: 81-114.

—. 2008. "Domestic Bonds, Credit Derivatives, and the Next Transformation of Sovereign Debt." Rutgers School of Law Research Paper Series Paper **No. 038**.

Gelpern, A. and M. Gulati (2007). "Public Symbol in Private Contract: A Case Study." Washington University Law Quarterly.

Germain, R. (1997). International Organization of Credit. New York, Cambridge University Press.

Ginsburg, T. and T. S. Ulen (2007). "Odious Debt, Odious Credit, Economic Development and Democratization." Law and Contemporary Problems 70: 115-136.

Goderis, B. and W. Wagner (October 2006). "Credit Derivatives and Sovereign Debt Crises." Available at SSRN: http://ssrn.com/abstract=826644.

Gold, J. (1984). Legal and Institutional Aspects of the International Monetary System. Selected Essays. Washington, D.C., International Monetary Fund.

Goodman, P. S. (December 23, 2004). China Invests Heavily in Sudan's Oil Industry. The Washington Post.

Gottlieb, G. (Spring 1983). "Relationism: Legal Theory for a Relational Society." The University of Chicago Law Review **50**(2).

Gulati, M. and S. J. Choi (2004). "Innovation in Boilerplate Contracts: An Empirical Examination of Sovereign Bonds." Emory Law Journal **53**: 930-996.

—. Guyana's Experience with Paris Club and Commercial Creditors (2006). Debt Negotiation and Renegotiation Seminar. Kingston, Jamaica.

Guzman, A. T. (2002). "Choice of Law: New Foundations." Georgetown Law Review 90: 883-940.

—. 2008. How International Law Works - A Rational Choice Theory, Oxford University Press.

Haas, P. M. (Winter 1992). "Introduction: Epistemic communities and International Policy Coordination." International Organization 46(1).

—. 2003. Lessons from Environmental Governance for Debt Forgiveness. Sovereign Debt: Origins, Management and Restructuring. V. Aggarwal and B. Gransville, Royal Institute of International Affairs Hanlon, J. (November 1998). Dictators and Debt. Jubilee Reports.

Hanlon, J. (2002) Defining "Illegitimate Debt" and asking when creditors should be liable for improper loans.

—. 2006. "Lenders, not borrowers are responsible for "illegitmate loans." Third World Quarterly 27(2).

Hanson, S. (June 6, 2008). "China, Africa and Oil." Backgrounder.

Hattori, T. (2008). The Moral Regulation of the State: The Constitution of Indebted States as Juridical Persons. Annual Conference of the International Association of Critical Realism. King's College, London, UK.

Herman, B. (2007). The Players and the Game of Sovereign Debt. Dealing Fairly with Developing Country Debt. C. Barry, B. Herman and L. Tomitova. Malden, MA, Blackwell Publishing: 9-39.

Hoeflich, M. H. (1982). "Through a Glass Darkly: Reflections upon the History of International Law of Public Debt in Connection with State Succession." University of Illinois Law Review **1**: 39-40.

Howse, R. (2007). The Concept of Odious Debt in Public International Law. United Nations Conference on Trade and Development. Geneva, Switzerland.

hoy.mec.ec. (2008). "Ecuador planea tribunal internacional que investigue deuda externa." Retrieved April 8th, 2009, 2009.

http://jubileeusa.typepad.com/blog_the_debt/2008/12/ecuador-defaults-on-illegitimate-debt.html)."(2008). Retrieved May 11, 2009.

"http://www.clubdeparis.org/en/presentation.php?BATCH=B01WP06."(2006). Retrieved May 13th, 2009.

Hughes-Verdier, P. (2004). Credit Derivatives and the Sovereign Debt Restructuring Process. Program on International Financial Systems. Cambridge, MA, Harvard Law School. **LL.M.**

Hyde, C. (1945). International Law Chiefly as Interpreted and Applied in the United States 2nd Ed. Boston, Little Brown.

Jayachandran, S. and M. Kremer (2002). Odious Debt. Conference on Macroeconomic Policies and Poverty Reduction. IMF, Washington.

—. 2006. "Odious Debt." The American Economic Review **96**(1): 82-92.

Jèze, G. (1921). La partage des dettes publiques au cas démembrement de territoire. Paris, M. Giard.

—.1922. Théorie du crédit public, 6e éd. . Paris, M. Giard.

Kaiser, J. and A. Queck (2004) VerabscheuungswürdigeSchulden-verabscheuungswürdige Gläubiger - Die deutschen Forderungen an den Irak nach Saddam Hussein. **Volume,** DOI:

—; — March 2004. Odious Debts - Odious Creditors? International Claims on Iraq. Dialogue on Globalization - Occasional Papers. Friedrich Ebert Stiftung.

Kapstein, E. B. (1994). Governing the Global Economy - International Finance and the State. Cambridge, Harvard University Press.

Katz, A. W. (March 2004). "The Economics of Form and Substance in Contract Interpretation." Columbia Law Review **104**(2).

Khalfan, A., J. King, et al. (2003). Advancing the Odious Debt Doctrine CISDL Working Paper. Montreal, Centre for International Sustainable Development Law.

Kindleberger, C. P. (1984). A Financial History of Western Europe. London, George Allen & Unwin Ltd.

King, J. (2003). "The doctrine of odious debt under international law: definition, evidence and issues concerning application." CISDL Working Paper: Advancing the Odious Debt Doctrine.

—. 2007. "Odious Debt: The Terms of the Debate." North Carolina Journal of International Law and Commercial Regulation **32**: 605-668.

Kletzer, K. M. (1994). Sovereign Immunity and International Lending. Handbook of International Macroeconomics. F. v. d. Ploeg. Oxford, Blackwell: 439-479.

Kofele -Kale, N. (2005). The International Law of Responsibility for Economic Crimes, Ashgate.

Krugman, P. (2009). The Return of Depression Economics and the Crisis of 2008. London, W.W. Norton&Company.

Kueffner, S. (December 12th, 2008). "Correa Defaults on Ecuador Bonds, Seeks Restructuring."

Laurenti, J. (2009). "Arrest warrant in Sudan may force Obama's hand." Retrieved April 7th, 2009.

Lienau, O. (2008). "Who is the "Sovereign" in Sovereign Debt?: Reinterpreting a Rule-of-Law Framework from the Early Twentieth Century." The Yale Journal of International Law **33**: 63.

Lipson, C. (1981). "The international Organization of Third World Debt." International Organization **35**(4): 603-31.

Lispey, R. G. and K. Lancaster (1956). "The General Theory of Second Best." Review of Economic Studies **24**(11).

Ludington, S., G. Mitu, et al. (Draft March, 17th, 2009). "Applied Legal Theory: Demistifying the Doctrine of Odious Debts." Duke Public Law and Legal Theory Research Series (No. 236).

Macmillan, R. (1995). "Towards a Sovereign Debt Work-out System." Northwestern Journal of International Law and Business 16: 57, 80-84.

Mailath, G. J. and L. Samuelson (2001). "Who Wants a Good Reputation?" Review of Economic Studies **68**(2): 415-41.

—; —. 2006. Repeated Games and Reputations: Long Run Relationships. Oxford.

Majot, J. (1994). "The Doctrine of Odious Debts." Fifty Years is Enough: The Case Against the World Bank and the International Monetary Fund **35**.

McClintock, L. H. (1948). Handbook of the Principles of Equity.

McGreal, C. (February 8th, 2007). Chinese Aid to Africa May Do More Harm Than Good Warns Benn. The Guardian.

Mercer, J. (1996). Reputation and International Politics. Ithaca, N.Y.

Michalowski, S. (2007). Unconstitutional Regimes and the Validity of Sovereign Debt. Hampshire, Ashgate Publishing Limited.

Mitchener, K. J., M. D. Weidenmier (2005). "Supersanctions and Sovereign Debt Repayment." NBER Working Paper **No. 11472**.

Mitra-Kahn, B. H. (2008). IMF's rhetorical U-turn. The Mint.

Moody's (December 22nd, 2008). Ecuador default not likely to affect payments to CAF.

Nehru, V. (2007). The Concept of Odious Debt: Some Considerations, Economic Policy and Debt Department of the World Bank

Nehru, V., W. Bank, et al. (2008). Meeting Notes. Round Table on Conceptual and Operational Issues of Lender Responsibility for Sovereign Debt, World Bank, Washington D.C. .

Nishio (11 June, 2008). Risks and Opportunities for lending to LICs, and IDA's role, International Development Association Resources Mobilization. Paris Club Meeting with the Private Sector.

Norway takes historic step. (2006) www.odiousdebts.org

O'Connell (1967). State Succession in International Law and Municipal Law.

—. Panel on New Expertise on Odious Debts (2008). World Bank.

Ochoa, C. (2007). "From Odious Debt to Odious Finance: Avoiding the Externalities of a Functional Odious Debt Doctrine." Law and Contemporary Problems 70.

Outcome document (2008). International Symposium on Illegitimate External Debt, Oslo, Norway.

Packer, F. and C. Suthiphongchai (2003). "Sovereign credit default swaps." BIS Quarterly Review (December).

Palzer, K. A. (1988). "Relational Contract Theory and Sovereign Debt." Northwestern Journal of International Law and Business **8**(Winter): 727.

Paris Club (2007) Paris Club Annual Report

Paulus, C. G. (2007). Background Paper: The Concept of "Odious Debts": A Historical Survey, The World Bank: 1-72.

Penn, J. D. (1996). "Moving Someone Else to the End of the Line." American Bankruptcy Institute Journal **36**.

Pérez, L. A. and D. M. Weissman (2007). "Public Power and Private Purpose: Odious Debt and the Political Economy of Hegemony." North Carolina Journal of International Law and Commercial Regulation **32**.

Petersen, M. A. (2004). Information: Hard and Soft.

Pimentel, L. (June 16th, 2009). "Ecuador Plays Bond 'Market for Fools,' Aberdeen Says."

Porzecanski, A. C. (2005-2006). "From Rogue Creditors to Rogue Debtors: Implications of Argentina's Default." Chicago Journal of International Law **6**.

Posner, E. A. (2007). "Review of Robert E. Scott and Paul B. Stephan, The Limits of Leviathan: Contract Theory and the Enforcement of International Law." American Journal of International Law **101**(509).

Power, H. and H. Sigurdardottir (October 21, 2008). Iceland agrees $6 billion deal with IMF. The Times.

Pufendorf, S. (1964). The Law of Nature and Nations. The Classics of International Law, James Brown Scott, 1345-6.

—: S. Africa Shuns Apartheid Lawsuits (November 27, 2002). Guardian.

—. 1967. Natural Law and the Law of Nations.

Raffer, K. (2007). "Risks of Lending and Liability of Lenders." Ethics and International Affairs **21.1**: 85 - 106.

Rajan, R. G. (1992). "Insiders and Outsiders: The Choice between Informed and Arm's Length Debt " The Journal of Finance **47**(4): 1367-1400.

—. December 2004 . Odious or Just Malodorous? Finance and Development.

—. 2005. "Has Financial Development Made the World Riskier?" NBER Working Paper **No. W11728**(November).

—: A Revolution Within: A Special Report on International Banking (May 14th, 2009). The Economist.

Ramasastry, A. (2007). "Odious Debt or Odious Payments? Using Anti-corruption Measures to Prevent Odious Debt." North Carolina Journal of International Law and Commercial Regulation 32: 819-839.

Rasmussen, R. K. (2007). Sovereign Debt Restructuring, Odious Debt and the Politics of Debt Relief.

Raustalia, K. (July 2005). "Form and Substance in International Agreements." American Journal of International Law.

Reina, V. (2004). "Iraq's Delictual and Contractual Liabilities: would Politics or International Law Provide for Better Resolution of Successor State Responsibility?" Berkeley Journal of International Law 22.

Rogoff, K. S. (January 22nd, 2003). Emerging Market Debt. What is the Problem? Sovereign Debt Restructuring Mechanism Conference, International Monetary Fund. Washington D.C.

Rowling, M. (August 9th, 2005). Bond issue sounds ethical alarm. BBC News.

Sack, A. N. (1927). Les Effets des Transformations des Etats sur leurs Dettes Publiques et Autres Obligations Financieres, Recueil Sirey.

—. 1938. "Diplomatic Claims Against the Soviets." NYU Legal Quarterly Review **1**(7).

Scott, H. S. and P. A. Wellons (2002). International Finance: Transactions, Policy and Regulation.

Scott, R. E. and P. B. Stephan (2006). The Limits of Leviathan: Contract Theory and the Enforcement of International Law. New York, Cambridge University Press.

Security Council Resolution No 1483 UN Doc S/RES/1483 (May 22, 2003). 1483.

Settling the China Question: A Caribbean Challenge (May 2nd, 2008). The Commonwealth.

Sgard, J. (2004). "IMF in Theory: Sovereign Debts, Judicialisation and Multilateralism." CEPII **no 2004-21**.

Shafter, J. (2007). The Due Diligence Model: A New Approach to the Problem of Odious Debts. Dealing Fairly with Developing Country Debt. C. B. Barry, Herman. Lydia,Tomitova. Malden, Massachussetts, Blackwell Publishing Inc. for Carnegie Council: 275-295.

Shavell, S. (1984). "Liability for Harm versus Regulation of Safety." Journal of Legal Studies 13(2): 357-374.

Shavell, S. (2004). Foundations of the Economic Analysis of Law. Cambridge, Massachussetts, Harvard University Press.

Slaughter, A.-M. (2004). A New World Order. Princenton, NJ, Princeton University Press.

Stephan, P. B. (2007). "The Institutionalist Implications of an Odious Debt Doctrine." Law and Contemporary Problems **70**: 213-232.

Stiglitz, J. (November 2003). Odious Rulers, Odious Debts. Atlantic Monthly.

Sturzenegger, F. and J. Zettelmeyer (2006). Debt Defaults and Lessons from a Decade of Crises. London, England, Massachusetts Institute of Technology.

Subramanian, K. (January 27, 2006). Has the IMF lost its relevance? The Hindu Business Line.

Sudan Arrest Warrant: Aid Organizations Kicked out of the Country (2009) Huffington Post DOI: http://www.huffingtonpost.com/2009/03(04sudan-arrest-prof_n_171768.html

Tanaka, M. (2006). "Bank Loans Versus Bond Finance: Implications for Sovereign Debtors." The Economic Journal **116**(510).

Tarullo, D. K. (2001). "Rules, Discretion and Authority in International Financial Reform." journal of International Economic Law **4**.

Tarullo, D. K. (2007). "Odious Debt in Retrospect." Law and Contemporary Problems 70.

The Economist (April 24th, 1999) South Africa's Debt: Unforgivable

The Economist. (April 25th, 2009) Springing into action.

The Guardian. (November 27, 2002) S. Africa Shuns Apartheid Lawsuits Guardian.

The President Ex Order 13,303 Protecting the Developing Fund for Iraq and Certain Other Property in Which Iraq has an Interest (May 28th, 2003). 68 Fed Reg 31931.

The President, Exec Order 13, 364 Modifying the Protection Granted to the Development Fund for Iraq and Certain Property in which Iraq has an Interest and Protecting the Central Bank of Iraq (November 29th, 2004). 69 Fed Reg 70177

The Vienna Convention on the Law of Treaties (May 23,1969). United Nations. **Treaty Series vol. 1155**: 331.

The Washington Post (November 30, 1979). Somoza's Legacy: Plundered Economy

Tomz, M. (August, 2004). Finance and Trade: Issue Linkage and the Enforcement of International Debt Contracts. American Political Science Association. Chicago.

—. 2005. Democratic Default: Domestic Audiences and Compliance with International Agreements, Stanford University.

—. 2007. Reputation and International Cooperation - Sovereign Debt across Three Centuries. Princeton, Princeton University Press.

Trachtman, J. L. D. a. J. P. (1999). "Economic Analysis of International Law." Yale Journal of International Law **24**(1).

Triantis, G. and M. Gulati (2007). "Contracts Without Law: Sovereign versus Corporate Debt." Duke Law School Legal Studies Research Paper Series **Research Paper No. 152.**

Truman, E. M. (January 22, 2009). The IMF and the Global Crisis: Role and Reform. Remarks delivered to the Tulsa Committee on Foreign Relations, Peterson Institute for International Economics.

Turner, A. (2009). The Turner Review: A regulatory response to the global banking crisis, Financial Services Authority: 70-76.

Udombana, N. J. (2005). "The summer has ended and we are not saved: Towards a transformative agenda for Africa's development." San Diego International Law Journal 7: 5-60.

UNCTAD (April 2010), Responsible Sovereign Lending and Borrowing, Discussion Papers No. 198 available at: http://www.unctad.org/en/docs/osgdp20102_en.pdf Last retrieved May 10, 2011

UNITAR (2007). Chapter 12: Eurobonds. Online Course on Negotiations of Financial Transactions, United Nations Institute for Training and Research.

Van Zyl, L. (2001). Investor Relations Practices by Leading Emerging Market Authorities South Africa. Investor Relations: A tool for Crisis Prevention. International Monetary Fund, Washington, D.C., International Monetary Fund.

Vasquez, I. (1996). "The Brady Plan and Market Based Solutions to Debt Crises." Cato Journal **16**: 233-43.

Veer, v. d. K. and d. E. Jong (August 2006). Paris Club Involvement: Helping or hurting the IMF's attempts to catalyze private capital flows?, Department of Economics, Radboud University Nijmegen, The Netherlands.

Weiss, M. A. (2006). "Iraq's Debt Relief: Procedure and Potential Implications for International Debt Relief." CRS Report for Congress Order Code RL33376.

Westlake, J. (1904). International Law. Cambridge, University Press.

World Bank (2008) Panel on New Expertise on Odious Debts.

Wright, M. L. J. (2002). Reputations and Sovereign Debt. Palo Alto, CA, Stanford University.

www.barackobama.com (2007) Strengthening our Common Security by Investing in our Common Humanity. Volume, DOI: http://www.barackobama.com/pdf/issues/Fact_Sheet_Foreign_Policy_Democratization_and_Development_FINAL.pdf Last retrieved May 11, 2009

www.eurodad.org. (2009). "Harvard conference considers odious debt proposals." Last retrieved April 8th, 2009.

—. 2011. "AFRODAD launches borrowing charter" Last Retrieved May 10, 2011

www.hacer.org. (2008). http://www.hacer.org/report/2008/10/ecuador-correa-warns-over-illegitimate.html.

www.odiousdebt.org."http://www.odiousdebts.org/odiousdebts/index.cfm?DSP=content&ContentID=18718)." Last retrieved May 11, 2009.

www.politifact.com. (2009). "Barack Obama Campaign Promise no. 211." Last retrieved April 8th, 2009.

Zeledon, M. (2009). Ecuador: Chronicles of a Default Foretold, Seeking Alpha.

FSC
www.fsc.org
MIX
Papier | Fördert
gute Waldnutzung
FSC® C083411

Kolibri 360 GmbH
Ferdinand-Jühlke-Straße 7
99095 Erfurt, Deutschland
produktsicherheit@kolibri360.de